Oxford Beginner's Italian Dictionary

First edition

OXFORD
UNIVERSITY PRESS

OXFORD
UNIVERSITY PRESS

Great Clarendon Street, Oxford OX2 6DP

Oxford University Press is a department of the University of Oxford.
It furthers the University's objective of excellence in research, scholarship,
and education by publishing worldwide in

Oxford New York

Auckland Cape Town Dar es Salaam Hong Kong Karachi
Kuala Lumpur Madrid Melbourne Mexico City Nairobi
New Delhi Shanghai Taipei Toronto

With offices in

Argentina Austria Brazil Chile Czech Republic France Greece
Guatemala Hungary Italy Japan Poland Portugal Singapore
South Korea Switzerland Thailand Turkey Ukraine Vietnam

Oxford is a registered trade mark of Oxford University Press
in the UK and in certain other countries

Published in the United States
by Oxford University Press Inc., New York

British Library Cataloguing in Publication Data
Data available

Library of Congress Cataloging in Publication Data
Data available

ISBN 0-19-929855-6
ISBN 978-0-19-929855-6

10 9 8 7 6 5 4 3

Typeset in Swift and Arial
Printed in Italy by Legoprint S.p.A.

Contents

Contributors

Chief Editor
Colin McIntosh

Editors
Francesca Logi
Francesca Moy
Loredana Riu
Paola Tite

Appendices
Lexus Ltd.

Proprietary terms

This dictionary includes some words which are, or are asserted to be, proprietary names or trade marks. Their inclusion does not imply that they have acquired for legal purposes a non-proprietary or general significance, nor is any other judgement implied concerning their legal status. In cases where the editor has some evidence that a word is used as a proprietary name or trade mark, this is indicated by the symbol ®, but no judgement concerning the legal status of such words is made or implied thereby.

Introduction

This dictionary represents a major departure from traditional dictionaries on several fronts: it looks different; it provides essential information in a totally new way; the two sides of the dictionary have very distinct functions. In all, the dictionary approaches the needs of the English-speaking learner of Italian from a very different angle, making it a uniquely accessible and user-friendly introduction to the Italian language.

It looks different

The dictionary page is uncluttered, with a streamlined typeface providing a consistent structure for the information, both in English and in Italian. Subdivisions are clearly indicated, using bullet points and numbers. The move from one language to another is explicitly indicated with = signs. Points of basic grammar are reinforced using the **!** sign, informal Italian usage is marked with the **✗** symbol, and **☞** indicates words to be used with special care.

It provides information in a new way

Every effort has been made to approach the foreign language from the point of view of the beginner who may be unfamiliar with the conventions of the more traditional bilingual dictionary.

Parts of speech and grammatical terms are given in full, not in abbreviated form, with a glossary providing explanations of all the terms used. Basic grammatical issues and specific points of usage are dealt with in short notes at appropriate points in the text.

Sets of words which behave in a similar way are treated in a consistent manner, and the user is encouraged to cross-refer to different parts of the dictionary, for example to verb tables and usage notes dealing with such concepts as jobs, illnesses, and telling the time.

The language used in examples and sense indicators (or signposts to the correct translation) has been carefully screened to ensure maximum clarity. The word list contains all the material a beginner would need and reflects current American and British English and Italian in clear, lively examples.

The two sides have different functions

Each side of the dictionary is shaped by its specific function. The English–Italian side is longer, providing the user with maximum help in expressing the message in the foreign language in the form of detailed coverage of essential grammar, clear signposts to the correct translation for a particular context, and a wide selection of example material.

The English–Italian side is designed to capitalize on what English speakers already know about their language, hence the more streamlined presentation of English-language information. From irregular verb forms to common idiomatic usage, such as might be encountered in the media, the dictionary provides generous coverage of those aspects of Italian which are less easy to decipher for English speakers. Irregular verbs, adjectives, and plurals are all featured in the wordlist, referring the user to the base form where the translations are given.

How to use the dictionary

Every entry in the dictionary tells you whether that particular word is a noun, verb, adjective, or another part of speech. If you need to know what the parts of speech are, look them up in the glossary of grammatical terms.

If there is more than one part of speech within an entry, numbers are used to separate them. Within each part of speech, different senses are given bullet points (•):

bene	**Italian ▶ 199**
1 *adverb*	**1** *adjective*
= well	= italiano/italiana
stanno bene = they're well	**2** *noun*
bene! = good!	• (*the people*)
va bene! = OK!	**the Italians** = gli italiani
tutto bene? = is everything OK?	• (*the language*)
2 *noun, masculine*	**Italian** = l'italiano
i beni = possessions	

The English–Italian entries tend to be longer, in order to offer detailed guidance on how to write and speak correctly in Italian, so it is a good idea to scan the whole entry to find the sense which is closest to the one you need.

Each Italian verb entry is marked with a number pointing you to the table of Italian verbs at the back of the dictionary. The number refers to the model verb in the table where you can find the information you need about how to form the tenses.

perdonare *verb* ⊡
= to forgive

Cross-references are shown by an arrow ▶. These are especially useful for identifying verb forms, which you might not otherwise recognize:

so ▶ sapere

In examples, different words with which a phrase can be used are put in square brackets. This means that it is possible to substitute another word for the alternatives given in the dictionary.

little¹
1 *determiner*
= poco/poca
little [**sugar**	**wine**	**time**] = poco [zucchero	
vino	tempo]

Notes giving additional information are designed to help you produce correct Italian in areas where it is all too easy to forget important points of grammar or usage:

uovo *noun, masculine* (*plural* **uova**)	**actually** *adverb*
un uovo = an egg	**!** *Note that* **actually** *is not translated by*
! *Note that* **uova** *is feminine.*	**attualmente.**
	did she actually say that? = ha
	veramente detto così?
	actually, I'm rather tired = veramente sono
	piuttosto stanco

Boxed usage notes covering certain themes and sets of related words form a very useful feature of this dictionary. Topics covered include dates, the human body, illnesses, and the time of day. In relevant entries, a number refers you to the page with a note on the particular topic:

January *noun* ▶ <u>155</u>|
  January = gennaio

The structure of Italian–English entries

headword .... **iniziale** .... underlining of stressed syllable

numbers indicating **1** *adjective*
grammatical .... = initial
categories **2** *noun, feminine*
le iniziali = the initials .... translation clearly indicated by =

campione/campionessa *noun,*
masculine/feminine :................. feminine form
il campione/la campionessa = the of headword
champion

Ferragosto *noun, masculine*
explanatory gloss .... Ferragosto *Italian public holiday on*
August 15

carta *noun, feminine* .... part of speech plus
• la carta = paper gender
• una carta = a card
compounds ... • una carta = a map
presented in ... • **una carta di credito** = a credit card
block at end ... • **una carta d'identità** = an identity card
of entry ... • **la carta igienica** = toilet paper

importare *verb* 1 .... number of verb
information on .... • (**!** + *essere*) = to matter conjugation pattern
correct ... non m'importa = I don't care
grammatical usage ... • (**!** + *avere*) = to import

è ▶ essere .... cross-reference to headword

rimanere *verb* 56 (**!** + *essere*)
• = to stay
bullet points ... • = to be left
indicating ... me ne rimangono tre = I have three left
separate senses of ... • = to be
the headword sono rimasto deluso = I was disappointed
rimanere male = to be offended .... examples

symbol drawing ....
attention to **macello*** *noun, masculine*
register un macello = a mess

The structure of English–Italian entries

headword ······· **circus** *noun*
a circus = un circo

gender of Italian nouns made clear

part of speech made clear

narrow *adjective*
= stretto/stretta

feminine form of adjectives made clear

broke *adjective*
= al verde**✱**

symbol drawing attention to register

fire

numbers indicating grammatical categories

1 *noun*
a fire (*for heat*) = un fuoco
(*causing damage*) = un incendio
to catch fire = prendere fuoco

indicators which spell out the different senses of the headword

bullet points indicating separate senses of the headword

to be on fire = essere in fiamme
2 *verb*
• (*to shoot*) = sparare
• (*to dismiss*) = licenziare

fireman *noun* ▶ **281**
a fireman = un vigile del fuoco

page number cross-reference to a usage note

separate entries for compounds

fire station *noun*
a fire station = una caserma dei vigili de fuoco

translation clearly indicated by =

kick *verb*
to kick someone = dare un calcio a qualcuno
he kicked the ball = ha dato un calcio alla palla

phrasal verbs presented in independent blocks

kick off = dare il calcio d'inizio
kick out
to kick someone out = cacciare fuori qualcuno

need *verb*
• (*to have to*)
you don't need to ask permission = non c'è bisogno di chiedere il permesso
they'll need to come early = bisogna che vengano presto

basic structure to use as a model

information on correct grammatical usage

! Note that the subjunctive is used after bisogna che.

example indicating generative structure

• (*to want*) = avere bisogno di
they need [money | help | friends] = hanno bisogno di [soldi | aiuto | amici]

a (sometimes **ad** *before a vowel*)
preposition

> **!** *Note that* **a** *combines with* **il, la,** *etc.*
> **A** + **il** = **al**; **a** + **l'** = **all'**; **a** + **lo** = **allo**;
> **a** + **i** = **ai**; **a** + **gli** = **agli**; **a** + **la** = **alla**;
> **a** + **le** = **alle**.

• = to
  vado a Ravenna = I'm going to Ravenna
  l'ho dato a Luca = I gave it to Luca
• = at
  alla stazione = at the station
  alle quattro = at four o'clock
• = in
  a Perugia = in Perugia
• (*indicating distance*)
  a cinquanta chilometri da Torino = 50 km
  from Turin
• (*with the infinitive*)
  comincia a piovere = it's starting to rain
• (*indicating price, rate*)
  dieci euro al chilo = ten euros a kilo
  duecento chilometri all'ora = two
  hundred kilometres an hour

abbaiare *verb* ⑥
  = to bark

abbandonare *verb* ①
  = to abandon

abbassare *verb* ①
• = to lower
• (*the radio, TV*) = to turn down

abbastanza *adverb*
• = enough
  abbastanza soldi = enough money
  non è abbastanza caldo = it's not warm
  enough
• = quite, rather
  abbastanza noioso = rather boring
• = quite a lot (of), rather a lot (of)
  abbastanza traffico = quite a lot of traffic

abbia, abbiamo, etc ▶ **avere**

abbigliamento *noun, masculine*
  = clothing

abbonamento *noun, masculine*
• (*for a magazine*)
  un abbonamento = a subscription
• (*for public transport*)
  un abbonamento = a season ticket

abbonarsi *verb* ① (**!** + *essere*)
• (*to a magazine*)
  = to subscribe
• (*for public transport*) = to take out a
  season ticket

abbondante *adjective*
  = plentiful

abbracciare *verb* ②
  = to hug

abbraccio *noun, masculine* (*plural*
  abbracci)
• **un abbraccio** = a hug
• (*in a letter*)
  un abbraccio, Chiara = lots of love,
  Chiara

abbronzante *adjective*
  la crema abbronzante = suntan lotion

abbronzato/abbronzata *adjective*
  = tanned

abbronzatura *noun, feminine*
  un'abbronzatura = a tan

abile *adjective*
  = skil(l)ful

abilità *noun, feminine* (**!** *never changes*)
  un'abilità = a skill

abitante *noun, masculine/feminine*
  un abitante/un'abitante = an inhabitant

abitare *verb* ①
  = to live

abito *noun, masculine*
  un abito = a suit
  un abito = a dress
  gli abiti = clothes

abituale *adjective*
  = ususal

abituarsi *verb* ① (**!** + *essere*)
  abituarsi a = to get used to

abituato/abituata *adjective*
  abituato a = used to

abitudine *noun, feminine*
  un'abitudine = a habit

abolire *verb* ⑨
  = to abolish

aborto *noun, masculine*
  un aborto = an abortion

abusare *verb* ①
  abusare di = to abuse

abusivo/abusiva *adjective*
  = illegal

abuso *noun, masculine*
  un abuso = an abuse

accadde, accaddero, etc ▶
  accadere

accademia *noun, feminine*
  un'accademia = an academy

accademico/accademica *adjective*
  (*plural* **accademici/accademiche**)
  = academic

accadere verb 19 (! + *essere*)
= to happen

accanto
1 *adverb*
= nearby
qui accanto = near here
2 **accanto a** *preposition*
= next to

accappatoio noun, masculine (*plural*
accappatoi)
un accappatoio = a bathrobe

accelerare verb 1
= to accelerate

acceleratore noun, masculine
l'acceleratore = the accelerator

accendere verb 53
• (*when it's a fire*) = to light
• (*when it's a light, TV, etc*) = to turn on

accendino noun, masculine
un accendino = a lighter

accennare verb 1
accennare a = to mention

accento noun, masculine
un accento = an accent

accese, accesero, etc ▶
accendere

acceso/accesa
1 ▶ **accendere**
2 *adjective*
= on

accessorio noun, masculine (*plural*
accessori)
un accessorio = an accessory

accettabile adjective
= acceptable

accettare verb 1
= to accept

acciaio noun, masculine
l'acciaio = steel

accidenti✶ exclamation
accidenti! = damn!
= wow!

acciuga noun, feminine (*plural*
acciughe)
un'acciuga = an anchovy

accogliente adjective
= cosy, cozy

accoglienza noun, feminine
un'accoglienza = a welcome

accogliere verb 22
= to welcome

accolgo, accolse, etc ▶
accogliere

accoltellare verb 1
= to stab

accolto/accolta ▶ **accogliere**

accomodare verb 1
1 = to fix
2 **accomodarsi** (! + *essere*)
accomodarsi = to sit down
si accomodi! = take a seat!

accompagnare verb 1
= to accompany

acconto noun, masculine
un acconto = a deposit

accordo noun, masculine
• **un accordo** = an agreement
• **d'accordo!** = OK!
essere d'accordo = to agree
sono d'accordo con te = I agree with you
mettersi d'accordo = to agree
andare d'accordo = to get on well

accorgersi verb 59 (! + *essere*)
• **accorgersi di** = to notice
• **accorgersi che** = to realize that

accorse, accorto/accorta, etc ▶
accorgersi

accumulare verb 1
= to accumulate

accurato/accurata adjective
= careful

accusa noun, feminine
un'accusa = an accusation

accusare verb 1
= to accuse

aceto noun, masculine
l'aceto = vinegar

acido/acida
1 *adjective*
= sour
2 **acido** noun, masculine
l'acido = acid

acqua noun, feminine
l'acqua = water
l'acqua minerale = mineral water

acquaio noun, masculine (*plural* **acquai**)
l'acquaio = the sink

acquario noun, masculine
• (*plural* **acquari**)
un acquario = an aquarium
• **Acquario**
Acquario = Aquarius

acquisire verb 9
= to acquire

acquistare verb 1
= to purchase

acquisto noun, masculine
un acquisto = a purchase
fare acquisti = to go shopping

acuto/acuta adjective
• = sharp
• = acute

ad ▶ a

adattare verb [1]
1 = to adapt
2 **adattarsi** (! + *essere*)
    adattarsi a = to adapt to

adattatore noun, masculine
un adattatore = an adaptor

adatto/adatta adjective
= suitable
adatto a = suitable for

addio exclamation
addio! = goodbye!

addirittura
1 adverb
= even
addirittura cinque milioni = as much as
    five million
2 exclamation
addirittura! = really!

addizione noun, feminine
l'addizione = addition
un'addizione = a sum

addormentarsi verb [1] (! + *essere*)
= to fall asleep

addosso adverb
= on
senza niente addosso = without
    anything on
saltare addosso a qualcuno = to jump on
    someone

adeguato/adeguata adjective
= suitable

aderente adjective
= tight

aderire verb [9]
aderire a = to stick to

adesivo noun, masculine
un adesivo = a sticker

adesso adverb
= now

adolescente noun, masculine|feminine
un adolescente/un'adolescente = a
    teenager

adottare verb [1]
= to adopt

adulto/adulta noun, masculine|feminine
un adulto/un'adulta = an adult

aereo noun, masculine
un aereo = a plane

aeroporto noun, masculine
un aeroporto = an airport

affamato/affamata adjective
= hungry

affare noun, masculine
• gli affari = business
    per affari = on business
• un affare = a deal
• un affare = a bargain

affascinante adjective
= charming

affatto adverb
= at all
non mi piace affatto = I don't like it at all
niente affatto! = not at all!

affermare verb [1]
= to state

affermazione noun, feminine
un'affermazione = a statement

afferrare verb [1]
• = to grab
    = to catch
• = to understand

affettare verb [1]
= to slice

affettato noun, masculine
gli affettati = cold meat

affetto noun, masculine
l'affetto = affection

affettuoso/affettuosa adjective
= affectionate

affezionato/affezionata adjective
affezionato/affezionata a = fond of

affidabile adjective
= trustworthy

affinché conjunction
= so that

affittare verb [1]
• = to rent
• = to rent out

affitto noun, masculine
l'affitto = the rent

affogare verb [5] (! + *essere* or *avere*)
= to drown

affollato/affollata adjective
= crowded

affondare verb [1] (! + *essere* or *avere*)
= to sink

affrettarsi verb [1] (! + *essere*)
= to hurry

affrontare verb [1]
= to face

affumicato/affumicata adjective
= smoked

afoso/afosa adjective
= stiflingly hot

africano/africana adjective
= African

agenda noun, feminine
un'agenda = a diary

agente noun, masculine|feminine
un agente/un'agente = an agent

agenzia noun, feminine
un'agenzia = an agency
un'agenzia di viaggi = a travel agency

agganciare verb 2
• = to hook
= to hitch
• (*on the telephone*) = to hang up

aggiornamento noun, masculine
un aggiornamento = an update
un corso di aggiornamento = a refresher course

aggiornare verb 1
1 = to bring up to date
2 aggiornarsi (! + *essere*)
aggiornarsi = to keep up to date

aggiornato/aggiornata adjective
= up-to-date

aggiungere verb 48
= to add

aggiunse ▶ **aggiungere**

aggiunta noun, feminine
un'aggiunta = an addition

aggiunto/aggiunta ▶ **aggiungere**

aggiustare verb 1
= to fix

aggredire verb 9
= to attack

aggressione noun, feminine
un'aggressione = an attack

aggressivo/aggressiva adjective
= aggressive

agio noun, masculine
non mi sento a mio agio = I don't feel at ease

agire verb 9
= to act

agitare verb 1
1 = to wave
2 agitarsi (! + *essere*)
agitarsi = to get worked up

agli ▶ **a**

aglio noun, masculine
l'aglio = garlic

agnello noun, masculine
un agnello = a lamb
l'agnello = lamb

ago noun, masculine (*plural* **aghi**)
un ago = a needle

agosto noun, masculine
= August

agricoltura noun, feminine
l'agricoltura = agriculture

agro/agra adjective
= sour

ai ▶ **a**

aiutare verb 1
= to help

aiuto noun, masculine
l'aiuto = help

al ▶ **a**

ala noun, feminine (*plural* **ali**)
un'ala = a wing

alba noun, feminine
l'alba = dawn

albergo noun, masculine (*plural* **alberghi**)
un albergo = a hotel

albero noun, masculine
un albero = a tree

albicocca noun, feminine (*plural* **albicocche**)
un'albicocca = an apricot

alcol noun, masculine
l'alcol = alcohol

alcolico/alcolica adjective (*plural* **alcolici/alcoliche**)
= alcoholic

alcolizzato/alcolizzata adjective
= alcoholic

alcuni/alcune adjective
= some

alfabeto noun, masculine
l'alfabeto = the alphabet

alga noun, feminine (*plural* **alghe**)
le alghe = seaweed

ali ▶ **ala**

alimentari noun, masculine (! *never changes*)
un alimentari = a grocer's

alla ▶ **a**

allacciare verb 2
= to fasten

allagato/allagata adjective
= flooded

allargare verb 5
1 = to widen
2 allargarsi (! + *essere*)
allargarsi = to widen

allarme noun, masculine
un allarme = an alarm

alle ▶ **a**

alleanza noun, feminine
un'alleanza = an alliance

alleato/alleata
1 adjective
= allied
2 noun, masculine/feminine
un alleato/un'alleata = an ally

allegare verb 5
= to enclose

allegato noun, masculine
un allegato = an (email) attachment

allegria noun, feminine
l'allegria = cheerfulness

A

allegro/allegra *adjective*
= cheerful

allenamento *noun, masculine*
l'allenamento = training

allenarsi *verb* [1] (**!** + *essere*)
= to train

allenatore/allenatrice *noun,*
masculine/feminine
un allenatore/un'allenatrice = a trainer

allergia *noun, feminine* (*plural* **allergie**)
un'allergia = an allergy

allergico/allergica *adjective* (*plural*
allergici/allergiche)
allergico/allergica a = allergic to

allevare *verb* [1]
• (*when it's children*) = to bring up
• (*when it's animals*) = to breed

allo ▶ **a**

alloggio *noun, masculine* (*plural* **alloggi**)
un alloggio = accommodation

allontanare *verb* [1]
1 = to move away
2 allontanarsi (**!** + *essere*)
allontanarsi = to move away

allora *adverb*
• = then
= at that time
• = well
= so

almeno *adverb*
= at least

Alpi *noun, feminine*
le Alpi = the Alps

alpinismo *noun, masculine*
l'alpinismo = mountaineering

alpino/alpina *adjective*
= Alpine

alt *exclamation*
alt! = stop!

alternativo/alternativa *adjective*
= alternative

altezza *noun, feminine*
l'altezza = the height

alto/alta *adjective*
• = high
• (*when it's a person*) = tall

altrettanto/altrettanta
1 *adjective*
= as much, as many
cento adulti e altrettanti bambini = a
hundred adults and the same number
of children
2 altrettanto *adverb*
= equally

altrimenti *adverb*
• = otherwise
• = differently

altro/altra *adjective*
= other
un altro/un'altra = another

altrui *adjective* (**!** *never changes*)
= other people's

alunno/alunna *noun,*
masculine/feminine
un alunno/un'alunna = a pupil

alzare *verb* [1]
1 = to raise
alzare il volume = to turn up the volume
2 alzarsi (**!** + *essere*)
alzarsi = to stand up
= to get up

amante *noun, masculine/feminine*
un amante/un'amante = a lover

amare *verb* [1]
= to love

amaro/amara *adjective*
= bitter

ambasciata *noun, feminine*
un'ambasciata = an embassy

ambientale *adjective*
= environmental

ambientare *verb* [1]
= to set
il film è ambientato a Firenze = the film
is set in Florence

ambiente *noun, masculine*
l'ambiente = the environment

ambiguo/ambigua *adjective*
= ambiguous

ambizione *noun, feminine*
l'ambizione = ambition

ambizioso/ambiziosa *adjective*
= ambitious

ambulanza *noun, feminine*
un'ambulanza = an ambulance

ambulatorio *noun, masculine* (*plural*
ambulatori)
un ambulatorio = a doctor's surgery, a
doctor's office

americano/americana *adjective*
= American

amichevole *adjective*
= friendly

amicizia *noun, feminine*
l'amicizia = friendship

amico/amica *noun, masculine/feminine*
(*plural* **amici/amiche**)
un amico/un'amica = a friend
un amico mio = a friend of mine

ammalato/ammalata *adjective*
= ill, sick

ammattire *verb* [9] (**!** + *essere*)
= to go crazy

ammazzare verb [1]
= to kill

ammesso/ammessa ▶ **ammettere**

ammettere verb [40]
• = to admit
• = to allow (in)

amministrazione noun, feminine
l'amministrazione = the administration

ammirare verb [1]
= to admire

ammirazione noun, feminine
l'ammirazione = admiration

ammise ▶ **ammettere**

ammobiliato/ammobiliata
adjective
= furnished

amore noun, masculine
l'amore = love

ampio/ampia adjective (plural
ampi/ampie)
= wide

ampliare verb [6]
= to extend
= to expand

anagrafe noun, feminine
l'anagrafe = the registry

analcolico/analcolica adjective
(plural **analcolici/analcoliche**)
= non-alcoholic

analisi noun, feminine (**!** never changes)
un'analisi = an analysis

analizzare verb [1]
= to analyse, to analyze

analogo/analoga adjective (plural
analoghi/analoghe)
= similar

ananas noun, masculine (**!** never
changes)
un ananas = a pineapple

anatomia noun, feminine
l'anatomia = anatomy

anatra noun, feminine
un'anatra = a duck

anche conjunction
• = also
= too
ci vado anch'io = I'm going too
• = even
anche se = even if
= although

ancora adverb
• = still
è ancora a letto = he's still in bed
• = yet
non è ancora arrivata = she hasn't arrived
yet
• = even
ancora più difficile = even more difficult

• = again
ancora una volta = once again
• = more
ne vuoi ancora? = do you want some
more?

ancora noun, feminine
l'ancora = the anchor

andare
1 verb [13] (**!** + essere)
• = to go
andare via = to go away
andare a sciare = to go skiing
• come va? = how are things?
va bene! = OK!
• non mi va di uscire = I don't want to go
out
ti va bene? = is it OK for you?
• (with the past participle)
va fatto = it has to be done
2 andarsene verb [13] (**!** + essere)
andarsene = to go away
me ne vado = I'm off

andata noun, feminine
l'andata = the journey there
Siena, solo andata = a single to Siena, a
one-way ticket to Siena
Bologna, andata e ritorno = a return to
Bologna, a round-trip ticket to Bologna

andrà, andrò, etc ▶ **andare**

anello noun, masculine
un anello = a ring

angelo noun, masculine
un angelo = an angel

angolo noun, masculine
• un angolo = a corner
dietro l'angolo = (a)round the corner
• = an angle

angoscia noun, feminine
l'angoscia = anguish

anguria noun, feminine
un'anguria = a water melon

anima noun, feminine
l'anima = the soul

animale noun, masculine
un animale = an animal

animato/animata adjective
= lively

annaffiare verb [6]
= to water

annata noun, feminine
un'annata = a vintage

annegare verb [5] (**!** + essere or avere)
= to drown

anniversario noun, masculine (plural
anniversari)
un anniversario = an anniversary

anno noun, masculine
un anno = a year
tutti gli anni = every year   ····▶

quanti anni hai? = how old are you?
ho vent'anni = I'm twenty
gli anni 60 = the 60s
buon anno! = happy New Year!

annoiarsi *verb* 6 (! + *essere*)
= to get bored

annoiato/annoiata *adjective*
= bored

annuale *adjective*
= annual

annullare *verb* 1
= to cancel

annunciare *verb* 2
= to announce

annuncio *noun, masculine* (*plural* **annunci**)
- **un annuncio** = an advertisement
- = an announcement

annuo/annua *adjective*
= annual

ansia *noun, feminine*
l'ansia = anxiety
stare in ansia = to be worried

ansioso/ansiosa *adjective*
= anxious

Antartico *noun, masculine*
l'Antartico = the Antarctic Ocean

antenato/antenata *noun, masculine/feminine*
un antenato/un'antenata = an ancestor

antenna *noun, feminine*
un'antenna = an aerial

anteriore *adjective*
= front

antibiotico *noun, masculine* (*plural* **antibiotici**)
un antibiotico = an antibiotic

antichità *noun, feminine* (! *never changes*)
l'antichità = ancient times

anticipare *verb* 1
- = to bring forward
- = to advance

anticipo *noun, masculine*
- **un anticipo** = an advance
- **in anticipo** = in advance

antico/antica *adjective* (*plural* **antichi/antiche**)
- = ancient
- = antique

antiorario/antioraria *adjective* (*plural* **antiorari/antiorarie**)
in senso antiorario = anti-clockwise

antipasto *noun, masculine*
un antipasto = a starter, an appetizer

antipatico/antipatica *adjective* (*plural* **antipatici/antipatiche**)
= unpleasant
Elena mi è antipatica = I don't like Elena

antiquariato *noun, masculine*
l'antiquariato = antiques
un negozio di antiquariato = an antique shop

anzi *conjunction*
- **ci vado lunedì, anzi martedì** = I'm going on Monday, no, Tuesday
- = on the contrary

anziano/anziana *adjective*
= elderly

anziché *conjunction*
= rather than

anzitutto *adverb*
= first of all

ape *noun, feminine*
un'ape = a bee

aperitivo *noun, masculine*
un aperitivo = an aperitif

aperto/aperta
1 ▶ **aprire**
2 *adjective*
- = open
- (*when it's the gas, a tap, etc*) = on

apertura *noun, feminine*
l'apertura = the opening

apostrofo *noun, masculine*
un apostrofo = an apostrophe

appaio, appaiono, etc ▶ **apparire**

apparecchiare *verb* 6
= to set the table

apparecchio *noun, masculine* (*plural* **apparecchi**)
un apparecchio = a machine

apparentemente *adverb*
= apparently

apparire *verb* 14 (! + *essere*)
= to appear

apparso/apparsa ▶ **apparire**

appartamento *noun, masculine*
un appartamento = a flat, an apartment

appartenere *verb* 73
appartenere a = to belong to

appartengo, appartiene, apparterrà, etc ▶ **appartenere**

apparve, apparvi, etc ▶ **apparire**

appassionante *adjective*
= exciting

appassionato/appassionata *adjective*
- = passionate
- **appassionato/appassionata di** = keen on

appello *noun, masculine*
- **un appello** = an appeal
- **fare l'appello** = to call the register

A

appena
1 *adverb*
• = just
  sono appena arrivati = they've just arrived
• = scarcely
  ti sento appena = I can scarcely hear you
2 *conjunction*
  = as soon as
  appena finito = as soon as I've finished
  appena possibile = as soon as possible

appendere *verb* 53
  = to hang up

appendice *noun, feminine*
  un'appendice = an appendix
  l'appendice = the appendix

appendicite *noun, feminine*
  l'appendicite = appendicitis

appeso/appesa, appese, etc ▶ **appendere**

appetito *noun, masculine*
  l'appetito = the appetite

appiccicare *verb* 4
  = to stick

appiccicoso/appiccicosa *adjective*
  = sticky

applaudire *verb* 9
  = to clap

applauso *noun, masculine*
  l'applauso = clapping

applicare *verb* 4
  = to apply

appoggiare *verb* 3
1 = to lean
  = to put down
2 appoggiarsi (**!** + *essere*)
  appoggiarsi a = to lean on

appoggio *noun, masculine* (*plural* **appoggi**)
  l'appoggio = support

apposta *adverb*
  = on purpose

apprendere *verb* 53
  = to learn

apprensivo/apprensiva *adjective*
  = apprehensive

appreso/appresa, apprese, etc ▶ **apprendere**

apprezzare *verb* 1
  = to appreciate

approfittare *verb* 1
  approfittare di = to take advantage of

approfondire *verb* 9
  = to examine more closely
  = to go into detail

approfondito/approfondita *adjective*
  = close

approssimativo/approssimativa *adjective*
  = approximate

approvare *verb* 1
  = to approve (of)

approvazione *noun, feminine*
  l'approvazione = approval

appuntamento *noun, masculine*
  un appuntamento = an appointment

appunto
1 *noun, masculine*
  gli appunti = notes
2 *adverb*
  = exactly
  appunto! = exactly!

aprile *noun, masculine*
  = April

aprire *verb* 15
1 (**!** + *avere*)
• = to open
• (*when it's the gas, a tap, etc*) = to turn on
2 aprirsi (**!** + *essere*)
  aprirsi = to open

apriscatole *noun, masculine* (**!** *never changes*)
  un apriscatole = a tin opener, a can opener

aquila *noun, feminine*
  un'aquila = an eagle

arabo/araba *adjective*
  = Arabic

aragosta *noun, feminine*
  un'aragosta = a lobster

arancia *noun, feminine* (*plural* **arance**)
  un'arancia = an orange

aranciata *noun, feminine*
  l'aranciata = orangeade

arancione *adjective*
  = orange

arbitro *noun, masculine*
  l'arbitro = the referee

architetto *noun, masculine*
  un architetto = an architect

architettura *noun, feminine*
  l'architettura = architecture

arco *noun, masculine* (*plural* **archi**)
• **un arco** = an arch
• **un arco** = a bow

arcobaleno *noun, masculine*
  un arcobaleno = a rainbow

area *noun, feminine*
  l'area = the area

argento *noun, masculine*
  l'argento = silver

argomento *noun, masculine*
  = a topic
  cambiare argomento = to change the subject

A

aria noun, feminine
l'aria = air
all'aria aperta = in the open air

Ariete noun, masculine
= Aries

arma noun, feminine (plural **armi**)
• un'arma = a weapon
• le armi = arms

armadio noun, masculine (plural **armadi**)
• un armadio = a cupboard
• un armadio = a wardrobe, a closet

armato/armata adjective
= armed

armi ▶ **arma**

armonia noun, feminine
l'armonia = harmony

arrabbiarsi verb ⑥ (! + essere)
= to get angry

arrabbiato/arrabbiata adjective
= angry

arrampicarsi verb ④ (! + essere)
= to climb

arrestare verb ①
= to arrest

arrivare verb ① (! + essere)
= to arrive

arrivederci, arrivederla exclamation
arrivederci! = goodbye!

arrivo noun, masculine
l'arrivo = the arrival

arrogante adjective
= arrogant

arrossire verb ⑨ (! + essere)
= to blush

arrostire verb ⑨
= to roast

arrosto
1 adjective (! never changes)
= roast
agnello arrosto = roast lamb
2 noun, masculine
un arrosto = a roast

arrugginito/arrugginita adjective
= rusty

arte noun, feminine
l'arte = art

Artico noun, masculine
l'Artico = the Arctic Ocean

articolo noun, masculine
un articolo = an article

Artide noun, feminine
l'Artide = the Arctic

artificiale adjective
= artificial

artigiano/artigiana noun, masculine/feminine
un artigiano/un'artigiana = a craftsman/a craftswoman

artista noun, masculine/feminine (plural **artisti/artiste**)
un artista/un'artista = an artist

artistico/artistica adjective (plural **artistici/artistiche**)
= artistic

arto noun, masculine
un arto = a limb

ascensore noun, masculine
un ascensore = a lift, an elevator

asciugamano noun, masculine
un asciugamano = a towel

asciugare verb ⑤
= to dry

asciutto/asciutta adjective
= dry

ascoltare verb ①
= to listen to
ascoltami! = listen to me!

asiatico/asiatica adjective (plural **asiatici/asiatiche**)
= Asian

asilo noun, masculine
• l'asilo = nursery school, kindergarten
• l'asilo politico = political asylum

asino noun, masculine
un asino = a donkey

asma noun, feminine
l'asma = asthma

asparago noun, masculine (plural **asparagi**)
gli asparagi = asparagus

aspettare verb ①
1 = to wait for
aspettami! = wait for me!
2 aspettarsi (! + essere)
aspettarsi che = to expect that

aspetto noun, masculine
l'aspetto = the appearance

aspirapolvere noun, masculine (! never changes)
un aspirapolvere = a vacuum cleaner
passare l'aspirapolvere = to vacuum

aspirina noun, feminine
un'aspirina = an aspirin

aspro/aspra adjective
= sour

assaggiare verb ③
= to taste

assassinare verb ①
= to murder

assassino/assassina *noun,*
masculine/feminine
un assassino/un'assassina = a murderer

assegno *noun, masculine*
un assegno = a cheque, a check

assemblea *noun, feminine*
un'assemblea = an assembly

assente *adjective*
= absent

assenza *noun, feminine*
un'assenza = an absence

assessore *noun, masculine*
un assessore = a council(l)or

assicurare *verb* 1
• = to insure
• = to assure

assicurazione *noun, feminine*
l'assicurazione = the insurance

assistente *noun, masculine/feminine*
un assistente/un'assistente = an assistant

assistenza *noun, feminine*
= assistance

assistere *verb* 16
assistere a = to be present at

asso *noun, masculine*
un asso = an ace

associazione *noun, feminine*
un'associazione = an association

assolutamente *adverb*
• = absolutely
• assolutamente no = certainly not

assoluto/assoluta *adjective*
= absolute

assomigliare *verb* 6 (! + *essere* or
avere)
assomigliare a = to look like

assorbente
1 *adjective*
= absorbent
2 *noun, masculine*
un assorbente = a sanitary towel

assumere *verb* 17
• = to hire
• = to assume

assunse, assunto/assunta, etc ▶
assumere

assurdo/assurda *adjective*
= absurd

asta *noun, feminine*
• un'asta = an pole
• un'asta = an auction

astratto/astratta *adjective*
= abstract

astrologia *noun, feminine*
l'astrologia = astrology

astronomia *noun, feminine*
l'astronomia = astronomy

astuccio *noun, masculine (plural*
astucci)
un astuccio = a case
= a pencil case

atlante *noun, masculine*
un atlante = an atlas

Atlantico *noun, masculine*
l'Atlantico = the Atlantic

atleta *noun, masculine/feminine (plural*
atleti/atlete)
un atleta/un'atleta = an athlete

atletica *noun, feminine*
l'atletica = athletics

atmosfera *noun, feminine*
l'atmosfera = the atmosphere

attaccare *verb* 4
1 (! + *avere*)
• = to attack
• = to attach
= to stick
• = to hang up
2 attaccarsi (! + *essere*) = to stick

attacco *noun, masculine (plural*
attacchi)
un attacco = an attack

atteggiamento *noun, masculine*
un atteggiamento = an attitude

attendere *verb* 53
= to await

attentato *noun, masculine*
un attentato = an attack
un attentato contro qualcuno = an
attempt on someone's life

attento/attenta *adjective*
= careful
stai attento! = be careful!

attenzione *noun, feminine*
= attention
fai attenzione! = pay attention!

atterraggio *noun, masculine (plural*
atterraggi)
un atterraggio = a landing

atterrare *verb* 1 (! + *essere* or *avere*)
= to land

attesa *noun, feminine*
un'attesa = a wait

attese, atteso/attesa, etc ▶
attendere

attimo *noun, masculine*
un attimo = a moment
un attimo! = just a moment!

attirare *verb* 1
= to attract

attività *noun, feminine (! never changes)*
un'attività = an activity

attivo/**attiva** *adjective*
= active

atto *noun, masculine*
un atto = an act
un atto di trasferimento di proprietà
= (property) deed

attore/**attrice** *noun, masculine/feminine*
un attore/un'attrice = an actor/an actress

attorno ▶ **intorno**

attraente *adjective*
= attractive

attraversare *verb* [1]
= to cross

attraverso *preposition*
• = across
• = through

attrazione *noun, feminine*
un'attrazione = an attraction

attrezzatura *noun, feminine*
l'attrezzatura = the equipment

attrezzo *noun, masculine*
un attrezzo = a tool

attribuire *verb* [9]
= to attribute

attrice ▶ **attore**

attuale *adjective*
• = current

attualità *noun, feminine* (**!** *never changes*)
l'attualità = current affairs

attualmente *adverb*
= at present

augurare *verb* [1]
= to wish

auguri *noun, masculine plural*
gli auguri = best wishes
tanti auguri! = all the best!

aula *noun, feminine*
un'aula = a classroom

aumentare *verb* [1] (**!** + *essere* or *avere*)
= to increase

aumento *noun, masculine*
un aumento = an increase

austriaco/**austriaca** *adjective* (*plural* **austriaci**/**austriache**)
= Austrian

autentico/**autentica** *adjective* (*plural* **autentici**/**autentiche**)
= authentic

autista *noun, masculine/feminine* (*plural* **autisti**/**autiste**)
un autista/un'autista = a driver

auto (**!** *never changes*), **automobile** *noun, feminine*
un'auto = a car

autobus *noun, masculine* (**!** *never changes*)
un autobus = a bus

autogrill *noun, masculine* (**!** *never changes*)
un autogrill = a motorway café, a freeway diner

automatico/**automatica** *adjective* (*plural* **automatici**/**automatiche**)
= automatic

automobile ▶ **auto**

autonoleggio *noun, masculine* (*plural* **autonoleggi**)
= car hire, car rental

autore/**autrice** *noun, masculine/feminine*
un autore/un'autrice = an author

autorevole *adjective*
= authoritative

autorità *noun, feminine* (**!** *never changes*)
un'autorità = an authority

autorizzare *verb* [1]
= to authorize

autostop *noun, masculine*
fare l'autostop = to hitch-hike

autostrada *noun, feminine*
un'autostrada = a motorway, a freeway

autovelox *noun, masculine*
un autovelox = a speed camera

autrice ▶ **autore**

autunno *noun, masculine*
l'autunno = the autumn, the fall

avanti
1 *adverb*
• = forward
• (*when it's a clock*) = to be fast
2 *exclamation*
avanti! = come in!

avanzare *verb* [1] (**!** + *essere* or *avere*)
• = to advance
• = to be left over

avanzato/**avanzata** *adjective*
• = advanced
• = leftover

avanzi *noun, masculine plural*
gli avanzi = the leftovers

avaro/**avara** *adjective*
= miserly

avere *verb* [12] **▶ 12** See the boxed note.
quanti ne abbiamo oggi? = what's the date today?
che cos'hai? = what's wrong with you?

avere

1 avere functions as an ordinary verb:

= to have

    abbiamo un cane   = *we have a dog*

= to get

    ho avuto il messaggio   = *I got your message*

2 avere is used as an auxiliary verb to form other tenses. The perfect tense uses the present tense of **avere** + the past participle. It is used to talk about events in the fairly recent past or that have had an effect on the present:

    l'ho ricevuto ieri   = *I received it yesterday*
    ho già visto questo film   = *I've already seen this film*

The pluperfect tense uses the imperfect tense of **avere** + the past participle. It is used to talk about events that happened before the event that is the main focus of attention:

    l'avevo conosciuta prima = *I had met her before*

3 avere is used to talk about ages:

    quanti anni hai?   = *how old are you?*
    ho ventidue anni   = *I'm twenty-two*

4 avere is used to form many expressions such as **aver fame**. To find translations for these, look up the entry for the noun in the expression.

---

avesti, avrò, etc ▶ avere

avvelenare verb ⓵
= to poison

avvenimento noun, masculine
un avvenimento = an event

avvenga, avvengono, etc ▶
avvenire

avvenire verb ⑦⑧ (**!** + *essere*)
= to happen

avvenne, avvennero, etc ▶
avvenire

avventura noun, feminine
un'avventura = an adventure

avversario/avversaria noun,
masculine/feminine (plural
avversari/avversarie)
un avversario/un'avversaria = an
opponent

avvertimento noun, masculine
un avvertimento = a warning

avvertire verb ⑩
= to notify
= to warn

avviare verb ⑦
1 (**!** + *avere*)
= to start (up)
2 avviarsi (**!** + *essere*)
avviarsi = to set off

avvicinare verb ⓵
1 = to bring closer
2 avvicinarsi (**!** + *essere*)
avvicinarsi = to come closer
avvicinarsi a = to approach

avviene ▶ avvenire

avvisare verb ⓵
= to notify

avviso noun, masculine
un avviso = a notice

avvocato noun, masculine
un avvocato = a lawyer

azienda noun, feminine
un'azienda = a firm

azione noun, feminine
• un'azione = an action
• un'azione = a share

azzeccato/azzeccata adjective
= exactly right

azzurro/azzurra adjective
= blue

Bb

babbo noun, masculine
• il babbo = the dad
• Babbo Natale = Father Christmas, Santa
Claus

baccalà noun, masculine (**!** *never*
changes)
il baccalà = salt cod

baccano noun, masculine
fare baccano = to make a racket

bacchetta *noun, feminine*
- una bacchetta = a stick
  = a baton
- una bacchetta magica = a magic wand

baciare *verb* 2
1 = to kiss
2 **baciarsi** (**!** + *essere*)
baciarsi = to kiss (each other)

bacio *noun, masculine* (*plural* **baci**)
un bacio = a kiss

badare *verb* 1
- badare a = to look after
- badare a = to pay attention to

baffi *noun, masculine plural*
i baffi = a m(o)ustache

bagaglio *noun, masculine*
il bagaglio = the luggage
i bagagli = the luggage
fare i bagagli = to pack

bagnare *verb* 1
1 = to wet
2 **bagnarsi** (**!** + *essere*)
bagnarsi = to get wet

bagnato/bagnata *adjective*
= wet

bagnino/bagnina *noun,*
masculine/feminine
un bagnino/una bagnina = a lifeguard

bagno *noun, masculine*
- (*a room*)
  il bagno = the bathroom
- fare il bagno
  (*in a bathtub*) = to have a bath
  (*in the sea*) = to have a swim

bagnoschiuma *noun, masculine*
(**!** *never changes*)
il bagnoschiuma = bubble bath

baia *noun, feminine*
una baia = a bay

balcone *noun, masculine*
un balcone = a balcony

balena *noun, feminine*
una balena = a whale

ballare *verb* 1
= to dance

ballerino/ballerina *noun,*
masculine/feminine
un ballerino/una ballerina = a dancer

balletto *noun, masculine*
il balletto = ballet

ballo *noun, masculine*
un ballo = a dance
il ballo = dancing

balzo *noun, masculine*
un balzo = a jump

bambino/bambina *noun,*
masculine/feminine

un bambino/una bambina = a boy/a girl
= a child

bambola *noun, feminine*
una bambola = a doll

banale *adjective*
= banal

banca *noun, feminine* (*plural* **banche**)
una banca = a bank
andare in banca = to go to the bank
una banca etica = an ethical bank

bancarella *noun, feminine*
una bancarella = a stall

bancario/bancaria (*plural*
bancari/bancarie)
1 *adjective*
= bank
2 *noun, masculine/feminine*
un bancario/una bancaria = a bank clerk

bancarotta *noun, feminine*
la bancarotta = bankruptcy

banchiere *noun, masculine*
un banchiere = a banker

banco *noun, masculine* (*plural* **banchi**)
- (*at school*)
  un banco = a desk
- (*in a shop*)
  il banco = the counter

Bancomat® *noun, masculine* (**!** *never changes*)
un Bancomat = a cash machine

banconota *noun, feminine*
una banconota = a (bank)note, a bill

banda *noun, feminine*
una banda = a band
la banda larga = broadband

bandiera *noun, feminine*
una bandiera = a flag

barattolo *noun, masculine*
un barattolo = a jar
= a tin, a can

barba *noun, feminine*
- la barba = a beard
- farsi la barba = to shave

barbiere *noun, masculine*
un barbiere = a barber

barbone/barbona *noun,*
masculine/feminine
un barbone/una barbona = a tramp, a bum

barca *noun, feminine* (*plural* **barche**)
- una barca = a boat
- una barca di = loads of

barista *noun, masculine/feminine* (*plural* **baristi/bariste**)
un/una barista = a bartender

barriera *noun, feminine*
una barriera = a barrier

barzelletta *noun, feminine*
una barzelletta = a joke

basato/basata *adjective*
basato su = based on

base *noun, feminine*
una base = a base

basilico *noun, masculine*
il basilico = basil

basso/bassa *adjective*
• = low
• (*when it's a person*) = short

bastardo/bastarda* *noun, masculine/feminine*
un bastardo/una bastarda* = a bastard

bastare *verb* [1] (**!** + *essere*)
• = to be enough
basta così! = that's enough!
basta conoscere qualcuno = you just have to know someone
• basta che = as long as

bastone *noun, masculine*
un bastone = a stick

battaglia *noun, feminine* (*plural* **battaglie**)
una battaglia = a battle

battere *verb* [8]
• = to beat
• = to hit

batteria *noun, feminine*
• una batteria = a battery
• la batteria = the drums

battesimo *noun, masculine*
un battesimo = a christening

baule *noun, masculine*
• un baule = a trunk
• (*of a car*)
il baule = the boot, the trunk

bebè *noun, masculine* (**!** *never changes*)
un bebè = a baby

beccare *verb* [4]
• = to peck
• = to get
= to catch

becco *noun, masculine* (*plural* **becchi**)
il becco = the beak

Befana *noun, feminine*
• Befana = Epiphany (January 6)
• la Befana *an old woman who is supposed to bring presents to children on January 6*

begli, bei, bel ▶ **bello**

belga *adjective* (*plural* **belgi/belghe**)
= Belgian

Belgio *noun, masculine*
il Belgio = Belgium

bellezza *noun, feminine*
la bellezza = beauty

bello/bella *adjective*
! *Before masculine nouns beginning with z, ps, gn, or s + another consonant,* **bello** *is used in the singular and* **begli** *in the plural. Before masculine nouns beginning with other consonants,* **bel** *is used in the singular and* **bei** *in the plural. Before all nouns beginning with a vowel,* **bell'** *is used in the singular and* **begli** *(masculine) or* **belle** *(feminine) in the plural.*
• = beautiful
= good-looking
• = nice
un bel film = a good film
bello caldo = nice and warm

benché *conjunction*
= although

bene
1 *adverb*
= well
stanno bene = they're well
bene! = good!
va bene! = OK!
tutto bene? = is everything OK?
2 *noun, masculine*
i beni = possessions

bensì *conjunction*
= but

bentornato/bentornata *adjective*
bentornato! = welcome back!

benvenuto/benvenuta *adjective*
benvenuto! = welcome!

benzina *noun, feminine*
la benzina = petrol, gas(oline)

bere *verb* [18]
= to drink

berrà, berrò, etc ▶ **bere**

bersaglio *noun, masculine* (*plural* **bersagli**)
un bersaglio = a target

bestemmia *noun, feminine*
una bestemmia = a curse

bestia *noun, feminine*
una bestia = an animal

bevanda *noun, feminine*
una bevanda = a drink

beve, bevuto, bevve, etc ▶ **bere**

biancheria *noun, feminine*
la biancheria = linen
la biancheria intima = underwear

bianco/bianca *adjective* (*plural* **bianchi/bianche**)
= white

Bibbia *noun, feminine*
la Bibbia = the Bible

---

bibita noun, feminine
una bibita = a soft drink

biblioteca noun, feminine (plural biblioteche)
una biblioteca = a library
andare in biblioteca = to go to the library

bicchiere noun, masculine
un bicchiere = a glass
un bicchiere di plastica = a plastic cup

bici (! never changes), **bicicletta** noun, feminine
una bici = a bike
andare in bici = to cycle

bidello/bidella noun, masculine/feminine
un bidello/una bidella = a school caretaker, a janitor

bidone noun, masculine
il bidone dei rifiuti = the rubbish bin, the trashcan
fare il bidone a qualcuno* = to stand someone up

biglietto noun, masculine
• un biglietto = a ticket
• un biglietto = a note, a bill

bilancia noun, feminine (plural bilance)
• una bilancia = scales
• **Bilancia**
  Bilancia = Libra

bilancio noun, masculine (plural bilanci)
un bilancio = a balance

bilingue adjective
= bilingual

bimbo/bimba noun, masculine/feminine
un bimbo/una bimba = a boy/a girl
= a child

binario noun, masculine (plural binari)
un binario = a platform

biografia noun, feminine
una biografia = a biography

biologia noun, feminine
la biologia = biology

biondo/bionda adjective
= blond
= blonde

birichino/birichina adjective
= naughty

birra noun, feminine
una birra = a beer

bis
1 exclamation
bis! = encore!
2 noun, masculine (! never changes)
il bis = an encore

biscotto noun, masculine
un biscotto = a biscuit, a cookie

bisnonno/bisnonna noun, masculine/feminine
il bisnonno/la bisnonna = the great-grandfather/the great-grandmother
i bisnonni = the great-grandparents

bisognare verb [1]
bisogna [andare | aspettare | decidere]
= we/you have to [go | wait | decide]
bisogna che studino = they have to study

bisogno noun, masculine
aver bisogno di = to need
ho bisogno di tempo = I need time
non c'è bisogno che tu gridi = you don't need to shout

bistecca noun, feminine (plural bistecche)
una bistecca = a steak

bloccare verb [4]
1 = to block
2 bloccarsi (! + essere)
= to get stuck

bloccato/bloccata adjective
rimanere bloccato/bloccata = to be stuck

blocco noun, masculine (plural blocchi)
un blocco = a block

bloc-notes noun, masculine (! never changes)
un bloc-notes = a notepad

blu adjective (! never changes)
= blue

bocca noun, feminine (plural bocche)
• la bocca = the mouth
• in bocca al lupo! = good luck!

boccata noun, feminine
una boccata d'aria = a breath of fresh air

bocciare verb [2]
= to fail
= to reject
essere bocciato/bocciata = to fail

boccone noun, masculine
= a mouthful

bolla noun, feminine
una bolla = a bubble

bollente adjective
• = boiling
• = scalding

bolletta noun, feminine
una bolletta = a bill
la bolletta [della luce | del gas | del telefono]
= the [electricity | gas | telephone] bill

bollire verb [10]
= to boil

bollo noun, masculine
un bollo = a stamp

bomba noun, feminine
una bomba = a bomb

bombolone noun, masculine
un bombolone = a doughnut

bontà *noun, feminine*
la bontà = goodness

bordo *noun, masculine*
• il bordo = the edge
• salire a bordo = to go on board

borghese *adjective*
= middle-class

borghesia *noun, feminine*
la borghesia = the middle classes

borotalco *noun, masculine*
il borotalco = talcum powder

borsa *noun, feminine*
• una borsa = a handbag, a purse
= a bag
• **Borsa**
la Borsa = the Stock Exchange

borsaiolo/borsaiola *noun, masculine/feminine*
un borsaiolo/una borsaiola = a pickpocket

borsellino *noun, masculine*
un borsellino = a purse

bosco *noun, masculine (plural **boschi**)*
un bosco = a wood

botanico/botanica
1 *adjective (plural **botanici/botaniche**)*
un giardino/un orto botanico = botanical gardens
2 **botanica** *noun, feminine*
la botanica = botany

botta *noun, feminine*
una botta = a blow

botte *noun, feminine*
una botte = a barrel

bottega *noun, feminine (plural **botteghe**)*
una bottega = a shop

bottiglia *noun, feminine (plural **bottiglie**)*
una bottiglia = a bottle

bottone *noun, masculine*
un bottone = a button

boxe *noun, feminine (**!** never changes)*
la boxe = boxing

braccio *noun, masculine (plural **braccia**)*
> **!** Note that **braccia** is feminine.

il braccio = the arm

brace *noun, feminine*
la brace = embers
alla brace = grilled

brano *noun, masculine*
un brano = a passage

bravo/brava *adjective, exclamation*
= good
bravo a [disegnare | cantare | spiegare]
= good at [drawing | singing | explaining]
bravo/brava! = well done!

breve *adjective*
= short

brezza *noun, feminine*
una brezza = a breeze

briciola *noun, feminine*
una briciola = a crumb

brillante *adjective*
• = shiny
• = brilliant

brillare *verb [1]*
= to shine

brina *noun, feminine*
la brina = frost

brindare *verb [1]*
= to toast

brindisi *noun, masculine (**!** never changes)*
fare un brindisi = to drink a toast

britannico/britannica *adjective (plural **britannici/britanniche**)*
= British

brivido *noun, masculine*
un brivido = a shiver

brocca *noun, feminine (plural **brocche**)*
una brocca = a jug

brodo *noun, masculine*
il brodo = stock
= broth

brontolare *verb [1]*
= to grumble

bronzo *noun, masculine*
il bronzo = bronze

bruciare *verb [2]*
1 (**!** + avere)
• = to burn
• = to be very hot
2 **bruciarsi** (**!** + essere)
bruciarsi = to burn oneself

brufolo *noun, masculine*
un brufolo = a pimple

bruno/bruna *adjective*
= dark

brutto/brutta *adjective*
• = ugly
• = horrible

buca *noun, feminine (plural **buche**)*
una buca = a hole
la buca delle lettere = the postbox, the mailbox

bucare *verb [4]*
= to make a hole in

bucato/bucata
1 *adjective*
= full of holes
2 **bucato** *noun, masculine*
il bucato = the washing

buccia *noun, feminine (plural **bucce**)*
la buccia = the peel
= the skin

buco *noun, masculine (plural **buchi**)*
un buco = a hole

budino *noun, masculine*
un budino = a pudding

bufera *noun, feminine*
una bufera = a storm

buffo/buffa *adjective*
= funny

bugia *noun, feminine (plural **bugie**)*
dire una bugia = to tell a lie

bugiardo/bugiarda
1 *adjective*
= lying
2 *noun, masculine/feminine*
un bugiardo/una bugiarda = a liar

buio/buia
1 *adjective (plural **bui/buie**)*
= dark
2 buio *noun, masculine*
il buio = the dark

buonanotte *exclamation*
buonanotte! = good night!

buonasera *exclamation*
buonasera! = good evening!

buongiorno *exclamation*
buongiorno! = good morning!

buono/buona *adjective*
1 *adjective*

> **!** *Before masculine singular nouns beginning with z, ps, gn, or s + another consonant, **buono** is used. Before masculine singular nouns beginning with other letters, **buon** is used. Before feminine singular nouns beginning with a vowel, **buon'** is used.*

= good
2 buono *noun, masculine*
un buono = a voucher

burattino *noun, masculine*
un burattino = a puppet

burocrazia *noun, feminine*
la burocrazia = bureaucracy

burro *noun, masculine*
il burro = butter

bussare *verb* [1]
= to knock

bussola *noun, feminine*
una bussola = a compass

busta *noun, feminine*
una busta = an envelope
= a bag

bustarella *noun, feminine*
una bustarella = a bribe

bustina *noun, feminine*
una bustina = a bag
= a packet

buttare *verb* [1]
= to throw (out)

Cc

cabina *noun, feminine*
una cabina = a cabin
= a beach hut
una cabina telefonica = a phone box

cacao *noun, masculine*
il cacao = cocoa

caccia *noun, feminine*
la caccia = shooting, hunting
andare a caccia = to go shooting, to go hunting

cacciare *verb* [2]
• *(when it's animals)* = to shoot, to hunt
• *(when it's a person)* = to throw out

cacciatore/cacciatrice *noun, masculine/feminine*
un cacciatore/una cacciatrice = a hunter

cacciavite *noun, masculine*
un cacciavite = a screwdriver

cadavere *noun, masculine*
un cadavere = a corpse

cadde, **caddero**, etc ▶ **cadere**

cadere *verb* [19] (**!** + *essere*)
= to fall
lasciar cadere = to drop

cadrà, **cadrò**, etc ▶ **cadere**

caffè *noun, masculine* (**!** *never changes*)
un caffè = a coffee

calamaro *noun, masculine*
un calamaro = a squid

calamita *noun, feminine*
una calamita = a magnet

calare *verb* [1] (**!** + *essere*)
= to go down

calciatore *noun, masculine*
un calciatore = a footballer, a soccer player

calcio *noun, masculine*
• il calcio = football, soccer
• *(plural **calci**)*
un calcio = a kick

calcolare *verb* [1]
= to calculate

calcolatrice *noun, feminine*
una calcolatrice = a calculator

calcolo *noun, masculine*
un calcolo = a calculation

caldaia *noun, feminine*
una caldaia = a boiler

caldo/calda
1 *adjective*
= hot
= warm
2 caldo *noun, masculine*
il caldo = the heat
aver caldo = to be hot
far caldo = to be hot

calendario *noun, masculine* (*plural* **calendari**)
un calendario = a calendar

calma *noun, feminine*
la calma = calm
mantenere la calma = to stay calm

calmare *verb* [1]
1 = to calm
2 calmarsi (**!** + *essere*)
calmarsi = to calm down

calmo/calma *adjective*
= calm

calo *noun, masculine*
un calo = a drop

calore *noun, masculine*
il calore = heat
= warmth

caloria *noun, feminine*
una caloria = a calorie

calvo/calva *adjective*
= bald

calza *noun, feminine*
le calze = stockings
= tights, pantyhose

calzino *noun, masculine*
un calzino = a sock

cambiamento *noun, masculine*
un cambiamento = a change
il cambiamento climatico = climate change

cambiare *verb* [6] (**!** + *essere* or *avere*)
1 = to change
cambiare casa = to move house
2 cambiarsi (**!** + *essere*)
cambiarsi = to get changed

cambio *noun, masculine*
• il cambio = the exchange
• il tasso di cambio = the rate of exchange

camera *noun, feminine*
una camera = a room
= a bedroom

cameriere/cameriera *noun,*
masculine/feminine
un cameriere/una cameriera = a waiter/a waitress

camicetta *noun, feminine*
una camicetta = a blouse

camicia *noun, feminine* (*plural* **camicie**)
una camicia = a shirt

camion *noun, masculine* (**!** *never changes*)
un camion = a lorry, a truck

camionista *noun, masculine/feminine*
(*plural* **camionisti/camioniste**)
un/una camionista = a lorry driver, a trucker

camminare *verb* [1]
= to walk

campagna *noun, feminine*
• la campagna = the countryside
in campagna = in the country
• una campagna = a campaign

campana *noun, feminine*
una campana = a bell

campanello *noun, masculine*
un campanello = a bell
suonare il campanello = to ring the bell

campeggio *noun, masculine* (*plural* **campeggi**)
un campeggio = a campsite, a campground
andare in campeggio = to go camping

campionato *noun, masculine*
il campionato = the championship

campione/campionessa *noun,*
masculine/feminine
il campione/la campionessa = the champion

campo *noun, masculine*
• un campo = a field
• un campo di calcio = a football pitch, a soccer field

canadese *adjective*
= Canadian

canale *noun, masculine*
• un canale = a channel
• un canale = a canal

cancellare *verb* [1]
= to erase

cancelletto *noun, masculine*
un cancelletto = a hash sign

cancello *noun, masculine*
un cancello = a gate

cancro *noun, masculine*
1 il cancro = cancer
avere un cancro = to have cancer
2 Cancro
Cancro = Cancer

candela *noun, feminine*
una candela = a candle

candidato/candidata *noun,*
masculine/feminine
un candidato/una candidata = a candidate

cane *noun, masculine*
un cane = a dog

canestro *noun, masculine*
un canestro = a basket

cannuccia *noun, feminine* (*plural* **cannucce**)
una cannuccia = a straw

canoa *noun, feminine*
una canoa = a canoe

canottaggio *noun, masculine*
il canottaggio = rowing

canottiera *noun, feminine*
una canottiera = a vest, an undershirt

canotto *noun, masculine*
un canotto = a dinghy

cantante *noun, masculine/feminine*
un/una cantante = a singer

cantare *verb* [1]
= to sing

cantiere *noun, masculine*
un cantiere = a building site

cantina *noun, feminine*
la cantina = the cellar

canto *noun, masculine*
il canto = singing

cantone *noun, masculine*
un cantone = a canton

canzone *noun, feminine*
una canzone = a song

caos *noun, masculine*
il caos = chaos

caotico/caotica *adjective* (*plural* **caotici/caotiche**)
= chaotic

capace *adjective*
capace di = capable of

capacità *noun, feminine* (**!** *never changes*)
la capacità = the ability

capello *noun, masculine*
un capello = a hair
i capelli = the hair
ha i capelli neri = she has black hair

capire *verb* [9]
= to understand
ho capito = I see
capito? = you see?

capitale *noun, feminine*
una capitale = a capital

capitano *noun, masculine*
il capitano = the captain

capitare *verb* [1] (**!** + *essere*)
= to turn up
= to happen

capito ▶ **capire**

capitolo *noun, masculine*
un capitolo = a chapter

capo *noun, masculine*
• il capo = the boss
• il capo = the head

capodanno *noun, masculine*
= New Year's (Day)

capolavoro *noun, masculine*
un capolavoro = a masterpiece

cappella *noun, feminine*
una cappella = a chapel

cappello *noun, masculine*
un cappello = a hat

cappotto *noun, masculine*
un cappotto = a coat

cappuccio *noun, masculine* (*plural* **cappucci**)
un cappuccio = a hood

capra *noun, feminine*
una capra = a goat

capriccio *noun, masculine* (*plural* **capricci**)
• un capriccio = a whim
• fare i capricci = to be naughty

Capricorno *noun, masculine*
= Capricorn

carabiniere *noun, masculine*
un carabiniere = a policeman

caramella *noun, feminine*
una caramella = a sweet, a candy

carattere *noun, masculine*
il carattere = the character

caratteristica *noun, feminine* (*plural* **caratteristiche**)
una caratteristica = a characteristic

carbone *noun, masculine*
il carbone = coal

carcere *noun, masculine*
un carcere = a prison

carciofo *noun, masculine*
un carciofo = an artichoke

caricare *verb* [4]
• = to load
• = to charge

carico/carica *adjective* (*plural* **carichi/cariche**)
• = loaded
• = charged

carino/carina *adjective*
= nice

carne *noun, feminine*
la carne = meat

carnevale *noun, masculine*
il carnevale = carnival

caro/cara *adjective*
- = dear
  caro Flavio = dear Flavio
- = expensive

carota *noun, feminine*
  una carota = a carrot

carrello *noun, masculine*
  un carrello = a trolley, a cart

carriera *noun, feminine*
  una carriera = a career

carrozzina *noun, feminine*
  una carrozzina = a pram, a baby carriage

carta *noun, feminine*
- la carta = paper
- una carta = a card
- una carta = a map
  una carta di credito = a credit card
  una carta fedeltà = a loyalty card
  una carta d'identità = an identity card
  la carta igienica = toilet paper
  una carta SIM = a SIM card

cartello *noun, masculine*
  un cartello = a sign

cartoleria *noun, feminine*
  una cartoleria = a stationer's, an office
    supply store

cartolina *noun, feminine*
  una cartolina = a postcard

cartone *noun, masculine*
- il cartone = cardboard
- un cartone = a carton
  un cartone animato = a cartoon

casa *noun, feminine*
  una casa = a house
  a casa = at home
  andare a casa = to go home

casalinga *noun, feminine (plural*
  casalinghe)
  una casalinga = a housewife

cascare *verb* [4] (**!** + *essere*)
  = to fall

casco *noun, masculine (plural* **caschi)**
  un casco = a helmet

caserma *noun, feminine*
  una caserma = barracks

casino *noun, masculine*
- un casino = a mess
  che casino! = what a mess!
- un casino = a racket

casinò *noun, masculine* (**!** *never*
  changes)
  un casinò = a casino

caso *noun, masculine*
  un caso = a case
  a caso = at random
  per caso = by chance

---

cassa *noun, feminine*
- una cassa = a crate
- la cassa
  (*in a supermarket*) = the checkout
  (*in a bank*) = the cashier's desk
- una cassa = a speaker

cassaforte *noun, feminine*
  una cassaforte = a safe

casseruola *noun, feminine*
  una casseruola = a saucepan

cassetta *noun, feminine*
  una cassetta = a cassette
  la cassetta delle lettere = the letter box,
    the mailbox

cassetto *noun, masculine*
  un cassetto = a drawer

castagna *noun, feminine*
  una castagna = a chestnut

castano/castana *adjective*
  = brown

castello *noun, masculine*
  un castello = a castle

casuale *adjective*
  = chance

catalogo *noun, masculine (plural*
  cataloghi)
  un catalogo = a catalog(ue)

catasto *noun, masculine*
  il catasto = the land registry

catastrofe *noun, feminine*
  una catastrofe = a catastrophe

categoria *noun, feminine*
  una categoria = a category

catena *noun, feminine*
  una catena = a chain

cattedra *noun, feminine*
  la cattedra = the teacher's desk

cattedrale *noun, feminine*
  la cattedrale = the cathedral

cattivo/cattiva *adjective*
- = bad

cattolico/cattolica *adjective (plural*
  cattolici/cattoliche)
  = Catholic

catturare *verb* [1]
  = to capture

causa *noun, feminine*
  una causa = a cause

causare *verb* [1]
  = to cause

cautela *noun, feminine*
  la cautela = caution

cauto/cauta *adjective*
  = cautious

cava *noun, feminine*
  una cava = a quarry

---

cavallo *noun, masculine*
un cavallo = a horse

cavarsela *verb* [1] (**!** + *essere*)
= to get on
= to get by
me la cavo bene = I'm getting on well

cavatappi *noun, masculine*
un cavatappi = a corkscrew

caviglia *noun, feminine*
la caviglia = the ankle

cavo/cava *adjective*
= hollow

cavolfiore *noun, masculine*
il cavolfiore = cauliflower

cavolo *noun, masculine*
• un cavolo = a cabbage
• che cavolo vuoi?✶ = what the heck do
  you want?

cazzo *exclamation*
che cazzo vuoi?✶ = what the hell do you
want?

cella *noun, feminine*
una cella = a cell

cellula *noun, feminine*
una cellula = a cell

cellulare *noun, masculine*
un cellulare = a mobile phone, a cellular
phone

cemento *noun, masculine*
il cemento = cement

cena *noun, feminine*
la cena = dinner

cenere *noun, feminine*
la cenere = the ash

cent *noun, masculine*
un cent = a cent

centesimo/centesima
1 *adjective*
= hundredth
2 centesimo *noun, masculine*
un centesimo = a cent

centimetro *noun, masculine*
un centimetro = a centimetre, a
centimeter

centinaio *noun, masculine* (*plural*
centinaia)

> **!** *Note that* **centinaia** *is feminine.*

un centinaio = about a hundred
centinaia di persone = hundreds of
people

cento *number*
= a hundred

centrale *adjective*
= central

centralino *noun, masculine*
il centralino = the switchboard

centro *noun, masculine*
il centro = the centre, the center
un centro benessere = a wellness
centre, center

cera *noun, feminine*
la cera = wax

cerca *noun, feminine*
in cerca di = in search of

cercare *verb* [4]
• = to look for
• cercare di fare qualcosa = to try to do
  something

cerchio *noun, masculine* (*plural* **cerchi**)
un cerchio = a circle

cerimonia *noun, feminine*
una cerimonia = a ceremony

cerotto *noun, masculine*
un cerotto = a plaster, a Band-Aid®

certamente *adverb*
= certainly

certezza *noun, feminine*
la certezza = certainty

certificato *noun, masculine*
un certificato = a certificate

certo/certa *adjective*
• = certain
• certo! = sure!

cervello *noun, masculine*
il cervello = the brain

cespuglio *noun, masculine* (*plural*
cespugli)
un cespuglio = a bush

cessare *verb* [1] (**!** + *essere* or *avere*)
= to cease

cestino *noun, masculine*
• un cestino = a basket
• un cestino = a waste-paper basket, a
  wastebasket

cesto *noun, masculine*
un cesto = a basket

chattare *verb*
(*on the Internet*) = to chat

che
1 *pronoun*
• (*in questions*) = what
  che fai? = what are you doing?
• (*in relative clauses*) = who
  = which
  = that
  la macchina che ho comprato = the car I
  bought
2 *conjunction*
= that
mi ha detto che non viene = he told me
he's not coming

chi *pronoun*
• = who
  chi è? = who is it?   ····▶

di chi sono queste scarpe? = whose shoes are these?
- = anyone who
  ci saranno problemi per chi deve viaggiare = there will be problems for anyone who has to travel

chiacchierare verb [1]
= to chat

chiacchierata noun, feminine
una chiacchierata = a chat

chiacchierone/chiacchierona adjective
= talkative

chiamare verb [1]
1 = to call
2 **chiamarsi** (! + essere)
chiamarsi = to be called
come ti chiami? = what's your name?
mi chiamo Elisa = my name's Elisa

chiamata noun, feminine
una chiamata = a call

chiaramente adverb
= clearly
= obviously

chiarezza noun, feminine
la chiarezza = clarity

chiarire verb [9]
= to clarify

chiaro/chiara adjective
- = clear
  è chiaro? = is that clear?
- = light
  verde chiaro = light green

chiasso noun, masculine
un chiasso = a din

chiave noun, feminine
una chiave = a key

chicco noun, masculine (plural **chicchi**)
un chicco di riso = a grain of rice
un chicco di caffè = a coffee bean
un chicco d'uva = a grape

chiedere verb [20]
1 (! + avere)
= to ask
chiedere il conto = to ask for the bill
chiedere a qualcuno di fare qualcosa = to ask someone to do something
chiedere di qualcuno = to ask about someone
2 **chiedersi** (! + essere)
chiedersi = to wonder

chiesa noun, feminine
una chiesa = a church

chiese, chiesto/chiesta, etc ▶ chiedere

chilo, chilogrammo noun, masculine
un chilo = a kilo

chilometro noun, masculine
un chilometro = a kilometre, a kilometer

chimica noun, feminine
la chimica = chemistry

chimico/chimica (plural **chimici/ chimiche**)
1 adjective
= chemical
2 noun, masculine/feminine
un chimico/una chimica = a chemist

chiocciola noun, feminine
- **una chiocciola** = a snail
- **una chiocciola** = an at sign

chiodo noun, masculine
un chiodo = a nail

chirurgia noun, feminine
la chirurgia = surgery

chirurgo noun, masculine (plural **chirurghi**)
un chirurgo = a surgeon

chissà adverb
= who knows

chitarra noun, feminine
una chitarra = a guitar

chiudere verb [21]
1 = to close, to shut
2 **chiudersi** (! + essere)
= to close, to shut

chiunque pronoun
= anyone

chiuse, chiusero, etc ▶ chiudere

chiuso/chiusa
1 ▶ chiudere
2 adjective
= closed, shut

ci (**ce** before lo/la, li/le, and ne)
1 pronoun
- = us
  = to us
  ci hanno visto = they've seen us
  vuole conoscerci = he wants to meet us
- = to it
  ci penso = I'll think about it
2 adverb
= here
= there
non ci vado = I'm not going
Flavio c'è? = is Flavio there?
c'è molto da fare = there's a lot to do
ce n'erano troppi = there were too many of them

ciao exclamation
- (when arriving)
  ciao! = hi!
- (when leaving)
  ciao! = bye!

ciascuno/ciascuna adjective, pronoun

> ! Note that before masculine nouns beginning with z, ps, gn, or s + another consonant **ciascuno** is used. **Ciascun** is used before all other masculine nouns.

····▶

= each
ciascuno di voi = each one of you

cibo *noun, masculine*
il cibo = food

cicatrice *noun, feminine*
una cicatrice = a scar

ciclismo *noun, masculine*
il ciclismo = cycling

cieco/cieca *adjective (plural **ciechi/cieche**)*
= blind

cielo *noun, masculine*
• il cielo = the sky
• il cielo = heaven

cifra *noun, feminine*
una cifra = a figure

ciglio *noun, masculine (plural **ciglia**)*
> **!** Note that **ciglia** is feminine.

il ciglio = the eyelash

ciliegia *noun, feminine (plural **ciliege**)*
una ciliegia = a cherry

cima *noun, feminine*
la cima = the top

cimitero *noun, masculine*
un cimitero = a cemetery

Cina *noun, feminine*
la Cina = China

cincin *exclamation*
cincin! = cheers!

cinema *noun, masculine*
il cinema = the cinema, the movie theater

cinese *adjective*
= Chinese

cinghiale *noun, masculine*
un cinghiale = a wild boar

cinico/cinica *adjective (plural **cinici/ciniche**)*
= cynical

cinquanta *number*
= fifty

cinquantesimo/cinquantesima *adjective*
= fiftieth

cinquantina *noun, feminine*
una cinquantina di chili = about fifty kilos

cinque *number*
= five

cinquecento
1 *number*
= five hundred
2 **Cinquecento** *noun, masculine*
il Cinquecento = the 16th century

cintura *noun, feminine*
una cintura = a belt
una cintura di sicurezza = a seat belt

ciò *pronoun*
= this
= that
ciò che fai non è giusto = what you're doing isn't right

cioccolata *noun, feminine,*
cioccolato *noun, masculine*
la cioccolata = chocolate

cioccolatino *noun, masculine*
un cioccolatino = a chocolate

cioè *conjunction*
= that is
= I mean

cipolla *noun, feminine*
una cipolla = an onion

circa *adverb*
= about, around

circo *noun, masculine (plural **circhi**)*
il circo = the circus

circolare
1 *adjective*
= circular
2 *verb* [1]
= to circulate

circondato/circondata *adjective*
circondato/circondata da = surrounded by

circostanza *noun, feminine*
una circostanza = a circumstance

citare *verb* [1]
= to quote

citazione *noun, feminine*
una citazione = a quotation

citofono *noun, masculine*
un citofono = an entry phone

città *noun, feminine (**!** never changes)*
una città = a town
= a city

cittadinanza *noun, feminine*
la cittadinanza = citizenship

cittadino/cittadina *noun, masculine/feminine*
un cittadino/una cittadina = a citizen

civile *adjective*
= civilized

civiltà *noun, feminine (**!** never changes)*
la civiltà = civilization

clacson *noun, masculine (**!** never changes)*
il clacson = the horn

clamoroso/clamorosa *adjective*
= outrageous

clandestino/clandestina *noun, masculine/feminine*
un clandestino/una clandestina = an illegal immigrant

classe noun, feminine
- una classe = a class, a grade
- una classe = a classroom

classico/classica adjective (plural **classici/classiche**)
= classic
= classical

cliccare verb
= to click

cliente noun, masculine|feminine
un/una cliente = a customer

clima noun, masculine
il clima = the climate

climatizzato/climatizzata adjective
= air-conditioned

clinica noun, feminine (plural **cliniche**)
una clinica = a clinic

cocco noun, masculine
il cocco = coconut
una noce di cocco = a coconut

coccodrillo noun, masculine
un coccodrillo = a crocodile

coccolare verb [1]
= to hug

cocomero noun, masculine
un cocomero = a water melon

coda noun, feminine
- la coda = the tail
- una coda = a queue, a line

codice noun, masculine
un codice = a code

coetaneo/coetanea adjective
sono coetanei = they're the same age

cofano noun, masculine
il cofano = the bonnet, the hood

cogli ▶ con

cogliere verb [22]
= to pick

coglioni◆ noun, masculine plural
i coglioni = balls

cognato/cognata noun, masculine|feminine
il cognato/la cognata = the brother-in-law/the sister-in-law

cognome noun, masculine
un cognome = a surname

coi ▶ con

coincidenza noun, feminine
- una coincidenza = a coincidence
- (on the train)
  una coincidenza = a connection

coinvolgere verb [59]
= to involve

coinvolse, coinvolto/coinvolta, etc ▶ coinvolgere

◆ may be considered offensive

col ▶ con

colare verb [1] (**!** + essere)
= to drip

colazione noun, feminine
la colazione = breakfast
fare colazione = to have breakfast

colgo, colgono, etc ▶ cogliere

colino noun, masculine
un colino = a strainer

colla ▶ con

colla noun, feminine
la colla = glue

collaborazione noun, feminine
la collaborazione = collaboration

collana noun, feminine
una collana = a necklace

collant noun, masculine
i collant = tights, pantyhose

collasso noun, masculine
un collasso = a collapse

colle ▶ con

collega noun, masculine|feminine (plural **colleghi/colleghe**)
un/una collega = a colleague

collegamento noun, masculine
un collegamento = a connection

collegare verb [5]
= to link
essere collegato/collegata a = to be linked to

colletto noun, masculine
un colletto = a collar

collezionare verb [1]
= to collect

collezione noun, feminine
una collezione = a collection

collina noun, feminine
una collina = a hill

collo ▶ con

collo noun, masculine
il collo = the neck

colloquio noun, masculine (plural **colloqui**)
un colloquio di lavoro = a job interview

colomba noun, feminine
una colomba = a dove

colonia noun, feminine
una colonia = a colony

colonna noun, feminine
una colonna = a column

colorare verb [1]
= to colo(u)r (in)

colorato/colorata adjective
= colo(u)red

colore *noun, masculine*
un colore = a colo(u)r

colpa *noun, feminine*
• la colpa = the blame
dare la colpa a qualcuno = to blame
someone
• è colpa tua = it's your fault

colpevole *adjective*
= guilty

colpire *verb* 9
= to hit
= to strike

colpo *noun, masculine*
un colpo = a blow
un colpo di fortuna = a stroke of luck
un colpo di telefono = a phone call

colsi, colse, etc ▶ **cogliere**

coltello *noun, masculine*
un coltello = a knife

colto/colta
1 ▶ cogliere
2 *adjective*
= cultured

combattere *verb* 8
= to fight

combinazione *noun, feminine*
una combinazione = a combination

come

> **!** *Note that before* è, era, *etc* com' *is used.*

1 *adverb*
• (*in questions*) = how
come si dice 'pizza' in inglese? = how do
you say 'pizza' in English?
come stai? = how are you?
com'è la casa? = what is the house like?
come? = what?
• (*in exclamations*)
com'è freddo! = it's so cold!
2 *conjunction*
(*in comparisons*) = like
= as
era come un sogno = it was like a dream
come sai = as you know
lavoro come barista = I work as a
bartender
come sempre = as usual

comico/comica *adjective* (*plural*
comici/comiche)
= funny
un film comico = a comedy

cominciare *verb* 2 (**!** + *essere* or
avere)
= to start
il film è cominciato = the film has started
cominciare a fare qualcosa = to start
doing something

commedia *noun, feminine*
una commedia = a play

commento *noun, masculine*
un commento = a comment

commerciale *adjective*
= commercial

commercialista *noun,*
masculine/feminine (*plural*
commercialisti/commercialiste)
un/una commercialista = an accountant

commercio *noun, masculine*
il commercio = trade

commesso/commessa
1 ▶ commettere
2 *noun, masculine/feminine*
un commesso/una commessa = a shop
assistant, a salesclerk

commestibile *adjective*
= edible

commettere *verb* 40
= to commit

commise, commisero, etc ▶
commettere

commissione *noun, feminine*
la commissione = commission

comò *noun, masculine* (**!** *never changes*)
un comò = a chest of drawers

comodo/comoda *adjective*
• = comfortable
• = convenient

compagnia *noun, feminine*
• una compagnia = a company
• fare compagnia a qualcuno = to keep
someone company

compagno/compagna *noun,*
masculine/feminine
un compagno/una compagna = a
companion
un compagno di classe = a classmate

compaio, compaiono, etc ▶
comparire

comparire *verb* 14 (**!** + *essere*)
= to appear

comparso/comparsa, comparve,
etc ▶ **comparire**

competente *adjective*
= competent

competizione *noun, feminine*
una competizione = a competition

compito *noun, masculine*
• un compito = a task
= a duty
• un compito in classe = a class test
i compiti = homework

compleanno *noun, masculine*
un compleanno = a birthday
buon compleanno! = happy birthday!

complessivo/complessiva
adjective
= total

complesso/complessa *adjective*
= complex

completamente *adverb*
= completely

completare *verb* [1]
= to complete

completo/completa *adjective*
• = complete
• = full up

complicato/complicata *adjective*
= complicated

complicazione *noun, feminine*
una complicazione = a complication

complimento *noun, masculine*
un complimento = a compliment

compongo, compone, etc ▶
comporre

comporre *verb* [50]
• = to compose
• (*using the telephone*) = to dial

comportamento *noun, masculine*
il comportamento = the behavio(u)r

comportarsi *verb* [1] (**!** + *essere*)
= to behave
comportati bene! = behave yourself!

compose, composi, etc ▶
comporre

compositore/compositrice *noun,*
masculine/feminine
un compositore/una compositrice = a
composer

composizione *noun, feminine*
una composizione = a composition

composto/composta
1 ▶ comporre
2 *adjective*
= compound

comprare *verb* [1]
= to buy

comprendere *verb* [53]
• = to include
• = to understand

comprensibile *adjective*
= understandable

comprensione *noun, feminine*
la comprensione = understanding

comprensivo/comprensiva
adjective
= understanding

comprese, compresi, etc ▶
comprendere

compreso/compresa
1 ▶ comprendere
2 *adjective*
= including

compromesso *noun, masculine*
un compromesso = a compromise

comunale *adjective*
= council
= municipal
il consiglio comunale = the town council

comune
1 *adjective*
= common
2 *noun, masculine*
il comune = the town council
= the town hall

comunicare *verb* [4]
= to communicate

comunicazione *noun, feminine*
la comunicazione = communication

comunione *noun, feminine*
la comunione = (first) communion

comunista *adjective* (*plural*
comunisti/comuniste)
= communist

comunità *noun, feminine* (**!** *never*
changes)
una comunità = a community

comunque
1 *adverb*
= anyway
2 *conjunction*
= however

con *preposition*
= with

> **!** Note that **con** sometimes combines
> with **il, la**, etc. Con + il = col; con + l'
> = coll'; con + lo = collo; con + i = coi;
> con + gli = cogli; con + la = colla;
> con + le = colle.

concentrarsi *verb* [1] (**!** + *essere*)
= to concentrate

concentrato/concentrata
1 *adjective*
• = concentrated
• = immersed
2 **concentrato** *noun, masculine*
il concentrato di pomodoro = tomato
purée

concentrazione *noun, feminine*
la concentrazione = concentration

concepire *verb* [9]
• = to conceive
• = to understand

concerto *noun, masculine*
un concerto = a concert

concessionaria *noun, feminine*
una concessionaria = a dealer

concetto *noun, masculine*
un concetto = a concept

conchiglia *noun, feminine*
una conchiglia = a shell

concludere *verb* 21
1 = to conclude
= to achieve
2 **concludersi** (**!** + *essere*)
concludersi = to end

concluse, **conclusi**, **etc** ▶
concludere

conclusione *noun, feminine*
una conclusione = a conclusion

concluso/conclusa ▶ concludere

concorrente *noun, masculine/feminine*
un/una concorrente = a competitor

concorrenza *noun, feminine*
la concorrenza = the competition

concorso *noun, masculine*
un concorso = a competition

concreto/concreta *adjective*
= concrete

condanna *noun, feminine*
una condanna = a sentence

condire *verb* 9
= to season
condire l'insalata = to dress the salad

condizione *noun, feminine*
una condizione = a condition

condominio *noun, masculine* (*plural* **condomini**)
un condominio = a block of flats, an apartment building

condotta *noun, feminine*
la condotta = conduct

condotto/condotta, **conduce**, **etc** ▶ condurre

condurre *verb* 54
• = to lead
• = to conduct

condusse, **condussi**, **etc** ▶
condurre

conferenza *noun, feminine*
• una conferenza = a lecture
• una conferenza = a conference
una conferenza stampa = a press conference

conferma *noun, feminine*
una conferma = a confirmation

confermare *verb* 1
= to confirm

confessare *verb* 1
= to confess

confessione *noun, feminine*
una confessione = a confession

confetto *noun, masculine*
un confetto = a sugared almond

conficcare *verb* 4
= to drive

confidare *verb* 1
= to confide

confidenza *noun, feminine*
una confidenza = a secret

confine *noun, masculine*
un confine = a border

conflitto *noun, masculine*
un conflitto = a conflict

confondere *verb* 24
1 = to confuse
2 **confondersi** (**!** + *essere*)
confondersi = to get confused

confrontare *verb* 1
= to compare

confronto *noun, masculine*
un confronto = a comparison

confuse, **confusi**, **etc** ▶
confondere

confusione *noun, feminine*
• la confusione = confusion
• una confusione = a mess
= a racket

confuso/confusa
1 ▶ confondere
2 *adjective*
• = confused
• = confusing

congelato/congelata *adjective*
= frozen

congelatore *noun, masculine*
il congelatore = the freezer

congratulazioni *exclamation*
congratulazioni! = congratulations!

congresso *noun, masculine*
un congresso = a conference

coniglio *noun, masculine* (*plural* **conigli**)
un coniglio = a rabbit

cono *noun, masculine*
un cono = a cone

conobbe, **conobbi**, **etc** ▶
conoscere

conoscenza *noun, feminine*
la conoscenza = knowledge

conoscere *verb* 25
• = to know
• = to meet

conosciuto/conosciuta
1 ▶ conoscere
2 *adjective*
= well-known

conquista *noun, feminine*
una conquista = a conquest

conquistare verb [1]
= to conquer

consapevole adjective
consapevole di = aware of

consegna noun, feminine
una consegna = a delivery

consegnare verb [1]
= to deliver

conseguenza noun, feminine
una conseguenza = a consequence

consentire verb [10]
= to consent

conservante noun, masculine
un conservante = a preservative

conservare verb [1]
= to keep

conservatore/conservatrice
adjective
= conservative

conservatorio noun, masculine (plural
conservatori)
un conservatorio = a music school

considerare verb [1]
= to consider

considerazione noun, feminine
la considerazione = consideration
prendere qualcosa in considerazione = to
take something into consideration

consigliare verb [6]
• consigliare a qualcuno di fare qualcosa
= to advise someone to do something
• = to recommend

consiglio noun, masculine (plural
consigli)
un consiglio = a piece of advice
dei consigli = some advice

consistere verb [16] (! + essere)
consistere di/in = to consist of

consolato noun, masculine
un consolato = a consulate

consonante noun, feminine
una consonante = a consonant

consulente noun, masculine/feminine
un/una consulente = a consultant

consultare verb [1]
= to consult

consumare verb [1]
• = to consume
= to use up
• = to wear out

consumatore/consumatrice noun,
masculine/feminine
un consumatore/una consumatrice = a
consumer

contabile noun, masculine/feminine
un/una contabile = an accountant

contabilità noun, feminine
la contabilità = accountancy

contadino/contadina noun,
masculine/feminine
un contadino/una contadina = a peasant

contaminare verb [1]
= to contaminate

contanti noun, masculine plural
i contanti = cash

contare verb [1]
= to count

contattare verb [1]
= to contact

contatto noun, masculine
il contatto = contact
mettersi in contatto con qualcuno = to
get in touch with someone

contemporaneo/contemporanea
adjective
= contemporary

contenere verb [73]
= to contain

contengo, contengono, etc ▶
contenere

contenitore noun, masculine
un contenitore = a container

contento/contenta adjective
= pleased

contenuto/contenuta
1 ▶ contenere
2 contenuto noun, masculine
il contenuto = the content

contesto noun, masculine
il contesto = the context

contiene, contieni, etc ▶
contenere

continente noun, masculine
un continente = a continent

continuare verb [1] (! + essere or
avere)
= to continue
= to carry on

continuazione noun, feminine
la continuazione = the continuation
in continuazione = constantly

continuo/continua adjective
= continuous
= continual

conto noun, masculine
• il conto = the bill
• un conto = an account
• un conto = a calculation
• rendersi conto di qualcosa = to realize
something

contorno noun, masculine
un contorno = a side dish

contrabbando *noun, masculine*
  il contrabbando = smuggling

contraccettivo *noun, masculine*
  un contraccettivo = a contraceptive

contraddizione *noun, feminine*
  una contraddizione = a contradiction

contrae, contraggo, etc ▶
  contrarre

contrario/contraria (*plural* **contrari/
  contrarie**)
  1 *adjective*
  = opposite
  2 **contrario** *noun, masculine*
  il contrario = the opposite

contrarre *verb* 74
  1 = to contract
  2 **contrarsi** (**!** + *essere*)
  = to contract

contrasse, contrassero, etc ▶
  contrarre

contrasto *noun, masculine*
  un contrasto = a contrast

contratto/contratta
  1 ▶ contrarre
  2 **contratto** *noun, masculine*
  un contratto = a contract

contribuente *noun, masculine/feminine*
  un/una contribuente = a taxpayer

contribuire *verb* 9
  = to contribute

contributo *noun, masculine*
  un contributo = a contribution

contro *preposition*
  = against

controllare *verb* 1
  = to check

controllo *noun, masculine*
  un controllo = a check

controllore *noun, masculine*
  un controllore = a ticket inspector

convegno *noun, masculine*
  un convegno = a conference

convenga, convengono, etc ▶
  convenire

conveniente *adjective*
  = cheap

convenire *verb* 78 (**!** + *essere*)
  • conviene aspettare = it's best to wait
    ti conviene non dire niente = you'd better
    not say anything
  • = to be cheaper

convento *noun, masculine*
  un convento = a convent

conversazione *noun, feminine*
  una conversazione = a conversation

conviene, convieni ▶ convenire

convincere *verb* 79
  = to convince
  convincere qualcuno a fare qualcosa = to
    persuade someone to do something

convinse, convinsi, etc ▶
  convincere

convinto/convinta
  1 ▶ convincere
  2 *adjective*
  essere convinto/convinta = to be sure

coperchio *noun, masculine* (*plural*
  coperchi)
  un coperchio = a lid

coperta *noun, feminine*
  una coperta = a blanket

copertina *noun, feminine*
  una copertina = a cover

coperto/coperta
  1 ▶ coprire
  2 *adjective*
  • coperto/coperta di neve = covered with
    snow

copertura di rete *noun, feminine*
  (*of mobile phone network*) = coverage

copia *noun, feminine*
  una copia = a copy

copiare *verb* 6
  = to copy

coppa *noun, feminine*
  • la coppa = the cup

coppia *noun, feminine*
  una coppia = a couple

coprire *verb* 15
  = to cover

coque *noun, feminine*
  un uovo alla coque = a soft-boiled egg

coraggio *noun, masculine*
  il coraggio = courage

coraggioso/coraggiosa *adjective*
  = brave

corallo *noun, masculine*
  il corallo = coral

corda *noun, feminine*
  una corda = a rope

corna ▶ corno

cornetta *noun, feminine*
  la cornetta = the receiver

cornice *noun, feminine*
  una cornice = a frame

corno *noun, masculine*
  un corno = a horn

  > **!** When **corno** refers to the horns of an
  > animal the plural is **corna** (*feminine*).

corona *noun, feminine*
  una corona = a crown

corpo *noun, masculine*
  un corpo = a body

correggere *verb* 39
  = to correct

corrente
1 *adjective*
  • = current
  • = fluent
2 *noun, feminine*
  una corrente = a current
  una corrente d'aria = a draught, a draft

correre *verb* 26 (**!** + *essere* or *avere*)
  = to run

corresse, corressi, etc ▶
  correggere

corretto/corretta
1 ▶ **correggere**
2 *adjective*
  = correct

correzione *noun, feminine*
  una correzione = a correction

corridoio *noun, masculine (plural*
  corridoi)
  un corridoio = a corridor

corrotto/corrotta *adjective*
  = corrupt

corruzione *noun, feminine*
  la corruzione = corruption

corsa *noun, feminine*
  una corsa = a race
  di corsa = quickly

corse, corsi, etc ▶ **correre**

corsia *noun, feminine*
  una corsia = a lane

corso/corsa
1 ▶ **correre**
2 **corso** *noun, masculine*
  un corso = a course

corte *noun, feminine*
  una corte = a court

cortese *adjective*
  = polite

cortesia *noun, feminine*
  una cortesia = a favo(u)r
  per cortesia = please

cortile *noun, masculine*
  un cortile = a yard

corto/corta *adjective*
  = short

cosa
1 *noun, feminine*
  una cosa = a thing
  dove sono le mie cose? = where are my
    things?
2 *pronoun*
  = what

(che) cosa è successo? = what
  happened?

coscia *noun, feminine (plural **cosce**)*
  • (*of a person*)
    la coscia = the thigh
  • (*of a chicken*)
    una coscia = a leg

coscienza *noun, feminine*
  la coscienza = the conscience

così
1 *adverb*
  • = like this
    = like that
    fallo così = do it like this
  • = so
    così grande = so big
    un film così lungo = such a long film
2 *conjunction*
  = so
  ho fatto tardi e così ho perso l'inizio del
    film = I was late so I missed the
    beginning of the film

cosiddetto/cosiddetta *adjective*
  = so-called

coso/cosa *noun, masculine/feminine*
  ho parlato con coso/cosa = I spoke to
    what's-his-name/what's-her-name

cosse, cossi, etc ▶ **cuocere**

costa *noun, feminine*
  la costa = the coast

costante *adjective*
  = constant

costare *verb* 1 (**!** + *essere*)
  = to cost

costo *noun, masculine*
  il costo = the cost

costola *noun, feminine*
  una costola = a rib

costoletta *noun, feminine*
  una costoletta = a cutlet

costoso/costosa *adjective*
  = expensive

costretto/costretta ▶ **costringere**

costringere *verb* 71
  costringere qualcuno a fare qualcosa
    = to force someone to do something
  fui costretto a fermarmi = I had to stop

costrinse, costrinsi, etc ▶
  costringere

costruire *verb* 9
  = to build

costume *noun, masculine*
  • un costume = a costume
  • un costume = a custom

cotoletta *noun, feminine*
  una cotoletta = a chop, a cutlet

cotone *noun, masculine*
  il cotone = cotton

cotto/cotta
1 ▶ **cuocere**
2 *adjective*
 = ready

cottura *noun, feminine*
 la cottura = the cooking

cozza *noun, feminine*
 una cozza = a mussel

cravatta *noun, feminine*
 una cravatta = a tie

creare *verb* ☐1
 = to create

crebbe, crebbi, etc ▶ **crescere**

credenza *noun, feminine*
 una credenza = a sideboard

credere *verb* ☐8
 = to believe
 = to think
 credo che sia vero = I think it's true
 crede di sapere tutto = he thinks he
  knows everything
 credo di sì = I think so
 credo di no = I don't think so
 non ci credo! = I don't believe it!

credito *noun, masculine*
 il credito = credit

crema *noun, feminine*
 • una crema = a cream
 • la crema = custard

crepa *noun, feminine*
 una crepa = a crack

crepare *verb* ☐1 (**!** + *essere*)
1 ✗ = to snuff it
2 **creparsi** (**!** + *essere*)
 creparsi = to crack

crescere *verb* ☐27 (**!** + *essere*)
 • = to grow
 • = to grow up

crescita *noun, feminine*
 la crescita = growth

cresciuto/cresciuta ▶ **crescere**

cretino/cretina *noun,*
 masculine/feminine
 un cretino/una cretina = a cretin

criminale *noun, masculine/feminine*
 un/una criminale = a criminal

criminalità *noun, feminine*
 la criminalità = crime

crimine *noun, masculine*
 un crimine = a crime

crisi *noun, feminine* (**!** *never changes*)
 una crisi = a crisis

cristallo *noun, masculine*
 un cristallo = a crystal

cristianesimo *noun, masculine*
 il cristianesimo = Christianity

cristiano/cristiana *adjective*
 = Christian

criterio *noun, masculine* (*plural* **criteri**)
 un criterio = a criterion

critica *noun, feminine* (*plural* **critiche**)
 una critica = a criticism

criticare *verb* ☐4
 = to criticize

critico/critica (*plural* **critici/critiche**)
1 *adjective*
 = critical
2 *noun, masculine/feminine*
 un critico/una critica = a critic

croccante *adjective*
 = crunchy

croce *noun, feminine*
 una croce = a cross

crociera *noun, feminine*
 una crociera = a cruise

crollare *verb* ☐1 (**!** + *essere*)
 = to collapse

crollo *noun, masculine*
 un crollo = a collapse

crosta *noun, feminine*
 una crosta = a crust

cruciverba *noun, masculine* (**!** *never changes*)
 un cruciverba = a crossword

crudele *adjective*
 = cruel

crudeltà *noun, feminine*
 la crudeltà = cruelty

crudo/cruda *adjective*
 = raw

cubetto *noun, masculine*
 un cubetto di ghiaccio = an ice cube

cubo *noun, masculine*
 un cubo = a cube

cuccetta *noun, feminine*
 una cuccetta = a couchette

cucchiaino *noun, masculine*
 un cucchiaino = a teaspoon

cucchiaio *noun, masculine* (*plural* **cucchiai**)
 un cucchiaio = a spoon

cucciolo *noun, masculine*
 un cucciolo = a pup
 = a cub

cucina *noun, feminine*
 • la cucina = the kitchen
 • una cucina = a cooker, a stove
 • la cucina italiana = Italian cookery

cucinare *verb* ☐1
 = to cook

cucire *verb* ☐10
 = to sew

cucitrice noun, feminine
  una cucitrice = a stapler

cuffia noun, feminine
• una cuffia = a cap
• una cuffia = headphones

cugino/cugina noun, masculine/feminine
  un cugino/una cugina = a cousin

cui pronoun
• = whose
• = whom
  = which

culla noun, feminine
  una culla = a crib

culo⁎ noun, masculine
  il culo = the arse, the ass

cultura noun, feminine
  la cultura = culture

culturale adjective
  = cultural

culturismo noun, masculine
  il culturismo = body-building

cuocere verb 28
  = to cook

cuoco/cuoca noun, masculine/feminine
  (plural **cuochi/cuoche**)
  un cuoco/una cuoca = a cook

cuoio noun, masculine
  il cuoio = leather

cuore noun, masculine
  il cuore = the heart

cupola noun, feminine
  una cupola = a dome

cura noun, feminine
• una cura = a cure
• la cura = treatment
  prendersi cura di = to look after

curare verb 1
• = to treat
• = to cure

curiosità noun, feminine
  la curiosità = curiosity

curioso/curiosa adjective
  = curious

curriculum noun, masculine (**!** never
changes)
  un curriculum = a CV, a résumé

curva noun, feminine
  una curva = a bend
  = a curve

cuscino noun, masculine
  un cuscino = a cushion
  = a pillow

custode noun, masculine/feminine
  un/una custode = a caretaker, a janitor

custodire verb 9
  = to guard

Dd

da preposition
> **!** Note that **da** combines with **il**, **la**, etc.
> Da + il = dal; da + l' = dall'; da + lo
> = dallo; da + i = dai; da + gli = dagli;
> da + la = dalla; da + le = dalle.

• = from
  da Roma a Milano = from Rome to Milan
• = at
  = to
  sarò da Giulia = I'll be at Giulia's
  vado dal dentista = I'm going to the
  dentist's
• = by
  è stata costruita dai pisani = it was built
  by the Pisans
• = for
  = since
  la conosco da anni = I've known her for
  years
  lavoro qui dal 1996 = I've been working
  here since 1996
• (other uses)
  qualcosa da mangiare = something to eat
  un francobollo da 0,41 euro = a 0·41
  euro stamp
  da bambino/bambina = as a child

dà, **da'** ▶ **dare**

dado noun, masculine
• un dado = a dice
• un dado = a stock cube

dagli ▶ **da**

dai
1 ▶ **dare**
2 ▶ **da**

dal, **dalla**, **dalle**, etc ▶ **da**

dammi ▶ **dare**

danese adjective
  = Danish

Danimarca noun, feminine
  la Danimarca = Denmark

danneggiare verb 3
  = to damage

danno
1 ▶ **dare**
2 noun, masculine
  fare un danno = to cause damage
  i danni = damage

dannoso/dannosa adjective
  = harmful

danza noun, feminine
  una danza = a dance

dappertutto adverb
  = everywhere

⁎ in informal situations ⁎ may be considered offensive

dare verb 29
- = to give
  dammi la chiave! = give me the key!
- **dare del tu a qualcuno** = to address
  someone using 'tu'
  dare del lei a qualcuno = to address
  someone using 'lei'
- **la finestra dà sulla piazza** = the window
  overlooks the square
- **dare un esame** = to take an exam
- **dare da mangiare a qualcuno** = to feed
  someone

data noun, feminine
  una data = a date

date ▶ dare

dato/data
1 ▶ dare
2 **dato** noun, masculine
  un dato = a piece of information
  i dati = information

datore/datrice noun,
masculine/feminine
  un datore/una datrice di lavoro = an
  employer

dattilografo/dattilografa noun,
masculine/feminine
  un dattilografo/una dattilografa = a typist

davanti
1 adverb
- = in front
  la macchina davanti = the car in front
- = opposite
  la stazione è davanti = the station is
  opposite
2 **davanti a** preposition
- = in front of
  incontriamoci davanti alla scuola = let's
  meet in front of the school
- = opposite
  la stazione è davanti alla chiesa = the
  station is opposite the church

davvero adverb
  = really

debito noun, masculine
  un debito = a debt

debole adjective
  = weak

decennio noun, masculine (plural
  decenni)
  un decennio = a decade

decente adjective
  = decent

decidere verb 30
  = to decide
  decidere di sposarsi = to decide to get
  married

decimo/decima adjective
  = tenth

decina noun, feminine
  una decina di studenti = about ten
  students

decisamente adverb
  = definitely

decise, decisi, etc ▶ decidere

decisione noun, feminine
  una decisione = a decision

deciso/decisa ▶ decidere

decollare verb 1
  = to take off

decollo noun, masculine
  un decollo = a take-off

decorare verb 1
  = to decorate

decorazione noun, feminine
  una decorazione = a decoration

dedicare verb 4
  = to dedicate

deduco, deduce, etc ▶ dedurre

dedurre verb 54
- = to deduct
- = to deduce

dedusse, dedotto/dedotta, etc ▶
  dedurre

deficiente✗ adjective
  = stupid

definire verb 9
  = to define

definito/definita adjective
  = definite

definizione noun, feminine
  una definizione = a definition

degli ▶ di

degno/degna adjective
  = worthy

dei, del ▶ di

delfino noun, masculine
  un delfino = a dolphin

delicato/delicata adjective
  = delicate

delitto noun, masculine
  un delitto = a crime

delizioso/deliziosa adjective
  = delicious

della, delle, dello ▶ di

deludere verb 21
  = to disappoint

deluse, delusero, etc ▶ deludere

delusione noun, feminine
  una delusione = a disappointment

deluso/delusa
1 ▶ deludere
2 adjective
  = disappointed

demo<u>cra</u>tico/demo<u>cra</u>tica
adjective (plural
demo<u>cra</u>tici/demo<u>cra</u>tiche)
= democratic

demo<u>cra</u>zia *noun, feminine*
la democrazia = democracy

demo<u>li</u>re *verb* 9
= to demolish

de<u>na</u>ro *noun, masculine*
il denaro = money

<u>den</u>te *noun, masculine*
un dente = a tooth

denti<u>fri</u>cio *noun, masculine*
il dentifricio = toothpaste

den<u>ti</u>sta *noun, masculine/feminine (plural*
den<u>ti</u>sti/den<u>ti</u>ste)
un/una dentista = a dentist

<u>den</u>tro *preposition, adverb*
= inside

de<u>nun</u>cia *noun, feminine (plural*
de<u>nun</u>cie)
una denuncia = a report

denun<u>cia</u>re *verb* 2
= to report

deodo<u>ran</u>te *noun, masculine*
il deodorante = deodorant

depli<u>ant</u> *noun, masculine (! never*
changes)
un depliant = a leaflet

de<u>po</u>sito *noun, masculine*
• **un deposito** = a deposit
• **deposito bagagli** = left luggage office

de<u>pres</u>so/de<u>pres</u>sa *adjective*
= depressed

depri<u>men</u>te *adjective*
= depressing

deru<u>ba</u>re *verb* 1
= to rob

de<u>scris</u>se, de<u>scrit</u>to/de<u>scrit</u>ta,
etc ▶ descrivere

de<u>scri</u>vere *verb* 65
= to describe

descri<u>zio</u>ne *noun, feminine*
una descrizione = a description

de<u>ser</u>to *noun, masculine*
un deserto = a desert

deside<u>ra</u>re *verb* 1
= to want

desi<u>de</u>rio *noun, masculine (plural*
desi<u>de</u>ri)
esprimere un desiderio = to make a wish

destina<u>ta</u>rio/destina<u>ta</u>ria *noun,*
*masculine/feminine (plural **destina<u>ta</u>ri/***
destina<u>ta</u>rie)
il destinatario/la destinataria = the
addressee

destina<u>zio</u>ne *noun, feminine*
una destinazione = a destination

de<u>sti</u>no *noun, masculine*
il destino = destiny

<u>de</u>stro/<u>de</u>stra
1 *adjective*
= right
la mano destra = the right hand
2 <u>de</u>stra *noun, feminine*
= right
a destra = on the right
girare a destra = to turn right

determina<u>zio</u>ne *noun, feminine*
la determinazione = determination

det<u>ta</u>glio *noun, masculine (plural*
det<u>ta</u>gli)
un dettaglio = a detail

<u>det</u>te, <u>det</u>ti, etc ▶ dare

<u>det</u>to/<u>det</u>ta ▶ dire

<u>de</u>ve, <u>de</u>vo, etc▶ dovere

di

> **!** *Note that* **di** *combines with* **il, la,** *etc.*
> **Di + il = del; di + l' = dell'; di + lo**
> **= dello; di + i = dei; di + gli = degli;**
> **di + la = della; di + le = delle.**

1 *preposition*
• = of
la capitale d'Italia = the capital of Italy
la porta della cucina = the kitchen door
la macchina di Renato = Renato's car
• = from
sono di Dublino = they're from Dublin
• = than
tu sei più alto di me = you're taller than
me
• = by
un libro di Calvino = a book by Calvino
• = made of
è di legno = it's made of wood
2 del/della *determiner*
= some

> **!** *Before masculine nouns beginning*
> *with z, ps, gn, or s + another*
> *consonant,* **dello** *is used in the singular*
> *and* **degli** *in the plural. Before*
> *masculine nouns beginning with other*
> *consonants,* **del** *is used in the singular*
> *and* **dei** *in the plural. Before all nouns*
> *beginning with a vowel,* **dell'** *is used in*
> *the singular and* **degli** *(masculine) or*
> **delle** *(feminine) in the plural.*

dell'acqua = some water
sono arrivate delle lettere = some letters
have arrived

di' ▶ dire

<u>di</u>a ▶ dare

dia<u>be</u>tico/dia<u>be</u>tica *adjective (plural*
dia<u>be</u>tici/dia<u>be</u>tiche)
= diabetic

diagnosi *noun, feminine* (**!** *never changes*)
  una diagnosi = a diagnosis

dialetto *noun, masculine*
  un dialetto = a dialect

dialogo *noun, masculine* (*plural* **dialoghi**)
  un dialogo = a dialogue

diamo ▶ **dare**

diapositiva *noun, feminine*
  una diapositiva = a slide

diario *noun, masculine* (*plural* **diari**)
  un diario = a diary

diavolo *noun, masculine*
  il diavolo = the devil

dibattito *noun, masculine*
  un dibattito = a debate

dica, dice, dicevo, etc ▶ **dire**

dichiarare *verb* $\boxed{1}$
  = to declare

dichiarazione *noun, feminine*
  una dichiarazione = a declaration

dici, diciamo ▶ **dire**

diciannove *number*
  = nineteen

diciannovenne *adjective*
  = nineteen-year-old

diciannovesimo/diciannovesima *adjective*
  = nineteenth

diciassette *number*
  = seventeen

diciassettenne *adjective*
  = seventeen-year-old

diciassettesimo/diciasettesima *adjective*
  = seventeenth

diciottenne *adjective*
  = eighteen-year-old

diciottesimo/diciottesima *adjective*
  = eighteenth

diciotto *number*
  = eighteen

dico, dicono ▶ **dire**

dieci *number*
  = ten

diede, diedi, etc ▶ **dare**

dieta *noun, feminine*
  una dieta = a diet
  mettersi a dieta = to go on a diet

dietro
1 *adverb*
  = behind
  = in/at the back

2 *noun, masculine*
  il dietro = the back
3 **dietro (a/di)** *preposition*
  = behind
  la macchina dietro di noi = the car behind us
  dietro alla stazione = behind the station

difendere *verb* $\boxed{53}$
  = to defend

difesa *noun, feminine*
  la difesa = defence, defense

difese, difeso/difesa, etc ▶ **difendere**

difetto *noun, masculine*
  un difetto = a defect

differente *adjective*
  = different

differenza *noun, feminine*
  una differenza = a difference

difficile *adjective*
  = difficult

difficilmente *adverb*
  = with difficulty

difficoltà *noun, feminine* (**!** *never changes*)
  una difficoltà = a difficulty

diffondere *verb* $\boxed{24}$
1 = to spread
2 **diffondersi** (**!** + *essere*)
  diffondersi = to spread

diffuso/diffusa, etc
1 ▶ **diffondere**
2 *adjective*
  = common

digitale *adjective*
  = digital

digiuno/digiuna *adjective*
  = on an empty stomach
  essere digiuno/digiuna = not to have eaten

dignità *noun, feminine*
  la dignità = dignity

dilettante *noun, masculine/feminine*
  un/una dilettante = an amateur

dimagrire *verb* (**!** + *essere*)
  = to lose weight

dimensione *noun, feminine*
  una dimensione = a dimension

dimenticare *verb* $\boxed{4}$
  = to forget

dimesso/dimessa ▶ **dimettersi**

dimettersi *verb* $\boxed{40}$
  = to resign

diminuire *verb* $\boxed{9}$ (**!** + *essere* or *avere*)
  = to decrease

dimise, dimisi, etc ▶ **dimettersi**

dimissioni *noun, feminine plural*
dare le dimissioni = to resign

dimmi ▶ **dire**

dimostrare *verb* 1
= to show

dimostrazione *noun, feminine*
una dimostrazione = a demonstration

dinamico/dinamica *adjective* (*plural* dinamici/dinamiche)
= dynamic

dintorni *noun, masculine plural*
i dintorni = the outskirts

dio/dea *noun, masculine/feminine* (*plural* dei/dee)
1 un dio/una dea = a god/a goddess
2 **Dio** *noun, masculine*
Dio = God

dipartimento *noun, masculine*
un dipartimento = a department

dipendente *noun, masculine/feminine*
un/una dipendente = an employee

dipendere *verb* 53 (**!** + *essere*)
dipendere da = to depend on
dipende = it depends

dipingere *verb* 48
= to paint

dipinse, dipinsi, etc ▶ **dipingere**

dipinto/dipinta
1 ▶ **dipingere**
2 dipinto *noun, masculine*
un dipinto = a painting

diploma *noun, masculine* (*plural* diplomi)
un diploma = a diploma

dire *verb* 31
= to say
= to tell
dire di sì/di no = to say yes/no
dimmi la verità! = tell me the truth!
dica! = yes?

diresse, diressi, etc ▶ **dirigere**

direttamente *adverb*
= directly
vado direttamente a casa = I'm going straight home

diretto/diretta
1 ▶ **dirigere**
2 *adjective*
= direct

direttore/direttrice *noun, masculine/feminine*
• un direttore/una direttrice = a director
= a manager
• un direttore/una direttrice = a headteacher, a principal

direzione *noun, feminine*
• una direzione = a direction
• la direzione = the management

dirigente *noun, masculine/feminine*
un/una dirigente = a leader
= a manager

dirigere *verb* 32
= to lead

diritto/diritta
1 *adjective*
= straight
2 diritto *noun, masculine*
un diritto = a right

disastro *noun, masculine*
un disastro = a disaster

discesa *noun, feminine*
la discesa = the descent

disciplina *noun, feminine*
la disciplina = discipline

disco *noun, masculine* (*plural* dischi)
un disco = a record
= a disc, a disk
un disco fisso = a hard disk

discorso *noun, masculine*
• un discorso = a speech
• che discorsi! = what a stupid thing to say!

discoteca *noun, feminine* (*plural* discoteche)
una discoteca = a club

discreto/discreta *adjective*
= not bad

discriminazione *noun, feminine*
la discriminazione = discrimination

discussione *noun, feminine*
una discussione = an argument

discusse, discussi, etc ▶ **discutere**

discusso/discussa
1 ▶ **discutere**
2 *adjective*
= controversial

discutere *verb* 33
= to discuss

disdetto/disdetta, disdico, etc ▶ **disdire**

disdire *verb* 31
= to cancel

disegnare *verb* 1
= to draw

disegno *noun, masculine*
un disegno = a drawing
= a design

disgrazia *noun, feminine*
una disgrazia = a terrible thing

disoccupato/disoccupata *adjective*
= unemployed

disoccupazione *noun, feminine*
la disoccupazione = unemployment

disordinato/disordinata *adjective*
= untidy

disordine *noun, masculine*
un disordine = a mess
in disordine = in a mess

disperato/disperata *adjective*
= desperate

disperazione *noun, feminine*
la disperazione = desperation

dispettoso/dispettosa *adjective*
= naughty

dispiacere
1 *verb* (**!** + *essere*)
• mi dispiace = I'm sorry
• se non le dispiace = if you don't mind
  ti dispiace abbassare la radio? = would
  you mind turning down the radio?
• non mi dispiace = I quite like it
2 *noun, masculine*
un dispiacere = a disappointment

dispiaciuto/dispiaciuta
1 ▶ dispiacere
2 *adjective*
= sorry

dispone, dispongo, etc ▶ disporre

disponibile *adjective*
• = available
• (*when it's a person*) = helpful

disponibilità *noun, feminine*
la disponibilità = availability

disporre *verb* 50
= to arrange

dispose, disposi, etc ▶ disporre

disposto/disposta
1 ▶ disporre
2 *adjective*
disposto/disposta a fare qualcosa
= willing to do something

disse, dissi, etc ▶ dire

distante *adjective*
= far away

distanza *noun, feminine*
la distanza = the distance

distinguere *verb* 34
= to distinguish
= to make out

distinse, distinsi, etc ▶
distinguere

distinto/distinta
1 ▶ distinguere
2 *adjective*
• = distinct
• = distinguished

distinzione *noun, feminine*
una distinzione = a distinction

distribuire *verb* 9
= to distribute
= to hand out

distribuzione *noun, feminine*
la distribuzione = the distribution

distruggere *verb* 39
= to destroy

distrussi, distrusse, etc ▶
distruggere

distrutto/distrutta
1 ▶ distruggere
2 *adjective*
= exhausted

distruzione *noun, feminine*
la distruzione = destruction

disturbare *verb* 1
= to disturb

disturbo *noun, masculine*
• un disturbo = a disturbance
• un disturbo di stomaco = a stomach
  upset

dita ▶ dito

dite ▶ dire

dito *noun, masculine* (*plural* **dita**)
  ! *Note that* **dita** *is feminine.*
un dito = a finger

ditta *noun, feminine*
una ditta = a firm

dittatore *noun, masculine*
un dittatore = a dictator

divano *noun, masculine*
un divano = a sofa
un divano letto = a sofa bed

diventare *verb* 1 (**!** + *essere*)
= to become

diverso/diversa *adjective*
• = different
• = several
  diverse volte = several times

divertente *adjective*
= enjoyable
= amusing

divertimento *noun, masculine*
il divertimento = fun

divertirsi *verb* 10 (**!** + *essere*)
= to have a good time

dividere *verb* 30
• = to divide
• = to share

divieto *noun, masculine*
un divieto = a ban

D

dovere

1 dovere functions as an ordinary verb:
= to owe

mi devi trenta euro	= *you owe me thirty euros*

2 dovere is used to talk about obligations and prohibitions:

devo andare	= *I have to go*
dobbiamo agire subito	= *we must do something at once*
abbiamo dovuto prendere un taxi	= *we had to get a taxi*
non si deve correre	= *you mustn't run*
non dovevi dirglielo	= *you weren't supposed to tell him*

3 dovere is used to make polite offers:

ti devo aiutare?	= *shall I help you?*

4 dovere is used when making a logical deduction:

ci deve essere una perdita	= *there must be a leak*
dev'essere il postino	= *it must be the postman*

5 dovere is used in the *conditional tense* to express the idea of 'ought to' or 'should'. The forms of this tense are:

dovrei
dovresti
dovrebbe
dovremmo
dovreste
dovrebbero

dovrei andare	= *I ought to go*
non dovrebbe fare quel rumore	= *it shouldn't make that noise*
dovrebbero arrivare alle undici	= *they should arrive at eleven*

---

divino/divina *adjective*
= divine

divisa *noun, feminine*
una divisa = a uniform

divise, divisi, etc ▶ **dividere**

divisione *noun, feminine*
una divisione = a division

diviso/divisa ▶ **dividere**

divorziato/divorziata *adjective*
= divorced

divorzio *noun, masculine (plural* **divorzi***)*
un divorzio = a divorce

dizionario *noun, masculine (plural* **dizionari***)*
un dizionario = a dictionary

do ▶ **dare**

dobbiamo ▶ **dovere**

doccia *noun, feminine (plural* **docce***)*
una doccia = a shower
fare una doccia = to have a shower, to take a shower

---

documentario *noun, masculine (plural* **documentari***)*
un documentario = a documentary

documento *noun, masculine*
un documento = a document

dodicenne *adjective*
= twelve-year-old

dodicesimo/dodicesima *adjective*
= twelfth

dodici *number*
= twelve

dogana *noun, feminine*
la dogana = customs

doganiere *noun, masculine*
un doganiere = a customs officer

dolce
1 *adjective*
• = sweet
• = gentle
2 *noun, masculine*
un dolce = a dessert
= a cake

dollaro *noun, masculine*
un dollaro = a dollar

dolore *noun, masculine*
un dolore = a pain

* in informal situations

domanda *noun, feminine*
  una domanda = a question
  fare una domanda = to ask a question
una domanda di lavoro = a job
    application

domandare *verb* [1]
1 = to ask
2 domandarsi (! + *essere*)
  domandarsi = to wonder

domani *adverb*
  = tomorrow
  domani l'altro = the day after tomorrow

domattina *adverb*
  = tomorrow morning

domenica *noun, feminine* (*plural*
  domeniche)
  = Sunday
  arrivo domenica = I'm arriving on Sunday
  la domenica = on Sundays

domestico/domestica *adjective*
  (*plural* **domestici/domestiche**)
  = household
  = domestic

donare *verb* [1]
  = to donate

donna *noun, feminine*
  una donna = a woman

dono *noun, masculine*
  un dono = a gift

dopo
1 *preposition*
  = after
2 *adverb*
  = afterward(s)

dopodomani *adverb*
  = the day after tomorrow

doppio/doppia *adjective*
  = double

dormire *verb* [10]
  = to sleep

dorso *noun, masculine*
  il dorso = the back

dose *noun, feminine*
  una dose = a dose

dottorato *noun, masculine*
  un dottorato = a doctorate

dottore/dottoressa *noun,*
  masculine/feminine
  un dottore/una dottoressa = a doctor

dove *adverb*
  = where
  dov'è Roberta? = where's Roberta?

dovere
1 *verb*
  = must

  = to have to
  devo andare = I have to go
2 *noun, masculine*
  il dovere = duty

dovette, **dovrà**, **dovrebbe**, etc ▶
dovere

dovunque *adverb*
  = everywhere

dozzina *noun, feminine*
  una dozzina = a dozen

dramma *noun, masculine* (*plural*
  drammi)
  un dramma = a drama

drammatico/drammatica *adjective*
  (*plural* **drammatici/drammatiche**)
  = dramatic

dritto/dritta *adjective*
  = straight
  sempre dritto = straight on

droga *noun, feminine* (*plural* **droghe**)
  una droga = a drug
  la droga = drugs

drogarsi *verb* [5] (! + *essere*)
  = to take drugs

drogato/drogata* *noun,*
  masculine/feminine
  un drogato/una droga = a junkie

dubbio *noun, masculine* (*plural* **dubbi**)
  un dubbio = a doubt
  senza dubbio = no doubt

dubitare *verb* [1]
  = to doubt

due *number*
  = two

duecento
1 *number*
  = two hundred
2 Duecento *noun, masculine*
  il Duecento = the 13th century

duemila *number*
  = two thousand
  il duemila = the year 2000

dunque *conjunction*
  = so

duomo *noun, masculine*
  il duomo = the cathedral

durante *preposition*
  = during

durare *verb* [1] (! + *essere*)
  = to last
  quanto dura? = how long does it last?

durata *noun, feminine*
  la durata = the length

duro/dura *adjective*
  = hard

e (sometimes **ed** *before a vowel*)
conjunction
= and
e gli altri? = what about the others?

è ▶ **essere**

ebbe, **ebbi**, etc ▶ **avere**

ebraico/ebraica *adjective* (*plural*
ebraici/ebraiche)
= Jewish

ebreo/ebrea *noun, masculine|feminine*
un ebreo/un'ebrea = a Jew

ecc *abbreviation*
= etc
eccellente *adjective*
= excellent

eccessivo/eccessiva *adjective*
= excessive

eccetera *adverb*
= et cetera

eccezionale *adjective*
= exceptional

eccezione *noun, feminine*
un'eccezione = an exception

eccitare *verb* [1]
= to arouse

ecco *adverb*
ecco! = here!
eccolo/eccola! = here he is/here she is!
eccomi! = here I am!

eco *noun, feminine* (*plural* **echi**)

> **!** *Note that* **echi** *is masculine.*

un'eco = an echo

ecologico/ecologica *adjective* (*plural*
ecologici/ecologiche)
• = ecological
• = green

economia *noun, feminine*
l'economia = the economy

economico/economica *adjective*
(*plural* **economici/economiche**)
= cheap

ed ▶ **e**

edicola *noun, feminine*
un'edicola = a newsagent's, a newsdealer's

edificio *noun, masculine* (*plural* **edifici**)
un edificio = a building

Edimburgo *noun*
= Edinburgh

editore/editrice *noun,*
masculine|feminine

un editore/un'editrice = a publisher

edizione *noun, feminine*
un'edizione = an edition

educare *verb* [4]
= to bring up

educato/educata *adjective*
= well-behaved

educazione *noun, feminine*
l'educazione = up-bringing

effettivamente *adverb*
= in fact

effettivo/effettiva *adjective*
= real

effetto *noun, masculine*
un effetto = an effect

efficace *adjective*
= effective

efficiente *adjective*
= efficient

egli *pronoun*
= he

egoista *adjective* (*plural*
egoisti/egoiste)
= selfish

elaborare *verb* [1]
= to work out

elefante *noun, masculine*
un elefante = an elephant

elegante *adjective*
= elegant
= smart, well-dressed

eleganza *noun, feminine*
l'eleganza = elegance

eleggere *verb* [39]
= to elect

elementare *adjective*
= elementary

elemento *noun, masculine*
un elemento = an element

elenco *noun, masculine* (*plural* **elenchi**)
un elenco = a list
l'elenco telefonico = the phone book

eletto/eletta ▶ **eleggere**

elettricista *noun, masculine|feminine*
(*plural* **elettricisti/elettriciste**)
un elettricista/un'elettricista = an
electrician

elettrico/elettrica *adjective* (*plural*
elettrici/elettriche)
= electric
= electrical

elettrodomestici *noun, masculine*
plural
gli elettrodomestici = electrical goods

elevato/elevata *adjective*
= high

elezione *noun, feminine*
un'elezione = an election

elicottero *noun, masculine*
un elicottero = a helicopter

eliminare *verb* $\boxed{1}$
= to eliminate

ella *pronoun*
= she

emarginato/emarginata *noun, masculine/feminine*
un emarginato/un'emarginata = an outcast

emergenza *noun, feminine*
un'emergenza = an emergency

emigrare *verb* $\boxed{1}$ (**!** + *essere*)
= to emigrate

emigrato/emigrata *noun, masculine/feminine*
un emigrato/un'emigrata = an emigrant

emittente *noun, feminine*
un'emittente = a station

emozionante *adjective*
= exciting

emozionato/emozionata *adjective*
• = excited
• = nervous

emozione *noun, masculine*
l'emozione = the emotion
= the excitement

enciclopedia *noun, feminine*
un'enciclopedia = an encyclopedia

energia *noun, feminine*
l'energia = energy

ennesimo/ennesima *adjective*
= umpteenth

enorme *adjective*
= huge

ente *noun, masculine*
un ente = a body

entrambi/entrambe *adjective*
= both

entrare *verb* (**!** + *essere*)
• = to come in
= to go in
entrare in = to enter
• = to fit
• che c'entra? = what's that got to do with it?

entrata *noun, feminine*
l'entrata = the entrance

entro *preposition*
entro il 5 maggio = by May 5

entusiasmo *noun, masculine*
l'entusiasmo = enthusiasm

entusiasta *adjective* (*plural* entusiasti/entusiaste)
= enthusiastic

epoca *noun, feminine* (*plural* **epoche**)
un'epoca = a time
a quell'epoca = at that time

eppure *conjunction*
= yet

equatore *noun, masculine*
l'equatore = the equator

equilibrio *noun, masculine*
l'equilibrio = balance

equipaggio *noun, masculine* (*plural* equipaggi)
l'equipaggio = the crew

equivalente *adjective*
= equivalent

equo/equa *adjective*
= fair

equosolidale *adjective*
= fair trade

era, **erano**, **eravamo**, etc ▶ **essere**

erba *noun, feminine*
• l'erba = grass
• un'erba = a(n) herb

erbaccia *noun, feminine* (*plural* erbacce)
un'erbaccia = a weed

ereditare *verb* $\boxed{1}$
= to inherit

eri, **ero** ▶ **essere**

eroe/eroina *noun, masculine/feminine*
un eroe/un'eroina = a hero/a heroine

eroina *noun, feminine*
l'eroina = heroin

errore *noun, masculine*
un errore = a mistake
fare un errore = to make a mistake

esagerare *verb* $\boxed{1}$
= to exaggerate

esame *noun, masculine*
un esame = an exam

esaminare *verb* $\boxed{1}$
= to examine

esatto/esatta
1 ▶ **esigere**
2 *adjective*
= exact
= correct
esatto! = exactly!

esaurito/esaurita *adjective*
• (*when it's a person*) = run-down
• (*when it's tickets, seats*) = sold out

esausto/esausta *adjective*
= exhausted

esca, **esce**, etc ▶ **uscire**

escludere *verb* $\boxed{21}$
= to exclude

E

essere

1 essere functions as an ordinary verb. It forms its perfect tense with **essere**:
= to be

è aperto	= *it's open*
sono io	= *it's me*
erano stanchi	= *they were tired*
dove sei stato?	= *where have you been?*

2 essere is used as an auxiliary verb to form other tenses of certain verbs, marked (**!** + **essere**) in this dictionary, and of all reflexive verbs. The perfect tense uses the present tense of **essere** + the past participle. It is used to talk about events that took place in the fairly recent past, or that have had an effect on the present:

siamo già passati di qua	= *we've already been this way*
ti sei divertita alla festa, Laura?	= *did you enjoy yourself at the party, Laura?*

The pluperfect tense uses the imperfect tense of **essere** + the past participle. It is used to talk about events that happened *before* the event that is the main focus of attention:

ci eravamo conosciuti prima = *we had met before*

3 essere is used to form the passive:

i motori sono fabbricati in Germania = *the engines are made in Germany*

4 essere is used with **ci** to mean 'there is', 'there are', etc.

c'è un problema	= *there's a problem*
ce n'erano troppi	= *there were too many*

---

escluse, **esclusi**, etc ▶ **escludere**

escluso/esclusa
1 ▶ **escludere**
2 *adjective*
martedì escluso = excluding Tuesdays

esco, **escono** ▶ **uscire**

eseguire *verb* [10]
= to carry out

esempio *noun, masculine* (*plural* **esempi**)
un esempio = an example
per esempio, ad esempio = for example

esente *adjective*
= exempt

esercito *noun, masculine*
l'esercito = the army

esercizio *noun, masculine* (*plural* **esercizi**)
un esercizio = an exercise

esigente *adjective*
= demanding

esigenza *noun, feminine*
un'esigenza = a need
= a demand

esigere *verb* [36]
= to demand

esistenza *noun, feminine*
l'esistenza = the existence

esistere *verb* [16] (**!** + *essere*)
= to exist

esitare *verb* [1]
= to hesitate

esotico/esotica *adjective* (*plural* **esotici/esotiche**)
= exotic

espansivo/espansiva *adjective*
= outgoing

esperienza *noun, feminine*
l'esperienza = experience

esperimento *noun, masculine*
un esperimento = an experiment

esperto/esperta *noun, masculine/feminine*
un esperto/un'esperta = an expert

esplodere *verb* [21] (**!** + *essere*)
= to explode
far esplodere una macchina = to blow up a car

esplorare *verb* [1]
= to explore

esplose, **esplosero**, etc ▶ **esplodere**

esplosione *noun, feminine*
un'esplosione = an explosion

esploso/esplosa ▶ **esplodere**

esportazione *noun, feminine*
l'esportazione = export

esposizione *noun, feminine*
un'esposizione = an exhibition

espressione *noun, feminine*
un'espressione = an expression

espresso/espressa
1 ▶ esprimere
2 *noun, masculine*
  un espresso = an espresso

esprimere *verb* 37
  = to express

essa ▶ esso

essenziale *adjective*
  = essential

essi/esse *pronoun*
  = they
  = them

essere ▶ 42 *See the boxed note.*
1 *verb* (! + *essere*)
  = to be
2 *noun, masculine*
  un essere = a being

esso/essa *pronoun*
  = it

est *noun, masculine*
  l'est = the east

estate *noun, feminine*
  l'estate = the summer
  d'estate = in summer

esterno/esterna *adjective*
  = outer

estero/estera
1 *adjective*
  = foreign
2 **estero** *noun, masculine*
  l'estero = overseas
  all'estero = abroad

esteso/estesa *adjective*
  = extensive

estetista *noun, masculine/feminine*
(*plural* **estetisti/estetiste**)
  un estetista/un'estetista = a beautician

estinto/estinta *adjective*
  = extinct

estivo/estiva *adjective*
  = summer

estrae, estraggo, etc ▶ estrarre

estrarre *verb* 74
  = to extract

estrasse, estrassero, etc ▶ estrarre

estratto/estratta
1 ▶ estrarre
2 **estratto** *noun, masculine*
  un estratto = an extract

estremamente *adverb*
  = extremely

estremo/estrema *adjective*
  = extreme

età *noun, feminine* (! *never changes*)
  l'età = age

etichetta *noun, feminine*
  un'etichetta = a label

etnico/etnica *adjective* (*plural* **etnici/etniche**)
  = ethnic

ettaro *noun, masculine*
  un ettaro = a hectare

etto *noun, masculine*
  un etto = a hundred grams

euro *noun, masculine*
  un euro = a euro

europeo/europea *adjective*
  = European

eventuale *adjective*
  = possible

eventualmente *adverb*
  eventualmente si può cambiare = you can change it if necessary

evidente *adjective*
  = obvious

evidentemente *adverb*
  = obviously

evidenza *noun, feminine*
  l'evidenza = the evidence

evitare *verb* 1
  = to avoid

evviva *exclamation*
  evviva! = hurray!

extracomunitario/extracomunitaria *noun, masculine/feminine*
  un extracomunitario/un extracomunitaria = a non-EU immigrant

Ff

fa
1 ▶ fare
2 *adverb*
  tre anni fa = three years ago
  quanto tempo fa? = how long ago?

fabbrica *noun, feminine* (*plural* **fabbriche**)
  una fabbrica = a factory

faccenda *noun, feminine*
  • una faccenda = a matter
  • fare le faccende = to do the housework

faccia *noun, feminine* (*plural* **facce**)
  la faccia = the face

faccia, facciamo ▶ fare

facciata *noun, feminine*
  la facciata = the façade

faccio, facemmo, faceva, etc ▶
fare

facile adjective
= easy

facoltà noun, feminine (**!** never changes)
una facoltà = a faculty

fagiolino noun, masculine
un fagiolino = a green bean

fagiolo noun, masculine
un fagiolo = a bean

fai ▶ fare

fai da te noun, masculine
il fai da te = DIY, do-it-yourself

falegname noun, masculine
un falegname = a carpenter

fallire verb 9 (**!** + essere)
• = to fail
• = to go out of business

fallito/fallita adjective
= unsuccessful

fallo noun, masculine
un fallo = a foul

falò noun, masculine (**!** never changes)
un falò = a bonfire

falso/falsa adjective
= false
= fake

fama noun, feminine
la fama = fame
avere la fama di = to have a reputation for

fame noun, feminine
la fame = hunger
aver fame = to be hungry

famiglia noun, feminine
una famiglia = a family

familiare adjective
= familiar

famoso/famosa adjective
= famous

fanale noun, masculine
un fanale = a light

fango noun, masculine
il fango = mud

fanno ▶ fare

fantascienza noun, feminine
la fantascienza = science fiction

fantasia noun, feminine
• la fantasia = imagination
• una fantasia = a fantasy

fantasma noun, masculine (plural fantasmi)
un fantasma = a ghost

fantastico/fantastica adjective (plural fantastici/fantastiche)
= fantastic

farcire verb 9
= to stuff

fare verb 38

> **!** You will find translations for phrases with fare such as fare colazione, fare una domanda, fare un errore etc under the words colazione, domanda, errore etc.

• = to make
fare un dolce = to make a cake
il vino si fa con l'uva = wine is made from grapes
• = to do
cosa fai? = what are you doing?
fare i compiti = to do one's homework
• = to have
fare una doccia = to have a shower, to take a shower
fare un picnic = to have a picnic
• (talking about the weather)
fa freddo = it's cold
fa bel tempo = it's nice weather
• (with the infinitive)
l'hai fatto piangere = you made him cry
mi hai fatto fare un errore = you've made me make a mistake
fammi parlare! = let me speak!
ho fatto riparare il cancello = I had the gate repaired
mi sono fatta fare un vestito = I had a dress made

farfalla noun, feminine
una farfalla = a butterfly

farina noun, feminine
la farina = flour

farmacia noun, feminine (plural farmacie)
una farmacia = a chemist's, a drugstore

faro noun, masculine
• un faro = a lighthouse
• i fari = the headlights

fascia noun, feminine (plural fasce)
una fascia = a band
= a bandage

fasciare verb 6
= to bandage

fascino noun, masculine
il fascino = charm

fascismo noun, masculine
il fascismo = Fascism

fascista adjective (plural fascisti/fasciste)
= Fascist

fase noun, feminine
una fase = a phase

fastidio noun, masculine
dare fastidio a = to annoy

fatale adjective
= fatal

fate ▶ fare

fatica noun, feminine
  una fatica = hard work

faticoso/faticosa adjective
  = tiring

fatto/fatta
1 ▶ fare
2 **fatto** noun, masculine
  un fatto = a fact
  = an event

fattore noun, masculine
• un fattore = a factor
• un fattore = a farmer

fattoria noun, feminine
  una fattoria = a farm

fattura noun, feminine
  una fattura = an invoice

favola noun, feminine
  una favola = a fairy tale

favoloso/favolosa adjective
  = fabulous

favore noun, masculine
  un favore = a favo(u)r
  per favore = please

favorevole adjective
  = favo(u)rable

fazzoletto noun, masculine
  un fazzoletto = a handkerchief

febbraio noun, masculine
  = February

febbre noun, feminine
  avere la febbre = to have a temperature

fece, feci, etc ▶ fare

fede noun, feminine
• la fede = faith
• una fede = a wedding ring

fedele adjective
  = faithful

fedeltà noun, feminine
  la fedeltà = loyalty

federa noun, feminine
  una federa = a pillowcase

fegato noun, masculine
  il fegato = the liver

felice adjective
  = happy

felicità noun, feminine
  la felicità = happiness

felpa noun, feminine
  una felpa = a sweatshirt

femmina
1 adjective
  = female
2 noun, feminine
  una femmina = a female
  = a girl

femminile adjective
  = female
  = feminine

feriale adjective
  un giorno feriale = a weekday

ferie noun, feminine plural
  le ferie = the holidays, the vacation
  in ferie = on holiday, on vacation

ferire verb ⑨
  = to injure
  = to wound

ferita noun, feminine
  una ferita = an injury
  = a wound

ferito/ferita
1 adjective
  = injured
  = wounded
2 noun, masculine/feminine
  un ferito/una ferita = an injured person
  i feriti = the injured

fermare verb ①
1 = to stop
2 **fermarsi** (! + essere)
  fermarsi = to stop

fermata noun, feminine
  una fermata = a stop

fermo/ferma adjective
  = stationary
  la macchina era ferma = the car wasn't moving
  stai fermo! = stay still!

feroce adjective
  = fierce

Ferragosto noun, masculine
  Ferragosto Italian public holiday on August 15

ferro noun, masculine
• il ferro = iron
• un ferro (da stiro) = an iron

ferrovia noun, feminine
  la ferrovia = the railway, the railroad

festa noun, feminine
• una festa = a holiday
• una festa = a party

festeggiare verb ③
  = to celebrate

festivo/festiva adjective
  un giorno festivo = a holiday

fetta noun, feminine
  una fetta = a slice

fiamma noun, feminine
  una fiamma = a flame

fiammifero noun, masculine
  un fiammifero = a match

fianco noun, masculine (plural fianchi)
• il fianco = the side
• i fianchi = the hips

F

fiasco noun, masculine (plural **fiaschi**)
• un fiasco di vino = a flask of wine
• un fiasco = a flop

fiato noun, masculine
il fiato = breath

ficcare verb [4]
= to put

fico noun, masculine (plural **fichi**)
un fico = a fig
= a fig tree

fidanzato/fidanzata
1 adjective
= engaged
2 noun, masculine|feminine
un fidanzato/una fidanzata = a fiancé/a fiancée

fidarsi verb [1] (! + essere)
fidarsi di qualcuno = to trust someone

fiducia noun, feminine
la fiducia = trust

fiera noun, feminine
una fiera = a fair

fiero/fiera adjective
= proud

figlio/figlia noun, masculine|feminine
(plural **figli/figlie**)
un figlio/una figlia = a son/a daughter
i figli = the children

figura noun, feminine
• una figura = a figure
• una figura = a picture

figurarsi verb [1] (! + essere)
= to imagine
figurati! = imagine that!

fila noun, feminine
• una fila = a row
• una fila = a queue, a line

film noun, masculine (! never changes)
un film = a film, a movie

filmare verb [1]
= to film

filo noun, masculine
• un filo = a string
= a thread
• un filo = a wire
senza fili = wireless

filosofia noun, feminine
la filosofia = philosophy

finale
1 adjective
= final
2 noun, feminine
la finale = the final
3 noun, masculine
il finale = the end

finalmente adverb
= finally

finanza noun, feminine
la finanza = finance

finché conjunction
= for as long as
finché dura = for as long as it lasts
finché (non) ne arrivano degli altri = until some more arrive

fine
1 noun, feminine
la fine = the end
2 noun, masculine
il fine = the aim
3 adjective
= fine

fine settimana noun, masculine
il fine settimana = the weekend

finestra noun, feminine
una finestra = a window

fingere verb [48]
= to pretend

finire verb [9] (! + essere or avere)
= to finish
hai finito di mangiare? = have you finished eating?

fino a preposition
= until
= as far as

finora adverb
= so far

finse, finsi, etc ▶ fingere

finta noun, feminine
fare finta di dormire = to pretend to be asleep

finto/finta
1 ▶ fingere
2 adjective
= false

fiocco noun, masculine (plural **fiocchi**)
• un fiocco = a bow
= a bow tie
• un fiocco = a flake

fioraio/fioraia noun, masculine|feminine
(plural **fiorai/fioraie**)
un fioraio/una fioraia = a florist

fiore noun, masculine
un fiore = a flower

fiorentino/fiorentina adjective
= Florentine

Firenze noun
= Florence

firma noun, feminine
una firma = a signature

firmare verb [1]
= to sign

fischiare verb [6]
= to whistle

fischio noun, masculine (plural **fischi**)
un fischio = a whistle

fisica noun, feminine
la fisica = physics

fisico/fisica adjective (plural
fisici/fisiche)
= physical

fissare verb 1
• = to fix
• = to stare at

fisso/fissa adjective
= fixed
= steady

fitto/fitta adjective
= thick

fiume noun, masculine
un fiume = a river

flauto noun, masculine
un flauto = a flute

fodera noun, feminine
la fodera = the lining

foglia noun, feminine
una foglia = a leaf

foglio noun, masculine (plural **fogli**)
un foglio = a sheet of paper

fogna noun, feminine
una fogna = a drain

folla noun, feminine
una folla = a crowd

folle adjective
= mad, crazy

follia noun, feminine
la follia = madness

fon noun, masculine (! never changes)
un fon = a hairdryer

fondamentale adjective
= basic

fondare verb 1
= to found

fondo noun, masculine
il fondo = the bottom
in fondo alla scatola = at the bottom of
the box
in fondo alla classe = at the back of the
classroom
in fondo al corridoio = at the end of the
corridor

fontana noun, feminine
una fontana = a fountain

fonte noun, feminine
• una fonte = a spring
• una fonte = a source

footing noun, masculine
fare footing = to go jogging

forbici noun, feminine plural
le forbici = scissors

forchetta noun, feminine
una forchetta = a fork

foresta noun, feminine
una foresta = a forest

forfora noun, feminine
la forfora = dandruff

forma noun, feminine
una forma = a form
= a shape
in forma = in good shape

formaggio noun, masculine (plural
formaggi)
il formaggio = cheese

formale adjective
= formal

formare verb 1
= to form

formica noun, feminine (plural **formiche**)
una formica = an ant

formidabile adjective
= tremendous

fornaio/fornaia noun,
masculine/feminine (plural **fornai/fornaie**)
un fornaio/una fornaia = a baker

fornire verb 9
= to supply

forno noun, masculine
un forno = an oven
un forno a microonde = a microwave

foro noun, masculine
un foro = a hole

forse adverb
= perhaps

forte
1 adjective
= strong
2 adverb
= hard
pioveva forte = it was raining heavily
parlare forte = to talk loudly

fortuna noun, feminine
la fortuna = luck
avere fortuna = to be lucky

fortunato/fortunata adjective
= lucky

forza noun, feminine
• la forza = strength
= force
• forza! = come on!

foschia noun, feminine
la foschia = mist

fossa noun, feminine
una fossa = a hole

fosso noun, masculine
un fosso = a ditch

fosti, **foste**, etc ▶ essere

F

foto *noun, feminine* (**!** *never changes*)
una foto = a photo
fare una foto a qualcuno = to take a photo of someone

fotocopia *noun, feminine*
una fotocopia = a photocopy

fotocopiare *verb* 6
= to photocopy

fotografare *verb* 1
= to photograph

fotografia *noun, feminine*
- **una fotografia** = a photograph
- **la fotografia** = photography

fotografo/fotografa *noun, masculine/feminine*
un fotografo/una fotografa = a photographer

foulard *noun, masculine* (**!** *never changes*)
un foulard = a scarf

fra, tra *preposition*
- = between
  = among
- **fra due anni** = in two years' time
  fra poco = soon

fragile *adjective*
= fragile

fragola *noun, feminine*
una fragola = a strawberry

frana *noun, feminine*
una frana = a landslide

francese *adjective*
= French

Francia *noun, feminine*
la Francia = France

franco/franca (*plural* **franchi/franche**)
1 *adjective*
= frank
2 **franco** *noun, masculine*
un franco = a franc

francobollo *noun, masculine*
un francobollo = a stamp

frase *noun, feminine*
una frase = a sentence

fratello *noun, masculine*
un fratello = a brother
i fratelli = brothers and sisters

frattempo *noun, masculine*
nel frattempo = meanwhile

frattura *noun, feminine*
una frattura = a fracture

fratturare *verb* 1
= to fracture

frazione *noun, feminine*
una frazione = a fraction

freccia *noun, feminine* (*plural* **frecce**)
- **una freccia** = an arrow
- (*on a car*)
  la freccia = the indicator

freddo/fredda
1 *adjective*
= cold
2 **freddo** *noun, masculine*
il freddo = cold
avere freddo = to be cold
fa freddo = it's cold

fregare *verb* 5
1 (**!** + *avere*)
- = to rub
- ✖ = to pinch, to swipe
- ✖ = to cheat

2 **fregarsene**✖ (**!** + *essere*)
me ne frego = I don't give a damn

frenare *verb* 1
= to brake

freno *noun, masculine*
un freno = a brake

frequentare *verb* 1
- = to go to
- = to hang around with

frequente *adjective*
= frequent

fresco/fresca *adjective* (*plural* **freschi/fresche**)
- = fresh
- = cool

fretta *noun, feminine*
avere fretta = to be in a hurry
in fretta = quickly

friggere *verb* 39
= to fry

frigorifero *noun, masculine*
un frigorifero = a fridge

frittata *noun, feminine*
una frittata = an omelet(te)

fritto/fritta
1 ▶ **friggere**
2 *adjective*
= fried

frizione *noun, feminine*
la frizione = the clutch

frizzante *adjective*
= fizzy

fronte
1 *noun, feminine*
la fronte = the forehead
2 *noun, masculine*
un fronte = a front
3 **di fronte a** *preposition*
= opposite
di fronte alla banca = opposite the bank

frontiera *noun, feminine*
la frontiera = the border

✖ in informal situations

frullato *noun, masculine*
un frullato = a milk shake

frutta *noun, feminine*
la frutta = fruit

fruttivendolo/fruttivendola *noun, masculine/feminine*
un fruttivendolo/una fruttivendola = a greengrocer

frutto *noun, masculine*
un frutto = a piece of fruit

fu ▶ **essere**

fucile *noun, masculine*
un fucile = a gun

fuga *noun, feminine (plural* **fughe***)*
• una fuga = an escape
• una fuga = a leak

fuggire *verb* [10] *(***!** *+ essere)*
= to flee

fui ▶ **essere**

fulminare *verb* [1]
1 essere fulminato = to be struck by lightning
2 fulminarsi (**!** *+ essere*)
si è fulminata la lampadina = the bulb has gone

fulmine *noun, masculine*
un fulmine = a flash of lightning
i fulmini = lightning

fumare *verb* [1]
= to smoke

fumatore/fumatrice *noun, masculine/feminine*
un fumatore/una fumatrice = a smoker
fumatori o non fumatori? = smoking or non-smoking?

fumetto *noun, masculine*
un fumetto = a cartoon

fummo ▶ **essere**

fumo *noun, masculine*
• il fumo = smoke
• il fumo = smoking

funerale *noun, masculine*
un funerale = a funeral

fungo *noun, masculine (plural* **funghi***)*
un fungo = a mushroom

funzionare *verb* [1]
= to work
far funzionare = to operate

funzione *noun, feminine*
una funzione = a function

fuoco *noun, masculine (plural* **fuochi***)*
un fuoco = a fire
dare fuoco a una casa = to set fire to a house
i fuochi d'artificio = fireworks

fuori *adverb*
= out
= outside
fuori dell'Italia = outside Italy

furbo/furba *adjective*
= clever, smart
= cunning

furgone *noun, masculine*
un furgone = a van

furono ▶ **essere**

furto *noun, masculine*
un furto = a theft

futuro/futura
1 *adjective*
= future
2 futuro *noun, masculine*
il futuro = the future

Gg

gabbia *noun, feminine*
una gabbia = a cage

gabinetto *noun, masculine*
il gabinetto = the toilet, the bathroom

galera✶ *noun, feminine*
in galera = in jail

galleggiare *verb* [3]
= to float

galleria *noun, feminine*
• una galleria = a gallery
• una galleria = a tunnel

Galles *noun, masculine*
il Galles = Wales

gallese *adjective*
= Welsh

gallina *noun, feminine*
una gallina = a hen

gallo *noun, masculine*
un gallo = a cock, a rooster

gamba *noun, feminine*
una gamba = a leg

gamberetto *noun, masculine*
un gamberetto = a shrimp

gambero *noun, masculine*
un gambero = a prawn, a shrimp

gancio *noun, masculine (plural* **ganci***)*
un gancio = a hook

gara *noun, feminine*
una gara = a race
= a competition

garantire verb [9]
= to guarantee

garanzia noun, feminine
una garanzia = a guarantee

gas noun, masculine (! never changes)
il gas = gas

gasolio noun, masculine
il gasolio = diesel

gassato/gassata adjective
= fizzy

gatto/gatta noun, masculine/feminine
un gatto/una gatta = a cat

gelare verb [1] (! + essere or avere)
= to freeze

gelateria noun, feminine
una gelateria = an ice cream parlo(u)r

gelato/gelata
1 adjective
= frozen
2 **gelato** noun, masculine
il gelato = ice cream

gelido/gelida adjective
= freezing

gelo noun, masculine
il gelo = frost

geloso/gelosa adjective
= jealous

gemello/gemella noun,
masculine/feminine
1 i gemelli = twins
2 **Gemelli**
= Gemini

generale
1 adjective
= general
2 noun, masculine
un generale = a general

generazione noun, feminine
una generazione = a generation

genere noun, masculine
un genere = a kind

genero noun, masculine
un genero = a son-in-law

generoso/generosa adjective
= generous

geniale adjective
= brilliant

genio noun, masculine (plural **geni**)
un genio = a genius

genitore noun, masculine
un genitore = a parent
i miei genitori = my parents

gennaio noun, masculine
= January

Genova noun
= Genoa

genovese adjective
= Genoese

gente noun, feminine (! never changes)
la gente = people
c'era troppa gente = there were too many
people

gentile adjective
= kind

gentilezza noun, feminine
la gentilezza = kindness

geografia noun, feminine
la geografia = geography

geometra noun, masculine/feminine
(plural **geometri/geometre**)
un/una geometra = a quantity surveyor

Germania noun, feminine
la Germania = Germany

gesso noun, masculine
il gesso = chalk

gestione noun, feminine
la gestione = the management

gestire verb [9]
= to run

gesto noun, masculine
un gesto = a gesture

gettare verb [1]
= to throw

gettone noun, masculine
un gettone = a telephone token

ghiaccio noun, masculine
il ghiaccio = ice

già adverb
= already
sono già partiti = they've already left

giacca noun, feminine (plural **giacche**)
una giacca = a jacket
una giacca a vento = a windcheater, a
windbreaker

giaccone noun, masculine
un giaccone = a jacket

giallo/gialla adjective
= yellow

Giappone noun, masculine
il Giappone = Japan

giapponese adjective
= Japanese

giardino noun, masculine
un giardino = a garden, a yard

gigante noun, masculine
un gigante = a giant

gilè noun, masculine (! never changes)
un gilè = a waistcoat, a vest

ginnastica noun, feminine
la ginnastica = gymnastics

ginocchio *noun, masculine (plural* **ginocchia***)*
> **!** *Note that* **ginocchia** *is feminine.*

un ginocchio = a knee

giocare *verb* 4
- • = to play
  giocare a tennis = to play tennis
- • = to bet
  = to gamble

giocatore/giocatrice *noun,*
masculine/feminine
- • un giocatore/una giocatrice = a player
- • un giocatore/una giocatrice = a gambler

giocattolo *noun, masculine*
un giocattolo = a toy

gioco *noun, masculine (plural* **giochi***)*
- • un gioco = a game
  fare un gioco = to play a game
- • il gioco = gambling
  i giochi olimpici = the Olympic Games
  i giochi paraolimpici = the Paralympic
  Games

gioia *noun, feminine*
la gioia = joy

gioielleria *noun, feminine*
una gioielleria = a jewel(l)er's shop

gioiello *noun, masculine*
un gioiello = a jewel
i gioielli = jewel(l)ery

giornalaio/giornalaia *noun,*
masculine/feminine (plural
giornalai/giornalaie*)*
un giornalaio/una giornalaia = a
newsagent, a newsdealer

giornale *noun, masculine*
un giornale = a newspaper

giornalismo *noun, masculine*
il giornalismo = journalism

giornalista *noun, masculine/feminine*
(plural **giornalisti/giornaliste***)*
un/una giornalista = a journalist

giornata *noun, feminine*
una giornata = a day

giorno *noun, masculine*
un giorno = a day

giovane
1 *adjective*
  = young
2 *noun, masculine/feminine*
un/una giovane = a young person
i giovani = the young

giovedì *noun, masculine (**!** never*
changes)
  = Thursday
il giovedì = on Thursdays

gioventù *noun, feminine*
la gioventù = youth

girare *verb* 1
1 (**!** + *avere*)

- • = to turn (over)
- • = to walk around
- • mi gira la testa = I feel dizzy
- • girare un film = to shoot a film
2 **girarsi** (**!** + *essere*)
  = to turn (around)

girasole *noun, masculine*
un girasole = a sunflower

giro *noun, masculine*
- • un giro = a tour
  fare il giro di = to go around
- • prendere in giro qualcuno = to make fun
  of someone

gironzolare *verb* 1
  = to hang around

gita *noun, feminine*
una gita = a trip

giù *adverb*
  = down
  porto giù la valigia = I'll take the case
  downstairs

giubbotto *noun, masculine*
un giubbotto = a jacket

giudicare *verb* 4
  = to judge

giudice *noun, masculine*
un giudice = a judge

giudizio *noun, masculine (plural* **giudizi***)*
un giudizio = a judg(e)ment

giugno *noun, masculine*
  = June

giungla *noun, feminine*
una giungla = a jungle

giurare *verb* 1
  = to swear

giuria *noun, feminine*
la giuria = the jury

giustizia *noun, feminine*
la giustizia = justice

giusto/giusta *adjective*
- • = right
- • = fair
  = just

gli ▶ il

gli/le *pronoun*
  = to him/to her
> **!** *Note that in spoken Italian* **gli** *is often*
> *used to mean 'to her' or 'to them'.*

gli ho detto la verità = I told
  him/her/them the truth
> **!** *When* **gli** *or* **le** *come immediately*
> *before* **lo/la, li/le,** *or* **ne,** *they combine*
> *to form* **glielo/gliela, glieli/gliele,** *and*
> **gliene.**

gliene ho dato un po' = I gave him some

glielo/gliela, glieli/gliele, gliene
  ▶ gli

G

goccia noun, feminine (plural **gocce**)
una goccia = a drop

goccio noun, masculine
un goccio di = a drop of

gocciolare verb ①
= to drip

gol noun, masculine (! never changes)
un gol = a goal

gola noun, feminine
la gola = the throat

golf noun, masculine (! never changes)
• il golf = golf
• un golf = a cardigan

golfo noun, masculine
un golfo = a gulf

goloso/golosa adjective
= greedy

gomito noun, masculine
il gomito = the elbow

gomma noun, feminine
• la gomma = rubber
• una gomma = an eraser
• una gomma = a tyre, a tire

gonfiare verb ⑥
1 = to inflate
2 gonfiarsi (! + essere)
= to swell (up)

gonfio/gonfia adjective
= swollen

gonna noun, feminine
una gonna = a skirt

gotico/gotica adjective (plural **gotici/gotiche**)
= Gothic

governo noun, masculine
il governo = the government

gradevole adjective
= pleasant

gradino noun, masculine
un gradino = a step

grado noun, masculine
un grado = a degree
trenta gradi = 30°C

graduale adjective
= gradual

graffiare verb ⑥
= to scratch

graffio noun, masculine (plural **graffi**)
un graffio = a scratch

grafico noun, masculine (plural **grafici**)
• un grafico = a graph
• un grafico = a graphic designer

grammatica noun, feminine
la grammatica = grammar

grammo noun, masculine
un grammo = a gram

gran ▶ **grande**

Gran Bretagna noun, feminine
la Gran Bretagna = Great Britain

granché pronoun
non era un granché = it was nothing special

granchio noun, masculine (plural **granchi**)
un granchio = a crab

grande adjective (! sometimes **gran** before a noun)
• = big
• = great
• = grown-up

grandezza noun, feminine
la grandezza = size

grandinare verb ①
= to hail

grandine noun, feminine
la grandine = hail

grano noun, masculine
• un grano = a grain
• il grano = wheat

granturco noun, masculine
il granturco = maize, corn

grappolo noun, masculine
un grappolo d'uva = a bunch of grapes

grasso/grassa adjective
• = fat
• = fatty
= greasy

gratis adverb
= free

grato/grata adjective
= grateful

grattugia noun, feminine (plural **grattugie**)
una grattugia = a grater

grattugiare verb ③
= to grate

gratuito/gratuita adjective
= free

grave adjective
= serious

gravidanza noun, feminine
la gravidanza = pregnancy

gravità noun, feminine
• la gravità = seriousness
• la gravità = gravity

grazia noun, feminine
la grazia = grace

grazie exclamation
grazie! = thank you!

grazioso/graziosa adjective
= pretty

Grecia noun, feminine
  la Grecia = Greece

greco/greca adjective (plural
  greci/greche)
  = Greek

grida ▶ **grido**

gridare verb [1]
  = to shout

grido noun, masculine (plural **grida**)
  ┌─────────────────────────────────┐
  │ **!** Note that **grida** is feminine. │
  └─────────────────────────────────┘
  un grido = a shout

grigio/grigia adjective (plural
  grigi/grigie)
  = grey, gray

griglia noun, feminine
  una griglia = a grill
  alla griglia = grilled

grillo noun, masculine
  un grillo = a cricket

grosso/grossa adjective
  = big

gruppo noun, masculine
  un gruppo = a group

guadagnare verb [1]
  = to earn

guaio noun, masculine (plural **guai**)
  un guaio = a problem
  essere nei guai = to be in trouble

guancia noun, feminine (plural **guance**)
  una guancia = a cheek

guanciale noun, masculine
  un guanciale = a pillow

guanto noun, masculine
  un guanto = a glove

guardare verb [1]
• = to look at
  = to watch
• guardare un bambino = to look after a
  child

guardia noun, feminine
  una guardia = a guard

guarire verb [9] (**!** + essere)
  = to get better

guasto/guasta
1 adjective
  = out of order
2 **guasto** noun, masculine
  un guasto = a fault

guerra noun, feminine
  una guerra = a war

gufo noun, masculine
  un gufo = an owl

guida noun, feminine
• una guida = a guide
• la guida = driving

guidare verb [1]
  = to drive

gusto noun, masculine
• il gusto = taste
• un gusto = a flavo(u)r

ha, **hai** ▶ **avere**

handicappato/handicappata
  adjective
  = handicapped

hanno, **ho** ▶ **avere**

Ii

i ▶ **il**

idea noun, feminine
  un'idea = an idea
  non ne ho idea = I've no idea

ideale adjective
  = ideal

identico/identica adjective (plural
  identici/identiche)
  = identical

identificare verb [4]
  = to identify

identità noun, feminine (**!** never
  changes)
  un'identità = an identity

idiota noun, masculine/feminine (plural
  idioti/idiote)
  un idiota/un'idiota = an idiot

idraulico noun, masculine (plural
  idraulici)
  un idraulico = a plumber

ieri adverb
  = yesterday
  ieri l'altro = the day before yesterday

igienico/igienica adjective (plural
  igienici/igieniche)
  = hygienic

ignorante adjective
  = ignorant

H
I

ignorare verb [1]
• = to ignore
• = not to know

il determiner

> ! Note that **il** can have the forms **lo, l',
> la, i, gli, le**. Look at the notes on **the,
> The human body,** and **Countries,
> cities, and continents** for more detailed
> information.

• = the
il Colosseo = the Colosseum
la Torre Pendente = the Leaning Tower
dove ho messo l'ombrello? = where did I
   put my umbrella?
non ho la macchina = I don't have a car
chiudi gli occhi! = close your eyes!

> ! Note that **il, la,** etc are sometimes not
> translated.

le sigarette sono care = cigarettes are
   expensive
non mi piace il vino = I don't like wine
la Francia = France
il Vesuvio = Vesuvius
• **il lunedì** = on Mondays
• **le tre** = three o'clock
sono le ventidue = it's 10 pm
• **nel 1265** = in 1265

illegale adjective
= illegal

illuminare verb [1]
= to light (up)

illusione noun, feminine
un'illusione = an illusion

imbarazzato/imbarazzata adjective
= embarrassed

imbarazzo noun, masculine
l'imbarazzo = embarrassment
mettere in imbarazzo = to embarrass

imbarco noun, masculine
l'imbarco = boarding

imbecille noun, masculine/feminine
un imbecille/un'imbecille = an idiot

imbiancare verb [4]
= to paint

imbrogliare verb [6]
= to cheat

imbroglio noun, masculine (plural
imbrogli)
un imbroglio = a trick

imbucare verb [4]
= to post, to mail

imitare verb [1]
= to imitate

imitazione noun, feminine
un'imitazione = an imitation

immaginare verb [1]
= to imagine

immaginazione noun, feminine
l'immaginazione = imagination

immagine noun, feminine
un'immagine = an image
= a picture

immediato/immediata adjective
= immediate

immenso/immensa adjective
= huge

immersione noun, feminine
un'immersione = a dive

immigrato/immigrata noun,
masculine/feminine
un immigrato/un'immigrata = an
   immigrant

imparare verb [1]
= to learn
imparare a guidare = to learn to drive

impaziente adjective
= impatient

impazzire verb [9] (! + essere)
= to go crazy

impedire verb [9]
• = to block
• **impedire a qualcuno di fare qualcosa**
   = to prevent someone from doing
   something

impegnarsi verb [1] (! + essere)
= to work hard

impegnato/impegnata adjective
• = busy
• = committed

impegno noun, masculine
• **un impegno** = a commitment
domani ho un impegno = I'm busy
   tomorrow
• **l'impegno** = determination
= effort

imperatore/imperatrice noun,
masculine/feminine
un imperatore/un'imperatrice = an
   emperor/an empress

impermeabile noun, masculine
un impermeabile = a raincoat

impero noun, masculine
un impero = an empire

impiccare verb [4]
= to hang

impiegare verb [5]
= to use

impiegato/impiegata noun,
masculine/feminine
un impiegato/un'impiegata = an office
   worker

impiego noun, masculine (plural
impieghi)
un impiego = a job
trovare impiego = to find work

imporre *verb* [50]
= to impose

importante *adjective*
= important

importanza *noun, feminine*
l'importanza = importance
non ha importanza = it's not important

importare *verb* [1]
• (**!** + *essere*) = to matter
non m'importa = I don't care
• (**!** + *avere*) = to import

importazione *noun, feminine*
un'importazione = an import

impossibile *adjective*
= impossible

imposta di successione *noun, feminine*
l'imposta di successione = inheritance tax

imprenditore/imprenditrice *noun,*
masculine/feminine
un imprenditore/un'imprenditrice = a
businessman/a businesswoman

impresa *noun, feminine*
un'impresa = a business

impressionante *adjective*
= shocking

impressione *noun, feminine*
un'impressione = an impression

imprevisto/imprevista
1 *adjective*
= unforeseen
2 imprevisto *noun masculine*
gli imprevisti = unexpected things

improbabile *adjective*
= improbable

improvvisamente *adverb*
= suddenly

improviso/improvisa *adjective*
= sudden
d'improvviso = suddenly

in *preposition*

> **!** *Note that* **in** *combines with* **il**, **la**, *etc.*
> **In** + **il** = **nel**; **in** + **l'** = **nell'**; **in** + **lo**
> = **nello**; **in** + **i** = **nei**; **in** + **gli** = **negli**;
> **in** + **la** = **nella**; **in** + **le** = **nelle**.

• = in
vivo in Italia = I live in Italy
• = to
vado in Francia = I'm going to France
• (*means of transport*) = by
in bicicletta = by bike
• siamo in nove = there are nine of us

inaccettabile *adjective*
= unacceptable

incantevole *adjective*
= charming

incapace *adjective*
= incapable

incazzato/incazzata⚈ *adjective*
= pissed off

incendio *noun, masculine* (*plural*
incendi)
un incendio = a fire

incertezza *noun, feminine*
l'incertezza = uncertainty

incerto/incerta *adjective*
= uncertain

inchiesta *noun, feminine*
un'inchiesta = an enquiry

inchiostro *noun, masculine*
l'inchiostro = ink

inciampare *verb* [1]
inciampare in = to stumble over

incidente *noun, masculine*
un incidente = an accident

incinta *adjective*
= pregnant

incirca *adverb*
all'incirca = approximately

incluso/inclusa *adjective*
= included
= including

incollare *verb* [1]
= to stick

incomprensibile *adjective*
= incomprehensible

incontrare *verb* [1]
= to meet
= to encounter

incontro *noun, masculine*
un incontro = a meeting

incoraggiare *verb* [3]
= to encourage

inconsciente *adjective*
= irresponsible

incredibile *adjective*
= incredible

incrocio *noun, masculine* (*plural*
incroci)
un incrocio = a junction

incubo *noun, masculine*
un incubo = a nightmare

indagare *verb* [5]
= to investigate

indagine *noun, feminine*
un'indagine = an investigation

indeciso/indecisa *adjective*
• = undecided
• = indecisive

indicare *verb* [4]
= to indicate

indicato/indicata *adjective*
= suitable

I

indicazione *noun, feminine*
- un'indicazione = an indication
- le indicazioni = directions

indice *noun, masculine*
- un indice = an index
- l'indice = the index finger

indietro *adverb*
essere indietro = to be behind
tornare indietro = to go back
all'indietro = backwards

indifferente *adjective*
= indifferent
per me è indifferente = it's all the same to me

indipendente *adjective*
= independent

indipendenza *noun, feminine*
l'indipendenza = independence

indiretto/indiretta *adjective*
= indirect

indirizzo *noun, masculine*
un indirizzo = an address
un indirizzo email = an email address

individuale *adjective*
= individual

individuare *verb* [1]
= to identify

individuo *noun, masculine*
un individuo = an individual

indizio *noun, masculine* (*plural* indizi)
un indizio = a clue

indossare *verb* [1]
= to wear

indovinare *verb* [1]
= to guess

industria *noun, feminine*
l'industria = industry

inevitabile *adjective*
= inevitable

infanzia *noun, feminine*
l'infanzia = childhood

infarto *noun, masculine*
un infarto = a heart attack

infastidire *verb* [9]
= to irritate

infatti *conjunction*
= indeed
infatti! = exactly!

infelice *adjective*
= unhappy

inferiore *adjective*
= lower
= inferior

infermiere/infermiera *noun, masculine/feminine*
un infermiere/un'infermiera = a nurse

inferno *noun, masculine*
l'inferno = hell

infezione *noun, feminine*
un'infezione = an infection

infine *adverb*
= finally

infinito/infinita *adjective*
= infinite

inflazione *noun, feminine*
l'inflazione = inflation

influenza *noun, feminine*
- un'inflenza = an influence
- l'influenza = flu

informale *adjective*
= informal

informare *verb* [1]
1 = to inform
2 informarsi (! + *essere*)
informarsi di = to find out about

informatica *noun, feminine*
l'informatica = information technology

informazione *noun, feminine*
un'informazione = a piece of information
l'informazione = information

ingannare *verb* [1]
= to trick

ingegnere *noun, masculine*
un ingegnere = an engineer

ingegneria *noun, feminine*
l'ingegneria = engineering

Inghilterra *noun, feminine*
l'Inghilterra = England

inghiottire *verb* [9]
= to swallow

inglese *adjective*
= English

ingrandimento *noun, masculine*
un ingrandimento = an enlargement

ingrassare *verb* [1] (! + *essere*)
= to put on weight

ingrediente *noun, masculine*
un ingrediente = an ingredient

ingresso *noun, masculine*
l'ingresso = the entrance

iniziale
1 *adjective*
= initial
2 *noun, feminine*
le iniziali = the initials

iniziare *verb* [6] (! + *essere* or *avere*)
= to start

inizio *noun, masculine* (*plural* inizi)
l'inizio = the beginning

innamorarsi verb [1] (**!** + *essere*)
= to fall in love

innamorato/innamorata *adjective*
essere innamorato/innamorata di
qualcuno = to be in love with someone

innocente *adjective*
= innocent

inoltre *adverb*
= besides

inquilino/inquilina *noun,*
masculine/feminine
un inquilino/un'inquilina = a tenant

inquinamento *noun, masculine*
l'inquinamento = pollution

inquinare verb [1]
= to pollute

insalata *noun, feminine*
l'insalata = salad

insegna *noun, feminine*
un'insegna = a sign

insegnamento *noun, masculine*
l'insegnamento = teaching

insegnante *noun, masculine/feminine*
un insegnante/un'insegnante = a teacher

insegnare verb [1]
= to teach

inserire verb [9]
= to insert

insetto *noun, masculine*
un insetto = an insect

insieme *adverb*
= together
insieme a noi = together with us

insistere verb [16]
insistere su = to insist on

insolito/insolita *adjective*
= unusual

insomma *adverb*
= well
insomma! = really!

insopportabile *adjective*
= unbearable

installare verb [1]
= to install

insultare verb
= to insult

intanto *adverb*
= meanwhile

integrale *adjective*
• = complete
• pane integrale = wholemeal bread

intelligente *adjective*
= intelligent

intendere verb [53]
• = to intend

= to mean
• = to understand

intenditore/intenditrice *noun,*
masculine/feminine
un intenditore/un'intenditrice = a
connoisseur

intensivo/intensiva *adjective*
= intensive

intenso/intensa *adjective*
= intense

intenzione *noun, feminine*
un'intenzione = an intention
ho intenzione di smettere = I intend to
stop

interessante *adjective*
= interesting

interessare verb [1]
= to interest

interesse *noun, masculine*
• l'interesse = interest
• (*in a bank*)
gli interessi = interest

interiore *adjective*
= inner

internazionale *adjective*
= international

Internet *noun, masculine*
l'Internet = the Internet

interno/interna
1 *adjective*
= internal
= inside
2 **interno** *noun, masculine*
l'interno = the inside

intero/intera *adjective*
= whole

interpretare verb [1]
= to interpret

interpretazione *noun, feminine*
un'interpretazione = an interpretation

interprete *noun, masculine/feminine*
• un interprete/un'interprete = an
interpreter
• un interprete/un'interprete = a performer

interrogare verb [5]
• = to interrogate
• (*in school*) = to test

interrompere verb [60]
= to interrupt

interrotto/interrotta, interruppe,
etc ▶ interrompere

interruttore *noun, masculine*
un interruttore = a switch

interruzione *noun, feminine*
un'interruzione = an interruption

interurbana *noun, feminine*
un'interurbana = a long-distance call

intervallo *noun, masculine*
  un intervallo = an interval, an intermission

intervengo, **intervengono**, etc ▶ intervenire

intervenire *verb* 78 (**!** + *essere*)
  = to intervene
  = to take part

intervento *noun, masculine*
  • **l'intervento** = the intervention
  • **un intervento chirurgico** = an operation

interviene, **intervenuto**/
  intervenuta, etc ▶ intervenire

intervista *noun, feminine*
  un'intervista = an interview

intervistare *verb* 1
  = to interview

intese, **inteso**/**intesa**, etc
1 ▶ intendere
2 *adjective*
  siamo intesi? = is that understood?

intimo/**intima** *adjective*
  = intimate

intorno
1 *adverb*
  = around
2 **intorno a** *preposition*
  = around
  intorno al tavolo = around the table

introdotto/**introdotta** ▶ introdurre

introdurre *verb* 54
  • = to introduce
  • = to insert

introdusse, **introdussero**, etc ▶
  introdurre

introduzione *noun, feminine*
  l'introduzione = the introduction

inutile *adjective*
  = useless
  è inutile che tu piangi = it's a waste of
    time crying

invadere *verb* 46
  = to invade

invasione *noun, feminine*
  un'invasione = an invasion

invase, **invaso**/**invasa**, etc ▶
  invadere

invecchiare *verb* 6 (**!** + *essere*)
  = to get old

invece *adverb*
  = instead
  invece di = instead of

inventare *verb* 1
  = to invent

invenzione *noun, feminine*
  un'invenzione = an invention

invernale *adjective*
  = winter

inverno *noun, masculine*
  l'inverno = winter
  d'inverno = in winter

investimento *noun, masculine*
  un investimento = an investment

investire *verb* 9
  • = to invest
  • = to knock down

inviare *verb* 7
  = to send

invidiare *verb* 6
  = to envy

invisibile *adjective*
  = invisible

invitare *verb* 1
  = to invite

invitato/**invitata** *noun,*
  masculine/feminine
  un invitato/**un'invitata** = a guest

invito *noun, masculine*
  un invito = an invitation

io *pronoun*
  = I
  sono io = it's me

ipotesi *noun, feminine* (**!** *never changes*)
  un'ipotesi = a hypothesis

Irlanda *noun, feminine*
  l'Irlanda = Ireland
  l'Irlanda del Nord = Northern Ireland

irlandese *adjective*
  = Irish

ironico/**ironica** *adjective* (*plural*
  ironici/**ironiche**)
  = ironic

irregolare *adjective*
  = irregular

irresistibile *adjective*
  = irresistible

irresponsabile *adjective*
  = irresponsible

irritare *verb* 1
  = to irritate

iscritto/**iscritta**
1 ▶ iscriversi
2 *noun, masculine/feminine*
  un iscritto/**un'iscritta** = a member

iscriversi *verb* 65 (**!** + *essere*)
  = to enrol(l)

iscrizione *noun, feminine*
  l'iscrizione = enro(l)lment

isola *noun, feminine*
  un'isola = an island

isolato/isolata
1 *adjective*
= isolated
2 **isolato** *noun, masculine*
un isolato = a block

ispettore/ispettrice *noun,*
masculine/feminine
un ispettore/un'ispettrice = an inspector

ispezione *noun, feminine*
un'ispezione = an inspection

ispirare *verb* 1
= to inspire

ispirazione *noun, feminine*
l'ispirazione = inspiration

istante *noun, masculine*
un istante = an instant

istinto *noun, masculine*
l'istinto = instinct

istituto *noun, masculine*
un istituto = an institute

istituzione *noun, feminine*
un'istituzione = an institution

istruzione *noun, feminine*
• l'istruzione = education
• le istruzioni = the instructions

Italia *noun, feminine*
l'Italia = Italy

italiano/italiana *adjective*
= Italian

IVA *noun, feminine*
l'IVA = VAT

Iugoslavia, etc ▶ Jugoslavia, etc

Jugoslavia *noun, feminine*
la Jugoslavia = Yugoslavia

jugoslavo/jugoslava *adjective*
= Yugoslavian

krapfen *noun, masculine* (**!** *never*
changes)
un krapfen = a doughnut

Ll

l'
1 ▶ il
2 ▶ lo/la

la
1 ▶ il
2 ▶ lo/la

là *adverb*
= there

labbro *noun, masculine* (*plural* **labbra**)
> **!** *Note that* **labbra** *is feminine.*

il labbro = the lip

lacca *noun, feminine*
la lacca = hairspray

laccio *noun, masculine* (*plural* **lacci**)
i lacci = shoelaces

lacrima *noun, feminine*
una lacrima = a tear

ladro/ladra *noun, masculine/feminine*
un ladro/una ladra = a thief

laggiù *adverb*
= down there
= over there

lago *noun, masculine* (*plural* **laghi**)
un lago = a lake

lama *noun, feminine*
una lama = a blade

lamentarsi *verb* 1 (**!** + *essere*)
= to complain

lametta *noun, feminine*
una lametta = a razor blade

lampada *noun, feminine*
una lampada = a lamp

lampadina *noun, feminine*
una lampadina = a bulb

lampo *noun, masculine*
un lampo = a flash of lightning
i lampi = lightning

lampone *noun, masculine*
un lampone = a raspberry

lana *noun, feminine*
la lana = wool

lanciare *verb* 2
• = to throw
• = to launch

larghezza *noun, feminine*
la larghezza = width

largo/larga *adjective* (*plural* **larghi/**
larghe)
= wide

J
K
L

lasciare verb 6
- = to leave
  lasciami stare! = leave me alone!
- = to let
  lasciami passare! = let me past!

lassù adverb
= up there

laterale adjective
= side

latino noun, masculine
il latino = Latin

lato noun, masculine
un lato = a side

latte noun, masculine
il latte = milk

lattina noun, feminine
una lattina = a can

laurea noun, feminine
una laurea = a degree

laurearsi verb 1 (! + essere)
= to graduate

laureato/laureata adjective
essere laureato/laureata in lingue = to
have a degree in languages

lavaggio noun, masculine (plural
lavaggi)
il lavaggio = washing
il lavaggio a secco = dry cleaning

lavagna noun, feminine
la lavagna = the board

lavandino noun, masculine
un lavandino = a sink

lavare verb 1
= to wash
mi sono lavato le mani = I washed my
hands

lavastoviglie noun, feminine (! never
changes)
una lavastoviglie = a dishwasher

lavatrice noun, feminine
una lavatrice = a washing machine

lavello noun, masculine
un lavello = a sink

lavorare verb 1
= to work

lavoratore/lavoratrice noun,
masculine/feminine
un lavoratore/una lavoratrice = a worker

lavoro noun, masculine
il lavoro = work
un lavoro = a job

le
1 ▶ **il**
2 ▶ **li/le**
3 ▶ **gli/le**

leccare verb 4
= to lick

lega noun, feminine (plural **leghe**)
- **una lega** = a league
- **una lega** = an alloy

legale adjective
= legal

legame noun, masculine
un legame = a link

legare verb 5
= to tie (up)

legge noun, feminine
la legge = the law

leggenda noun, feminine
una leggenda = a legend

leggere verb 39
= to read

leggermente adverb
= slightly

leggero/leggera adjective
- = light
- = slight

legno noun, masculine
il legno = wood
una sedia di legno = a wooden chair

lei pronoun
- = she
- = her
- = you

lente noun, feminine
una lente = a lens
una lente a contatto = a contact lens

lenticchia noun, feminine
una lenticchia = a lentil

lento/lenta adjective
= slow

lenzuolo noun, masculine (plural
lenzuola)

! Note that **lenzuola** is feminine.

un lenzuolo = a sheet

leone/leonessa noun,
masculine/feminine
1 **un leone/una leonessa** = a lion/a lioness
2 **Leone**
= Leo

lesse, **lessero**, etc ▶ **leggere**

lesso/lessa adjective
= boiled

lettera noun, feminine
una lettera = a letter

letteralmente adverb
= literally

letteratura noun, feminine
la letteratura = literature

lettino noun, masculine
un lettino = a cot, a crib

letto *noun, masculine*
un letto = a bed
andare a letto = to go to bed
un letto a una piazza = a single bed
un letto matrimoniale = a double bed

letto/letta ▶ leggere

lettore/lettrice *noun,*
masculine/feminine
un lettore/una lettrice = a reader
un lettore di compact disc = a CD player
un lettore di DVD = a DVD player

lettura *noun, feminine*
la lettura = reading

levare *verb* ①
= to remove

lezione *noun, feminine*
una lezione = a lesson

li/le *pronoun*
= them
li conosco benissimo = I know them
    really well
li ho mangiati tante volte = I've eaten
    them lots of times

> **!** *Note that* **li** *and* **le** *combine with the
> infinitive, the imperative and the
> gerund.*

voglio conoscerli = I want to meet them

> **!** *When the group referred to consists
> of males and females,* **li** *is always
> used.*

lì *adverb*
= there

liberare *verb* ①
1 = to free
2 liberarsi (**!** + *essere*)
liberarsi di qualcosa = to get rid of
    something

libero/libera *adjective*
= free

libertà *noun, feminine* (**!** *never changes*)
la libertà = freedom

libreria *noun, feminine*
una libreria = a bookshop, a bookstore

libro *noun, masculine*
un libro = a book

licenziare *verb* ⑥
= to sack

liceo *noun, masculine*
il liceo = secondary school, high school

lieto/lieta *adjective*
= glad
molto lieto/lieta! = pleased to meet you!

lieve *adjective*
= light

ligure *adjective*
= Ligurian

limitato/limitata *adjective*
= limited

limitazione *noun, feminine*
una limitazione = a limitation

limite *noun, masculine*
un limite = a limit

limonata *noun, feminine*
la limonata = lemonade

limone *noun, masculine*
un limone = a lemon

linea *noun, feminine*
una linea = a line
in linea = online

lingua *noun, feminine*
• la lingua = the tongue
• una lingua = a language

linguaggio *noun, masculine* (*plural*
linguaggi)
il linguaggio = language

linkare *verb*
= to link

lino *noun, masculine*
il lino = linen

liquidazione *noun, feminine*
una liquidazione = a sale

liquido *noun, masculine*
un liquido = a liquid

liquore *noun, masculine*
un liquore = a liqueur

lira *noun, feminine*
una lira = a lira

liscio/liscia *adjective* (*plural* **lisci/lisce**)
• = smooth
• avere i capelli lisci = to have straight hair

lista *noun, feminine*
una lista = a list

litigare *verb* ⑤
= to quarrel

litigio *noun, masculine* (*plural* **litigi**)
un litigio = a quarrel

litro *noun, masculine*
un litro = a litre, a liter

livello *noun, masculine*
il livello = the level

livido *noun, masculine*
un livido = a bruise

lo ▶ il

lo/la *pronoun* (*also* **l'** *before a vowel or
mute h*)
= him/her
= it
lo conosco benissimo = I know him
    really well
l'ho vista in città = I saw her in town

> **!** *Note that* **lo** *and* **la** *combine with the
> infinitive, the imperative and the
> gerund.*

voglio conoscerla = I want to meet her

locale
1 *adjective*
= local
2 *noun, masculine*
un locale = a club

logico/logica *adjective (plural **logici/logiche**)*
= logical

Lombardia *noun, feminine*
la Lombardia = Lombardy

lombardo/lombarda *adjective*
= Lombard

londinese *adjective*
= London

Londra *noun*
= London

lontano/lontana *adjective*
= far
= distant
è lontano dal mare = it's a long way from the sea

lordo/lorda *adjective*
= gross

loro
1 *pronoun*
= they
= them
= to them
loro stanno a casa = they're staying at home
vado con loro = I'm going with them
2 *determiner*
= their
il loro cane/la loro casa = their dog/their house

lotta *noun, feminine*
una lotta = a struggle
= a fight
la lotta = wrestling

lottare *verb* 1
= to struggle
= to fight

lotteria *noun, feminine*
una lotteria = a lottery

lucciola *noun, feminine*
una lucciola = a firefly, a glowworm

luce *noun, feminine*
la luce = light

lucertola *noun, feminine*
una lucertola = a lizard

lucidare *verb* 1
= to polish

lucido/lucida *adjective*
= shiny

luglio *noun, masculine*
= July

lui *pronoun*

= he
= him
lui è mio fratello = he's my brother
è per lui = it's for him

lumaca *noun, feminine*
una lumaca = a slug

luna *noun, feminine*
la luna = the moon

luna park *noun, masculine* (**!** *never changes*)
un luna park = a fair

lunedì *noun, masculine* (**!** *never changes*)
= Monday
arrivo lunedì = I'm arriving (on) Monday
il lunedì = on Mondays

lunghezza *noun, feminine*
la lunghezza = length

lungo/lunga (*plural **lunghi/lunghe**)*
1 *adjective*
= long
è lungo cinque metri = it's five metres long
2 **lungo** *preposition*
= along
lungo la spiaggia = along the beach

lungomare *noun, masculine*
il lungomare = the promenade

luogo *noun, masculine* (*plural **luoghi**)*
un luogo = a place
aver luogo = to take place

lupo *noun, masculine*
un lupo = a wolf

lusso *noun, masculine*
un lusso = a luxury

lussuoso/lussuosa *adjective*
= luxurious

lutto *noun, masculine*
il lutto = mourning

Mm

ma *conjunction*
= but

macchia *noun, feminine*
una macchia = a stain
= a spot

macchiare *verb* 6
= to stain

macchiato/macchiata
1 *adjective*
= stained
2 **macchiato** *noun, masculine*
un macchiato = an espresso with milk

macchina *noun, feminine*
* una macchina = a machine
* una macchina = a car
una macchina fotografica = a camera
una macchina da cucire = a sewing
  machine
una macchina da scrivere = a typewriter

macedonia *noun, feminine*
una macedonia = a fruit salad

macellaio/macellaia *noun,*
masculine/feminine (plural **macellai/**
macellaie*)*
un macellaio/una macellaia = a butcher

macelleria *noun, feminine*
una macelleria = a butcher's

macello* *noun, masculine*
un macello = a mess

macerie *noun, feminine plural*
le macerie = the rubble

macinapepe *noun, masculine (! never*
changes)
un macinapepe = a pepper mill

macinare *verb* [1]
= to mince, to grind

macinato *noun, masculine*
il macinato = mince, ground beef

madre *noun, feminine*
la madre = the mother

madrina *noun, feminine*
una madrina = a godmother

maestro/maestra *noun,*
masculine/feminine
un maestro/una maestra = a teacher

magari
1 *exclamation*
magari! = I wish!
2 *adverb*
= maybe

magazzino *noun, masculine*
un magazzino = a warehouse
= a store room
i grandi magazzini = a department store

maggio *noun, masculine*
= May

maggioranza *noun, feminine*
una maggioranza = a majority

maggiore *adjective*
* = elder
  = eldest
* la maggior parte di = most
  la maggior parte della gente = most
  people

maggiorenne *adjective*
essere maggiorenne = to be of age

magia *noun, feminine*
la magia = magic

magico/magica *adjective (plural*
magici/magiche*)*
= magic

maglia *noun, feminine*
* la maglia = knitting
  fare la maglia = to knit
* *(in sport)*
  una maglia = a shirt

maglietta *noun, feminine*
una maglietta = a T-shirt

maglione *noun, masculine*
un maglione = a sweater

magnifico/magnifica *adjective (plural*
magnifici/magnifiche*)*
= wonderful

mago/maga *noun, masculine/feminine*
(plural **maghi/maghe***)*
un mago/una maga = a magician

magro/magra *adjective*
= thin
= slim

mai *adverb*
* *(in negative sentences)* = never
  non ci sono mai stato = I've never been
  there
  non ci vado mai più = I'm never going
  there again
  non dice mai niente = he never says
  anything
* *(in questions)* = ever
  hai mai visto un lupo? = have you ever
  seen a wolf?
* come mai? = why?

maiale *noun, masculine*
un maiale = a pig
il maiale = pork

maionese *noun, feminine*
la maionese = mayonnaise

mais *noun, masculine*
il mais = maize, corn

maiuscolo/maiuscola *adjective*
= capital
S maiuscola = capital S

malato/malata *adjective*
= ill, sick

malattia *noun, feminine*
una malattia = an illness

male
1 *adverb*
= badly
è scritto male = it's spelt wrong
mi sento male = I don't feel well
2 *noun, masculine*
* il male = evil
* fare male = to hurt
  mi fanno male i piedi = my feet hurt
* un mal di testa = a headache

maledetto/maledetta *adjective*
= damned

maleducato/maleducata *adjective*
= badly-behaved

malgrado
1 *preposition*
= despite
2 *conjunction*
= although

maltempo *noun, masculine*
il maltempo = bad weather

mamma *noun, feminine*
la mamma = the mum, the mom

mancanza *noun, feminine*
• mancanza di = lack of
• sentire la mancanza di = to miss

mancare *verb* ④
• = to be lacking
= to be missing
chi manca? = who's missing?
ci manca il sale = there's not enough salt
• mancare di qualcosa = to lack something
• mancare a un appuntamento = to miss an
  appointment
• mi manca mia sorella = I miss my sister

mancia *noun, feminine (plural* **mance***)*
una mancia = a tip

manciata *noun, feminine*
una manciata di = a handful of

mancino/mancina *adjective*
= left-handed

mandare *verb* ①
= to send

mangiare *verb* ③
= to eat
a che ora si mangia? = what time are we
  having dinner?
dopo mangiato = after dinner

mani ▶ **mano**

manica *noun, feminine (plural* **maniche***)*
1 una manica = a sleeve
2 Manica
la Manica = the English Channel

manico *noun, masculine (plural* **manici***)*
un manico = a handle

maniera *noun, feminine*
• una maniera = a way
• le maniere = manners

manifestazione *noun, feminine*
una manifestazione = a demonstration

manifesto *noun, masculine*
un manifesto = a poster

maniglia *noun, feminine*
una maniglia = a handle

mano *noun, feminine (plural* **mani***)*
una mano = a hand
a mano = by hand
dare una mano a qualcuno = to give
  someone a hand

mansarda *noun, feminine*
una mansarda = an attic

mantenere *verb* ⑦③
= to keep

mantengo, **mantiene**, **etc** ▶
mantenere

manuale
1 *adjective*
= manual
2 *noun, masculine*
un manuale = a manual

mappa *noun, feminine*
una mappa = a map

marca *noun, feminine (plural* **marche***)*
una marca = a brand
= a make

marcia *noun, feminine (plural* **marce***)*
• una marcia = a march
• (*when it's a bicycle, car*)
una marcia = a gear
fare marcia indietro = to reverse

marciapiede *noun, masculine*
il marciapiede = the pavement, the
  sidewalk

marcio/marcia *adjective (plural*
marci/marce*)*
= rotten

marco *noun, masculine (plural* **marchi***)*
un marco tedesco = a German mark

mare *noun, masculine*
il mare = the sea
andare al mare = to go to the seaside

marea *noun, feminine*
la marea = the tide

margarina *noun, feminine*
la margarina = margarine

margherita *noun, feminine*
una margherita = a daisy

margine *noun, masculine*
• il margine = the edge
• un margine = a margin

marina *noun, feminine*
la marina = the navy

marinaio *noun, masculine (plural*
marinai*)*
un marinaio = a sailor

marinare *verb* ①
• = to marinade
• marinare la scuola = to play truant

marino/marina *adjective*
= marine
= sea

marito *noun, masculine*
il marito = the husband

marmellata *noun, feminine*
la marmellata = jam

marmo noun, masculine
il marmo = marble

marrone adjective
= brown (**!** never changes)

martedì noun, masculine (**!** never changes)
= Tuesday
il martedì = on Tuesdays

martello noun, masculine
un martello = a hammer

marzo noun, masculine
= March

maschera noun, feminine
• una maschera = a mask
• una maschera = fancy-dress, costume

mascherarsi verb ① (**!** + essere)
= to dress up

maschile adjective
= male
= masculine

maschio noun, masculine (plural
maschi)
un maschio = a male

massa noun, feminine
una massa = a mass

massimo/massima
1 adjective
= maximum
al massimo = at the most
2 **massima** noun, feminine
una massima = a maximum temperature

masterizzatore noun, masculine
(for CDs, DVDs)
un masterizzatore = a burner

masticare verb ④
= to chew

matematica noun, feminine
la matematica = mathematics

materasso noun, masculine
un materasso = a mattress

materia noun, feminine
• la materia = matter
• una materia = a subject

materiale noun, masculine
il materiale = material

materno/materna adjective
= maternal

matita noun, feminine
una matita = a pencil

matrigna noun, feminine
la matrigna = the stepmother

matrimonio noun, masculine (plural
matrimoni)
un matrimonio = a wedding
= a marriage

mattina noun, feminine, **mattino**
noun, masculine
la mattina = the morning

matto/matta adjective
= mad, crazy

mattone noun, masculine
un mattone = a brick

maturità noun, feminine
• la maturità = maturity
• la maturità = high school diploma

maturo/matura adjective
• = mature
• (when it's fruit) = ripe

maxischermo noun, masculine
un maxischermo = a wide screen

mazza noun, feminine
• (in golf) una mazza = a club
• (in baseball, cricket) una mazza = a bat

mazzo noun, masculine
un mazzo di fiori = a bunch of flowers
un mazzo di carte = a pack of cards, a
deck of cards

me pronoun
= me
= to me
vieni con me? = are you coming with
me?

meccanico/meccanica (plural
meccanici/meccaniche)
1 adjective
= mechanical
2 **meccanico** noun, masculine
un meccanico = a mechanic

medaglia noun, feminine
una medaglia = a medal

medesimo/medesima adjective
il medesimo/la medesima = the same

medicina noun, feminine
la medicina = medicine

medico/medica (plural **medici/
mediche**)
1 adjective
= medical
2 **medico** noun, masculine
un medico = a doctor

medievale adjective
= medieval

medio/media (plural **medi/medie**)
1 adjective
= average
2 **media** noun, feminine
• una media = an average
di media = on average
• le medie = middle school

Mediterraneo noun, masculine
il Mediterraneo = the Mediterranean

meglio adverb
= better
= best
Natascia guida meglio di me = Natascia
drives better than me
chi cucina meglio? = who cooks the best?

M

mela *noun, feminine*
una mela = an apple

melanzana *noun, feminine*
una melanzana = an aubergine, an
eggplant

melodia *noun, feminine*
una melodia = a tune

melone *noun, masculine*
un melone = a melon

membro *noun, masculine*
• (*plural* **membri**)
un membro = a member
• (*plural* **membra**)

! Note that **membra** is feminine.

un membro = a limb

memoria *noun, feminine*
la memoria = the memory

meno *adverb*
• = less
= least
è meno alto di me = he's not as tall as me
ho comprato le scarpe meno care = I
bought the least expensive shoes
mettici meno zucchero = put less sugar in
it
chi ha fatto meno errori? = who made the
fewest mistakes?
• 9 meno 6 = 9 minus 6
• fare a meno di qualcosa = to do without
something
• meno male! = thank goodness!
• a meno che = unless

mensa *noun, feminine*
una mensa = a canteen

mensile *adjective*
= monthly

menta *noun, feminine*
la menta = mint

mentale *adjective*
= mental

mentalità *noun, feminine*
una mentalità = a mentality

mente *noun, feminine*
la mente = the mind

mentire *verb* [9]
= to lie

mento *noun, masculine*
il mento = the chin

mentre *conjunction*
= while

menù *noun, masculine* (**!** *never changes*)
un menù = a menu

meraviglia *noun, feminine*
una meraviglia = a wonder

✦ may be considered offensive

meravigliarsi *verb* [6] (**!** + *essere*)
= to be amazed

meraviglioso/meravigliosa
adjective
= marvel(l)ous

mercato *noun, masculine*
un mercato = a market

merce *noun, feminine*
la merce = the goods

merceria *noun, feminine*
una merceria = a haberdasher's

mercoledì *noun, masculine* (**!** *never*
changes)
= Wednesday
il mercoledì = on Wednesdays

merda✦ *noun, feminine*
la merda = shit
merda! = shit!

merenda *noun, feminine*
una merenda = a snack

meridionale *adjective*
= southern

meritare *verb* [1]
= to deserve

mescolanza *noun, feminine*
una mescolanza = a mixture

mescolare *verb* [1]
= to mix

mese *noun, masculine*
un mese = a month
al mese = per month

messa *noun, feminine*
una messa = a mass

messaggiare *verb*
= to text

messaggio *noun, masculine* (*plural*
messaggi)
un messaggio = a (text) message

messo/messa ▶ **mettere**

mestiere *noun, masculine*
un mestiere = a trade

meta *noun, feminine*
una meta = a goal

metà *noun, feminine* (**!** *never changes*)
la metà della classe = half of the class
dividere qualcosa a metà = to cut
something in half

metallo *noun, masculine*
il metallo = metal

metodo *noun, masculine*
un metodo = a method

metro *noun, masculine*
• un metro = a metre, a meter
• un metro = a tape measure

metropolitana *noun, feminine*
  la metropolitana = the underground, the
  subway

mettere *verb* 40
1 (**!** + *avere*)
• = to put (on)
  metti le valigie qua = put the cases here
  mettere un CD = to put a CD on
  non so che mettermi = I don't know what
  to wear
• = to take
  quanto ci hai messo? = how long did you
  take?
  ci ho messo un'ora = I took an hour
2 **mettersi** (**!** + *essere*)
  si è messo a piovere = it's started to rain

mezzanotte *noun, feminine*
  = midnight

mezzo/mezza
1 *adjective*
  = half
  mezzo chilo di gamberetti = half a kilo of
  shrimps
  una mezz'ora = half an hour
2 **mezzo** *noun, masculine*
• il mezzo = the middle
  in mezzo alla piazza = in the middle of
  the square
• un mezzo = a means
  un mezzo di trasporto = a means of
  transport
• sono le tre e mezzo = it's half past three,
  it's three thirty

mezzogiorno *noun, masculine*
• = midday
• il mezzogiorno = the south

mi (**me** *before* **lo/la, li/le,** *and* **ne**) *pronoun*
  = me
  = to me
  = myself
  non mi ha creduto = he didn't believe me
  mi ha spiegato come funziona = he
  explained to me how it works
  non mi sono fatto male = I didn't hurt
  myself

mica *adverb*
  = not
  non è mica vero! = it's not true, you
  know!
  non vuoi mica andare a letto? = surely
  you don't want to go to bed?

microfono *noun, masculine*
  un microfono = a microphone

miei ▶ **mio**

miele *noun, masculine*
  il miele = honey

migliaio *noun, masculine (plural*
  migliaia)
  | **!** *Note that* **migliaia** *is feminine.* |

un migliaio di persone = about a
  thousand people
migliaia di insetti = thousands of insects

miglio *noun, masculine (plural* **miglia**)
  | **!** *Note that* **miglia** *is feminine.* |

un miglio = a mile

migliorare *verb* 1 (**!** + *essere* or *avere*)
  = to improve

migliore *adjective*
  = better
  = best
  la mia macchina nuova è migliore di
  quella vecchia = my new car is better
  than the old one
  il mio migliore amico = my best friend

-mila ▶ **mille**

Milano *noun*
  = Milan

miliardario/miliardaria *noun,*
  masculine/feminine (plural
  miliardari/miliardarie)
  un miliardario/una miliardaria = a
  millionaire

miliardo *number*
  un miliardo = a thousand million, a
  billion
  un miliardo di euro = a billion euros

milione *number*
  un milione = a million
  un milione di stelle = a million stars

militare
1 *adjective*
  = military
2 *noun, masculine*
  un militare = a soldier
  fare il militare = to do one's military
  service

mille *number (plural* **-mila**)
  = a thousand
  diecimila = ten thousand

millimetro *noun, masculine*
  un millimetro = a millimetre, a millimeter

minaccia *noun, feminine (plural*
  minacce)
  una minaccia = a threat

minacciare *verb* 2
  = to threaten

minatore *noun, masculine*
  un minatore = a miner

minerale *noun, masculine*
  un minerale = a mineral

minestra *noun, feminine*
  la minestra = soup

miniera *noun, feminine*
  una miniera = a mine

minimo/minima
1 *adjective*
  = minimum

····▶

M

2 minima noun, feminine
  una minima = a minimum temperature

ministero noun, masculine
  un ministero = a ministry

ministro noun, masculine
  un ministro = a minister

minoranza noun, feminine
  una minoranza = a minority

minore adjective
  = younger
  = youngest

minorenne adjective
  essere minorenne = to be under-age

minuscolo/minuscola adjective
  = small
  s minuscola = small s

minuto noun, masculine
  un minuto = a minute

mio/mia (plural miei/mie)
1 adjective
  = my
2 pronoun
  = mine
  il mio/la mia = my one

miracolo noun, masculine
  un miracolo = a miracle

mirare verb ☐1
  = to aim

mirtillo noun, masculine
  un mirtillo = a bilberry

mischiare verb ☐6
  = to mix (up)

mise ▶ mettere

miseria noun, feminine
  la miseria = poverty

misero, misi ▶ mettere

missile noun, masculine
  un missile = a missile
  = a rocket

missione noun, feminine
  una missione = a mission

misterioso/misteriosa adjective
  = mysterious

mistero noun, masculine
  un mistero = a mystery

misto/mista adjective
  = mixed

misura noun, feminine
• una misura = a size
• le misure = the measurements

misurare verb ☐1
  = to measure
  misurarsi la febbre = to take one's
    temperature

✱ in informal situations

mite adjective
  = mild

mito noun, masculine
  un mito = a myth

mittente noun, masculine/feminine
  il/la mittente = the sender

mobile
1 adjective
  = mobile
2 noun, masculine
  un mobile = a piece of furniture
  i mobili = furniture

moda noun, feminine
  la moda = fashion

modello noun, masculine
  un modello = a model

moderno/moderna adjective
  = modern

modesto/modesta adjective
  = modest

modificare verb ☐4
  = to modify

modo noun, masculine
  un modo = a way

modulo noun, masculine
  un modulo = a form

moglie noun, feminine (plural **mogli**)
  la moglie = the wife

mollare verb ☐1
• = to let go of
• (when it's a boyfriend or girlfriend)✱ = to
  dump

molle adjective
  = soft

molo noun, masculine
  un molo = a pier

moltiplicare verb ☐4
  = to multiply

molto/molta
1 adjective, pronoun
  molto/molta = much
  molti/molte = many
  c'era molto traffico = there was a lot of
    traffic
  hanno molti problemi = they have a lot of
    problems
  molto tempo fa = a long time ago
2 molto adverb
• = a lot
  leggo molto = I read a lot
• (with adjectives and adverbs) = very
  è molto caro = it's very expensive
• (with più) = much
  molto più grande = much bigger

momento noun, masculine
  un momento = a moment

monastero noun, masculine
  un monastero = a monastery

mondiale *adjective*
  = world

mondo *noun, masculine*
  il mondo = the world

moneta *noun, feminine*
• una moneta = a coin
• una moneta = a currency

montagna *noun, feminine*
  una montagna = a mountain
  la montagna = mountains

montare *verb* 1
• (**!** + *avere*) = to assemble
• (**!** + *essere*) = to get in
  = to get on

monte *noun, masculine*
  un monte = a mountain

monumento *noun, masculine*
  un monumento = a monument
  visitare i monumenti = to see the sights

moquette *noun, feminine* (**!** *never changes*)
  la moquette = fitted carpet

mora *noun, feminine*
  una mora = a blackberry

morale
  1 *adjective*
  = moral
  2 *noun, feminine*
  la morale = the moral
  3 *noun, masculine*
  il morale = morale

morbido/morbida *adjective*
  = soft

morbillo *noun, masculine*
  il morbillo = measles

mordere *verb* 45
  = to bite

morire *verb* 41 (**!** + *essere*)
  = to die
  morire di [fame | sete | noia] = to be dying
    of [hunger | thirst | boredom]

morse, morsi, etc ▶ **mordere**

morso/morsa
  1 ▶ **mordere**
  2 **morso** *noun, masculine*
  un morso = a bite

morte *noun, feminine*
  la morte = death

morto/morta
  1 ▶ **morire**
  2 *adjective*
  = dead

mosca *noun, feminine* (*plural* **mosche**)
  una mosca = a fly

Mosca *noun*
  = Moscow

mossa *noun, feminine*
  una mossa = a move

mosse, mossi, etc ▶ **muovere**

mosso/mossa
  1 ▶ **muovere**
  2 *adjective*
• (*when it's hair*) = wavy
• (*when it's the sea*) = rough

mostra *noun, feminine*
  una mostra = an exhibition

mostrare *verb* 1
  = to show

mostro *noun, masculine*
  un mostro = a monster

motivo *noun, masculine*
• un motivo = a reason
• un motivo = a pattern

moto
  1 *noun, masculine*
  il moto = movement
  fare del moto = to take some exercise
  2 *noun, feminine* (**!** *never changes*)
  una moto = a motorcycle

motore *noun, masculine*
  un motore = an engine
  = a motor

motorino *noun, masculine*
  un motorino = a moped

motoscafo *noun, masculine*
  un motoscafo = a motor boat

movimento *noun, masculine*
  un movimento = a movement

mucca *noun, feminine* (*plural* **mucche**)
  una mucca = a cow

mucchio *noun, masculine* (*plural* **mucchi**)
  un mucchio = a pile

mulino *noun, masculine*
  un mulino = a mill

multa *noun, feminine*
  una multa = a fine

municipio *noun, masculine* (*plural* **municipi**)
  il municipio = the town hall
  = the town council, the city council

muoio, muore, etc ▶ **morire**

muovere *verb* 42
  1 = to move
  2 **muoversi** (**!** + *essere*)
  muoversi = to move

mura *noun, feminine plural*
  le mura della città = the city walls

muratore *noun, masculine*
  un muratore = a builder

muro *noun, masculine*
  un muro = a wall

M

muscolo *noun, masculine*
un muscolo = a muscle

museo *noun, masculine*
un museo = a museum
= a gallery

musica *noun, feminine*
la musica = music

musicista *noun, masculine/feminine*
(*plural* **musicisti/musiciste**)
un/una musicista = a musician

muso *noun, masculine*
il muso
(*when it's an animal*) = the muzzle
(*when it's a person*)✱ = the face

musulmano/musulmana *noun,*
masculine/feminine
un musulmano/una musulmana = a
Muslim

mutande *noun, feminine plural*
le mutande = underpants

muto/muta *adjective*
• = dumb
• = silent

mutua *noun, feminine*
la mutua = the health service

mutuo *noun, masculine*
un mutuo = a mortgage

Nn

nacque, nacquero, etc ▶ nascere

napoletano/napoletana *adjective*
= Neapolitan

Napoli *noun*
= Naples

nascere *verb* 43 (**!** + *essere*)
= to be born
sono nato nel 1981 = I was born in 1981

nascita *noun, feminine*
una nascita = a birth

nascondere *verb* 58
1 (**!** + *avere*) = to hide
2 **nascondersi** (**!** + *essere*)
nascondersi = to hide

nascono ▶ nascere

nascose, nascosi, etc ▶
nascondere

nascosto/nascosta
1 ▶ **nascondere**
2 *adjective*

✱ in informal situations

= hiding
dov'era nascosta? = where was she
hiding?

naso *noun, masculine*
il naso = the nose

nastro *noun, masculine*
• un nastro = a ribbon
• un nastro = a tape

Natale *noun, masculine*
Natale = Christmas

nato/nata ▶ nascere

natura *noun, feminine*
la natura = nature

naturale *adjective*
= natural

naturalmente *adverb*
= of course

nave *noun, feminine*
una nave = a ship

nazionale *adjective*
= national

nazionalità *noun, feminine* (**!** *never*
changes)
una nazionalità = a nationality

nazione *noun, feminine*
una nazione = a nation

ne (**n'** *before* è, era, *etc*)
1 *pronoun*
= of it
= of them
ne ho tanti = I've got lots of them
quanto ce n'è? = how much is there?
non ne so niente = I don't know anything
about it
2 *adverb*
nessuno ne è uscito vivo = no one got
out of it alive
se n'è andato = he's gone away

né *conjunction*
né Carlo né Antonio = neither Carlo nor
Antonio

neanche *adverb*
• = neither
'non la conosco'—'neanch'io' = 'I don't
know her'—'neither do I'
• = not even
non mi ha neanche salutato = he didn't
even say hello

nebbia *noun, feminine*
la nebbia = fog

necessario/necessaria *adjective*
(*plural* **necessari/necessarie**)
= necessary

negare *verb* 5
= to deny

negativo/negativa *adjective*
= negative

negato/negata adjective
  essere negato/negata per qualcosa = to
  be useless at something

negli ▶ in

negozio noun, masculine (plural **negozi**)
  un negozio = a shop, a store

nei, nel, nella ▶ in

nemico/nemica noun,
  masculine/feminine (plural **nemici/
  nemiche**)
  un nemico/una nemica = an enemy

nemmeno ▶ neanche

neonato/neonata noun, masculine/
  feminine
  un neonato/una neonata = a newborn
  baby

neppure ▶ neanche

nero/nera adjective
  = black

nervo noun, masculine
  un nervo = a nerve

nervoso/nervosa adjective
  = on edge

nessuno/nessuna
1 adjective
  = no
  non c'è nessun dubbio = there's no doubt
  > ! Before masculine singular nouns
  > beginning with z, ps, gn, or s +
  > another consonant, **nessuno** is used.
  > Before masculine singular nouns
  > beginning with another consonant or a
  > vowel, **nessun** is used. Before feminine
  > singular nouns beginning with a vowel,
  > **nessun'** is used.

2 pronoun
  • = no one
  non ha chiamato nessuno = no one
    called
  • = none
  nessuno di noi può aiutare = none of us
    can help
  delle tre, nessuna era sposata = none of
    the three was married

neve noun, feminine
  la neve = snow

nevicare verb 4 (! + essere or avere)
  = to snow

nido noun, masculine
  un nido = a nest

niente pronoun
  • = nothing
  non è successo niente = nothing
    happened
  non voglio niente = I don't want anything
  niente di speciale = nothing special
  quasi niente = hardly anything
  • di niente! = you're welcome!

nipote noun, masculine/feminine
  • un/una nipote = a nephew/a niece
  • un/una nipote = a grandson/a
    granddaughter
  i nipoti = the grandchildren

no adverb
  = no
  dire di no = to say no
  lei è contenta ma io no = she's pleased
    but I'm not
  l'hai fatto, no? = you've done it, haven't
    you?

nocciola noun, feminine
  una nocciola = a hazelnut

nocciolina noun, feminine
  una nocciolina = a peanut

nocciolo noun, masculine
  un nocciolo = a stone, a pit

noce noun, feminine
  una noce = a walnut

nodo noun, masculine
  un nodo = a knot
  fare un nodo = to tie a knot

noi pronoun
  = we
  = us

noia noun, feminine
  la noia = boredom
  dare noia a qualcuno = to annoy
    someone

noioso/noiosa adjective
  = boring
  = annoying

noleggiare verb 3
  = to hire, to rent

nome noun, masculine
  un nome = a name
  = a first name
  un nome utente = a username

non adverb
  = not
  non fumo = I don't smoke
  non piangere! = don't cry!
  credo che non verrò = I don't think I'll
    come

nonno/nonna noun, masculine/feminine
  il nonno/la nonna = the grandfather/the
    grandmother
  i nonni = the grandparents

nono/nona adjective
  = ninth

nonostante
1 preposition
  = despite
2 conjunction
  = although

nord noun, masculine
  il nord = the north

N

nordest *noun, masculine*
il nordest = the north-east

nordovest *noun, masculine*
il nordovest = the north-west

normale *adjective*
= normal

nostalgia *noun, feminine*
la nostalgia = nostalgia
avere nostalgia di casa = to feel
homesick

nostro/nostra
1 *adjective*
= our
il nostro appartamento = our apartment
2 *pronoun*
= ours
il nostro/la nostra = our one

nota *noun, feminine*
una nota = a note

notare *verb* ⬛1⬛
• = to note
• = to notice

notevole *adjective*
= notable

notizia *noun, feminine*
una notizia = a piece of news
le notizie = the news

noto/nota *adjective*
= well-known

notte *noun, feminine*
una notte = a night
di notte = at night

novanta *number*
= ninety

novantesimo/novantesima
adjective
= ninetieth

nove *number*
= nine

novecento
1 *number*
= nine hundred
2 *Novecento noun, masculine*
il Novecento = the 20th century

novembre *noun, masculine*
= November

novità *noun, feminine* (! *never changes*)
una novità = a novelty

nozze *noun, feminine plural*
le nozze = the wedding

nubile *adjective*
= single

nucleare *adjective*
= nuclear

nudo/nuda *adjective*
= naked
= nude

nulla *pronoun*
= nothing
non vedo nulla = I can't see anything

numero *noun, masculine*
• un numero = a number
un numero di telefono = a phone number
• (*when talking about shoes*)
un numero = a size
un numero di identificazione personale
= PIN number

nuora *noun, feminine*
una nuora = a daughter-in-law

nuotare *verb* ⬛1⬛
= to swim

nuoto *noun, masculine*
il nuoto = swimming

nuovo/nuova *adjective*
• = new
• di nuovo = again

nuvola *noun, feminine*
una nuvola = a cloud

nuvoloso/nuvolosa *adjective*
= cloudy

Oo

o *conjunction*
= or
o domani o dopodomani = either
tomorrow or the day after

obbediente, ubbidiente *adjective*
= obedient

obbedire, ubbidire *verb* ⬛9⬛
obbedire a = to obey

obbligatorio/obbligatoria *adjective*
(*plural* obbligatori/obbligatorie)
= compulsory

obiettivo/obiettiva
1 *adjective*
= objective
2 *obiettivo noun, masculine*
• un obiettivo = an objective
• un obiettivo = a lens

obiezione *noun, feminine*
un'obiezione = an objection

oca *noun, feminine* (*plural* oche)
un'oca = a goose

occasione *noun, feminine*
• l'occasione = the opportunity
• un'occasione = an occasion
• un'occasione = a bargain

occhiali *noun, masculine plural*
gli occhiali = glasses
gli occhiali da sole = sunglasses

occhiata noun, feminine
  dare un'occhiata a qualcosa = to take a look at something

occhio noun, masculine (plural **occhi**)
  un occhio = an eye
  ha gli occhi azzurri = he has blue eyes
  tenere d'occhio qualcosa = to keep an eye on something

occidentale adjective
  = western

occidente noun, masculine
  l'occidente = the west

occorrere verb 26 (**!** + essere)
  = to be necessary
  ci occorre un chilo di farina = we need a kilo of flour

occupare verb 1
1 (**!** + avere)
  = to occupy
2 occuparsi (**!** + essere)
  occuparsi di = to deal with

occupato/occupata adjective
  = engaged, busy

oceano noun, masculine
  un oceano = an ocean

oculista noun, masculine/feminine (plural **oculisti/oculiste**)
  un oculista/un'oculista = an eye specialist

odiare verb 6
  = to hate

odio noun, masculine
  l'odio = hatred

odore noun, masculine
  un odore = a smell

offendere verb 53
1 (**!** + avere)
  = to offend
2 offendersi (**!** + essere)
  offendersi = to take offence, to take offense

offensivo/offensiva adjective
  = offensive

offerta noun, feminine
  un'offerta = an offer

offerto/offerta ▶ **offrire**

offese, offeso/offesa, etc ▶ **offendere**

officina noun, feminine
  un'officina = a garage = a workshop

offrire verb 15
1 (**!** + avere)
  = to offer
2 offrirsi (**!** + essere)
  offrirsi di fare qualcosa = to offer to do something

oggetto noun, masculine
  un oggetto = an object

oggi adverb
  = today

oggigiorno adverb
  = nowadays

ogni adjective
  = every
  ogni anno = every year
  ogni dieci anni = every ten years
  ogni tanto = every so often

ognuno/ognuna pronoun
• = each one
  ognuno di noi = every one of us
• **ognuno** = everyone

Olanda noun, feminine
  l'Olanda = the Netherlands

olandese adjective
  = Dutch

Olimpiadi noun, feminine plural
  le Olimpiadi = the Olympics

olio noun, masculine (plural **oli**)
  l'olio = oil

oliva noun, feminine
  un'oliva = an olive

oltre preposition
• = beyond
• = over
  oltre diciott'anni = over eighteen
• **oltre a** = as well as
  = apart from

ombra noun, feminine
• **un'ombra** = a shadow
• **l'ombra** = the shade
  ero seduto all'ombra = I was sitting in the shade

ombrello noun, masculine
  un ombrello = an umbrella

ombrellone noun, masculine
  un ombrellone = a beach umbrella

omesso/omessa ▶ **omettere**

omettere verb 40
  = to omit

omicida noun, masculine/feminine (plural **omicidi/omicide**)
  un omicida/un'omicida = a murderer

omicidio noun, masculine (plural **omicidi**)
  un omicidio = a murder

omise, omisi, etc ▶ **omettere**

omosessuale noun, masculine/feminine
  un omosessuale/un'omosessuale = a homosexual

onda noun, feminine
  un'onda = a wave

onestà noun, feminine
  l'onestà = honesty

onesto/onesta adjective
  = honest

O

onore noun, masculine
 un onore = an hono(u)r

ONU noun, feminine
 l'ONU = the United Nations

opera noun, feminine
 • un'opera = a work
  un'opera d'arte = a work of art
 • un'opera = an opera

operaio/operaia noun,
 masculine/feminine (plural
 operai/operaie)
 un operaio/un'operaia = a worker

operare verb 1
 • = to operate
 • operare qualcuno = to operate on
  someone

operazione noun, feminine
 un'operazione = an operation

opinione noun, feminine
 un'opinione = an opinion

oppone, oppongo, etc ▶ opporsi

opporsi verb 50 (! + essere)
 opporsi a qualcosa = to oppose
  something

oppose, opposi, etc ▶ opporsi

opportunità noun, feminine (! never
 changes)
 un'opportunità = an opportunity

opposizione noun, feminine
 l'opposizione = opposition

opposto/opposta
 1 ▶ opporsi
 2 adjective
 = opposite

oppure conjunction
 = or (else)

opuscolo noun, masculine
 un opuscolo = a brochure

ora
 1 noun, feminine
 • un'ora = an hour
  duecento chilometri all'ora = two
   hundred kilometres an hour
 • l'ora = the time
  che ore sono? = what's the time?
  l'ora di pranzo = lunchtime
 • non vedere l'ora di fare qualcosa = to
   look forward to doing something
  non vedo l'ora di andare in vacanza = I'm
   looking forward to going on holiday
  l'ora di punta = rush hour
 2 adverb
 = now

orale adjective
 = oral

orario/oraria (plural orari/orarie)
 1 adjective
 in senso orario = clockwise

2 **orario** noun, masculine
 un orario = a timetable

ordinare verb 1
 = to order
 ordinare a qualcuno di fare qualcosa = to
  order someone to do something

ordinario/ordinaria adjective (plural
 ordinari/ordinarie)
 = ordinary

ordinato/ordinata adjective
 = tidy

ordine noun, masculine
 • l'ordine = order
  mettere in ordine = to tidy up
 • un ordine = an order

orecchino noun, masculine
 un orecchino = an earring

orecchio noun, masculine (plural
 orecchie)
 | ! Note that orecchie is feminine. |
 un orecchio = an ear
 mi fanno male le orecchie = my ears hurt

organizzare verb 1
 = to organize

organizzazione noun, feminine
 un'organizzazione = an organization

organo noun, masculine
 un organo = an organ

orgoglio noun, masculine
 l'orgoglio = pride

orgoglioso/orgogliosa adjective
 = proud

orientale adjective
 = oriental
 = eastern

oriente noun, masculine
 l'oriente = the east

origano noun, masculine
 l'origano = oregano

originale adjective
 = original

origine noun, feminine
 l'origine = the origin

orizzontale adjective
 = horizontal

orizzonte noun, masculine
 l'orizzonte = the horizon

orlo noun, masculine
 • l'orlo = the edge
 • un orlo = a hem

ormai adverb
 = now
 = by now

oro noun, masculine
 l'oro = gold
 un anello d'oro = a gold ring

orologio *noun, masculine*
  un orologio = a watch
  = a clock

oroscopo *noun, masculine*
  un oroscopo = a horoscope

orrendo/orrenda *adjective*
  = horrible

orribile *adjective*
  = horrible

orrore *noun, masculine*
  l'orrore = horror

orso *noun, masculine*
  un orso = a bear

orto *noun, masculine*
  un orto = a vegetable garden

ortografia *noun, feminine*
  l'ortografia = spelling

osare *verb* 1
  = to dare
  come osi? = how dare you!

oscuro/oscura *adjective*
  = obscure

ospedale *noun, masculine*
  un ospedale = a hospital

ospitalità *noun, feminine*
  l'ospitalità = hospitality

ospitare *verb* 1
  ospitare qualcuno = to put someone up

ospite *noun, masculine/feminine*
  • un ospite/un'ospite = a host
  • un ospite/un'ospite = a guest

ossa ▶ osso

osservare *verb* 1
  = to observe

osservazione *noun, feminine*
  un'osservazione = a remark

ossigeno *noun, masculine*
  l'ossigeno = oxygen

osso *noun, masculine* (*plural* **ossi** *or* **ossa**)

> ! Note that **ossa** is feminine. It is used when referring to human bones.

  un osso = a bone
  mi fanno male le ossa = my bones hurt

ostacolo *noun, masculine*
  un ostacolo = an obstacle

ostaggio *noun, masculine* (*plural* **ostaggi**)
  un ostaggio = a hostage

ostello *noun, masculine*
  un ostello della gioventù = a youth hostel

ostile *adjective*
  = hostile

ostinato/ostinata *adjective*
  = obstinate

ostrica *noun, feminine* (*plural* **ostriche**)
  un'ostrica = an oyster

ottanta *number*
  = eighty

ottantesimo/ottantesima *adjective*
  = eightieth

ottavo/ottava *adjective*
  = eighth

ottenere *verb* 73
  = to obtain

ottengo, ottiene, etc ▶ ottenere

ottico *noun, masculine* (*plural* **ottici**)
  un ottico = an optician

ottimista (*plural* **ottimisti/ottimiste**)
1 *adjective*
  = optimistic
2 *noun, masculine/feminine*
  un ottimista/un'ottimista = an optimist

ottimo/ottima *adjective*
  = excellent

otto *number*
  = eight

ottobre *noun, masculine*
  = October

ottocento
1 *number*
  = eight hundred
2 Ottocento *noun, masculine*
  l'Ottocento = the 19th century

ovest *noun, masculine*
  l'ovest = the west

ovunque *adverb*
  = everywhere

ovvio/ovvia *adjective* (*plural* **ovvi/ovvie**)
  = obvious

Pp

pacchetto *noun, masculine*
  un pacchetto = a packet, a pack

pacco *noun, masculine* (*plural* **pacchi**)
  un pacco = a parcel, a package

pace *noun, feminine*
  la pace = peace

Pacifico *noun, masculine*
  il Pacifico = the Pacific

padella *noun, feminine*
  una padella = a frying pan

Padova *noun*
  = Padua

padovano/padovana adjective
= Paduan

padre noun, masculine
il padre = the father

padrino noun, masculine
un padrino = a godfather

padrone noun, masculine
un padrone = a master

paesaggio noun, masculine (plural
paesaggi)
il paesaggio = the landscape
= the scenery

paese noun, masculine
• un paese = a country
• un paese = a village

paga noun, feminine
la paga = the pay

pagamento noun, masculine
un pagamento = a payment

pagare verb [5]
= to pay (for)
pagare il conto = to pay the bill
non ho pagato i biglietti = I haven't paid
for the tickets

pagina noun, feminine
una pagina = a page

paglia noun, feminine
la paglia = straw

pagliaccio noun, masculine (plural
pagliacci)
un pagliaccio = a clown

pagnotta noun, feminine
una pagnotta = a loaf

paio noun, masculine (plural **paia**)
| ! Note that paia is feminine. |
• un paio di scarpe = a pair of shoes
• un paio d'anni fa = a couple of years ago

paiono ▶ parere

palazzo noun, masculine
• un palazzo = a palace
• un palazzo = a block of flats, an
apartment building

palcoscenico noun, masculine (plural
palcoscenici)
il palcoscenico = the stage

palestra noun, feminine
una palestra = a gym

palla noun, feminine
• una palla = a ball
• che palle!✖ = what a pain!
rompere le palle a qualcuno✖ = to get on
someone's nerves

pallacanestro noun, feminine
la pallacanestro = basketball

pallavolo noun, feminine
la pallavolo = volleyball

pallido/pallida adjective
= pale

pallina noun, feminine
una pallina = a ball

pallino noun, masculine
un pallino = a polka-dot
un vestito a pallini = a polka-dot dress

palloncino noun, masculine
un palloncino = a balloon

pallone noun, masculine
un pallone = a football

pallottola noun, feminine
una pallottola = a bullet

palma noun, feminine
una palma = a palm tree

palo noun, masculine
un palo = a pole
= a post

palude noun, feminine
una palude = a marsh

panca noun, feminine (plural **panche**)
una panca = a bench

pancetta noun, feminine
la pancetta = bacon

pancia noun, feminine (plural **pance**)
la pancia = the belly

pane noun, masculine
il pane = bread

panificio noun, masculine (plural
panifici)
un panificio = a bakery

panico noun, masculine
il panico = panic
farsi prendere dal panico = to panic

panino noun, masculine
un panino = a roll
un panino al formaggio = a cheese roll

panna noun, feminine
la panna = cream

panno noun, masculine
• un panno = a cloth
• i panni = the washing

pannolino noun, masculine
un pannolino = a nappy, a diaper

panorama noun, masculine (plural
panorami)
un panorama = a view

pantaloni noun, masculine plural
i pantaloni = trousers

papa noun, masculine (plural **papi**)
il Papa = the Pope

papà noun, masculine (! never changes)
il papà = the dad

✖ in informal situations

pappagallo *noun, masculine*
un pappagallo = a parrot

paradiso *noun, masculine*
il paradiso = paradise

paragonare *verb* [1]
= to compare

paragone *noun, masculine*
un paragone = a comparison

paragrafo *noun, masculine*
un paragrafo = a paragraph

paralizzato/paralizzata *adjective*
= paralysed, paralyzed

parallelo/parallela *adjective*
= parallel

parcheggiare *verb* [3]
= to park

parcheggio *noun, masculine (plural
parcheggi)*
un parcheggio = a car park, a parking lot
= a parking space

parco *noun, masculine (plural **parchi**)*
un parco = a park
un parco a tema = a theme park

parecchio/parecchia
1 *adjective (plural **parecchi/parecchie**)*
= quite a lot of
parecchio traffico = quite a lot of traffic
parecchie volte = several times
2 **parecchio** *adverb*
= quite a lot
mi è costato parecchio = it cost me quite
a lot

pareggio *noun, masculine (plural
pareggi)*
un pareggio = a draw

parente *noun, masculine/feminine*
un/una parente = a relative

parentesi *noun, feminine (**!** never
changes)*
fra parentesi = in brackets, in parentheses

parere
1 *verb* [44] (**!** + *essere*)
pare che = it seems that
mi pare che = I think that
mi pare [assurdo | giusto | logico] = I think
it's [absurd | right | logical]
a quanto pare = apparently
2 *noun, masculine*
un parere = an opinion
a mio parere = in my opinion

parete *noun, feminine*
una parete = a wall

pari *adjective (**!** never changes)*
= even
un numero pari = an even number

Parigi *noun*
= Paris

parlamentare
1 *adjective*
= parliamentary
2 *noun, masculine/feminine*
un/una parlamentare = a member of
parliament

parlamento *noun, masculine*
un parlamento = a parliament

parlare *verb* [1]
= to speak
= to talk
il libro parla della sua infanzia = the book
is about his childhood

parola *noun, feminine*
una parola = a word
le parole crociate = a crossword

parolaccia *noun, feminine (plural
parolacce)*
una parolaccia = a bad word

parrà, parranno ▶ **parere**

parrocchia *noun, feminine*
una parrocchia = a parish

parrucca *noun, feminine*
una parrucca = a wig

parrucchiere/parrucchiera *noun,
masculine/feminine*
un parrucchiere/una parrucchiera = a
hairdresser

parso/parsa ▶ **parere**

parte
1 *noun, feminine*
• una parte = a part
= a share
• da tutte le parti = everywhere
da nessuna parte = nowhere
2 a parte = apart from

partecipare *verb* [1]
partecipare a qualcosa = to take part in
something

partenza *noun, feminine*
la partenza = the departure

particolare
1 *adjective*
= particular
2 *noun, masculine*
un particolare = a detail

partire *verb* [10] (**!** + *essere*)
• = to leave
• a partire da lunedì = starting from
Monday

partita *noun, feminine*
una partita = a match, a game

partito *noun, masculine*
un partito politico = a political party

parve, parvero, etc ▶ **parere**

parziale *adjective*
= partial

P

Pasqua *noun, feminine*
Pasqua = Easter

Pasquetta *noun, feminine*
Pasquetta = Easter Monday

passaggio *noun, masculine (plural* passaggi*)*
• un passaggio = a passage
• dare un passaggio a qualcuno = to give someone a lift, a ride
un passaggio a livello = a level crossing, a grade crossing

passante *noun, masculine/feminine*
un/una passante = a passer-by

passaporto *noun, masculine*
un passaporto = a passport

passare *verb* 1
• (! + *avere*) = to pass
mi passi il sale? = can you pass the salt?
• (! + *avere*)
passare il tempo a fare qualcosa = to spend time doing something
• (! + *essere*) = to go past
è passato davanti alla banca = he went past the bank
non ci passo! = I can't get past!
passa di qua! = come this way!

passato *noun, masculine*
il passato = the past

passeggero/passeggera *noun, masculine/feminine*
un passeggero/una passeggera = a passenger

passeggiare *verb* 3
= to stroll

passeggino *noun, masculine*
un passeggino = a pushchair, a stroller

passione *noun, feminine*
la passione = passion

passo *noun, masculine*
un passo = a step
a due passi da qui = a stone's throw from here

pasta *noun, feminine*
• la pasta = pasta
• la pasta = pastry
= dough
• una pasta = a cake

pastasciutta *noun, feminine*
la pastasciutta = pasta

pasticceria *noun, feminine*
una pasticceria = a cake shop

pasticcio* *noun, masculine (plural* pasticci*)*
un pasticcio = a mess

pasto *noun, masculine*
un pasto = a meal

---

* in informal situations

pastore *noun, masculine*
un pastore = a shepherd

patata *noun, feminine*
una patata = a potato
le patate fritte = chips, French fries

patatina *noun, feminine*
una patatina = a crisp, a potato chip

patente *noun, feminine*
una patente di guida = a driving licence, a driver's license

patrigno *noun, masculine*
il patrigno = the stepfather

patrimonio *noun, masculine*
un patrimonio = a fortune

pattinaggio *noun, masculine*
il pattinaggio = skating

pattino *noun, masculine*
un pattino = a skate

paura *noun, feminine*
la paura = fear
ho paura dei ragni = I'm afraid of spiders

pausa *noun, feminine*
una pausa = a pause
fare una pausa = to have a break

pavimento *noun, masculine*
il pavimento = the floor

paziente
1 *adjective*
= patient
2 *noun, masculine/feminine*
un/una paziente = a patient

pazienza *noun, feminine*
la pazienza = patience
pazienza! = never mind!

pazzesco/pazzesca *adjective (plural* pazzeschi/pazzesche*)*
= crazy

pazzo/pazza *adjective*
= crazy

peccato *noun, masculine*
• un peccato = a sin
• che peccato! = what a pity!

Pechino *noun*
= Beijing

pecora *noun, feminine*
una pecora = a sheep

pedone *noun, masculine*
un pedone = a pedestrian

peggio *adverb*
= worse
= worst
poteva andare peggio = it could have been worse
i peggio pagati = the worst paid

peggiorare *verb* 1 *(! + essere)*
= to get worse

peggiore *adjective*
= worse
= worst
il clima è peggiore = the climate is worse
il momento peggiore = the worst time

pelato/pelata
1 *adjective*
= bald
2 pelati *noun, masculine plural*
i pelati = tinned tomatoes, canned tomatoes

pelle *noun, feminine*
• **la pelle** = the skin
• **la pelle** = leather

pelliccia *noun, feminine (plural* **pellicce***)*
una pelliccia = a fur

pellicola *noun, feminine*
una pellicola = a film

pelo *noun, masculine*
• **un pelo** = a hair
• **il pelo** = the coat
• **per un pelo** = by the skin of one's teeth

pena *noun, feminine*
• **la pena di morte** = the death penalty
• **valere la pena** = to be worth it

penisola *noun, feminine*
una penisola = a peninsula

penna *noun, feminine*
• **una penna** = a pen
• **una penna** = a feather

pennello *noun, masculine*
un pennello = a paintbrush

pensare *verb* $\boxed{1}$
= to think
che pensi della casa? = what do you think of the house?
stavo pensando alle vacanze = I was thinking about the holidays
penso di partire domani = I think I'll go tomorrow
penso di sì = I think so
penso di no = I don't think so

pensiero *noun, masculine*
un pensiero = a thought
stare in pensiero = to be worried

pensionato/pensionata *noun, masculine/feminine*
un pensionato/una pensionata = a pensioner

pensione *noun, feminine*
• **una pensione** = a boarding house
• **andare in pensione** = to retire
mezza pensione = half board
pensione completa = full board

pentirsi *verb* $\boxed{10}$ *(! + essere)*
pentirsi di aver fatto qualcosa = to regret doing something

pentola *noun, feminine*
una pentola = a pan

pepe *noun, masculine*
il pepe = pepper

peperoncino *noun, masculine*
un peperoncino = a chil(l)i

peperone *noun, masculine*
un peperone = a pepper

per *preposition*
• = for
è per te = it's for you
per tre notti = for three nights
• = in order to
per dormire = in order to sleep
• = times
tre per cinque = three times five

pera *noun, feminine*
una pera = a pear

perché
1 *adverb*
= why
perché non ti riposi? = why don't you have a rest?
perché no? = why not?
2 *conjunction*
= because

perciò *conjunction*
= therefore

perdere *verb* $\boxed{45}$
• = to lose
• = to miss
• = to leak
• **lascia perdere!** = forget it!

perdita *noun, feminine*
• **la perdita** = the loss
• **una perdita** = a leak
• **una perdita di tempo** = a waste of time

perdonare *verb* $\boxed{1}$
= to forgive

perfetto/perfetta *adjective*
= perfect

perfino *adverb*
= even

pericolo *noun, masculine*
il pericolo = danger

pericoloso/pericolosa *adjective*
= dangerous

periferia *noun, feminine*
la periferia di Varese = the outskirts of Varese

periodo *noun, masculine*
un periodo = a period

permanente *adjective*
= permanent

permanenza *noun, feminine*
una permanenza = a stay

P

permesso/permessa
1 ▶ permettere
2 permesso noun, masculine
• il permesso = permission
• un permesso = a permit

permettere verb 40
1 (! + avere)
permettere a qualcuno di fare qualcosa
= to allow someone to do something
permesso! = excuse me!
è permesso? = can I come in?
2 permettersi (! + essere)
non me lo posso permettere = I can't
afford it

però conjunction
= but
= however

perplesso/perplessa adjective
= perplexed

perse, **perso/persa**, etc ▶ perdere

persiana noun, feminine
una persiana = a shutter

persino ▶ perfino

persona noun, feminine
una persona = a person
trenta persone = thirty people

personaggio noun, masculine (plural
personaggi)
• un personaggio = a character
• un personaggio = a personality

personale
1 adjective = personal
2 noun, masculine
il personale = the staff

personalità noun, feminine (! never
changes)
la personalità = the personality

personalmente adverb
= personally

persuadere verb 46
= to persuade

pesante adjective
= heavy

pesare verb 1
= to weigh
quanto pesa? = how much does it weigh?

pesca¹ noun, feminine (plural pesche)
una pesca = a peach

pesca² noun, feminine
la pesca = fishing

pescare verb 4
= to fish
= to catch

pesce noun, masculine
• un pesce = a fish
mi piace il pesce = I like fish
• Pesci = Pisces

pescheria noun, feminine
una pescheria = a fishmonger's, a fish
shop

pescivendolo/pescivendola noun,
masculine/feminine
un pescivendolo/una pescivendola = a
fishmonger, a fish vendor

peso noun, masculine
il peso = the weight

pessimista (plural pessimisti/
pessimiste)
1 adjective
= pessimistic
2 noun, masculine/feminine
un/una pessimista = a pessimist

pessimo/pessima adjective
= dreadful

pestare verb 1
= to tread on

peste noun, feminine
• la peste = the plague
• una peste = a pest

petrolio noun, masculine
il petrolio = oil

pettinarsi verb 1 (! + essere)
= to comb one's hair

pettine noun, masculine
un pettine = a comb

petto noun, masculine
il petto = the chest
= the bust

pezzo noun, masculine
un pezzo = a piece

piaccia, **piacciono**, etc ▶ piacere

piacere
1 verb 47 (! + essere)
= to please
mi piace ballare = I like dancing
ti piacciono queste olive? = do you like
these olives?
2 noun, masculine
• il piacere = pleasure
piacere! = pleased to meet you!
• un piacere = a favo(u)r
per piacere = please

piacevole adjective
= pleasant

piaciuto/piaciuta, **piacque**, etc ▶
piacere

pianeta noun, masculine (plural pianeti)
un pianeta = a planet

piangere verb 48
= to cry

piano/piana
1 adjective
= level

····▶

2 piano noun, masculine
- **un piano** = a plan
- **un piano** = a piano
- **un piano** = a floor
  al piano terra (in Britain) = on the ground floor
  (in the US) = on the first floor
  al primo piano (in Britain) = on the first floor
  (in the US) = on the second floor

pianse, **piansi**, etc ▶ **piangere**

pianta noun, feminine
- **una pianta** = a plant
- **una pianta** = a plan

piantare verb [1]
- • = to plant
- •✘ = to ditch

pianterreno noun, masculine
  il pianterreno (in Britain) = the ground floor
  (in the US) = the first floor

pianto/pianta
1 ▶ **piangere**
2 pianto noun, masculine
  il pianto = crying

piattino noun, masculine
  un piattino = a saucer

piatto noun, masculine
  un piatto = a plate

piazza noun, feminine
  una piazza = a square

piccante adjective
  = spicy

picchiare verb [6]
  = to hit

piccolo/piccola adjective
  = small

piede noun, masculine
  un piede = a foot
  a piedi = on foot

piegare verb [5]
- • = to bend
- • = to fold

Piemonte noun, masculine
  il Piemonte = Piedmont

piemontese adjective
  = Piedmontese

pieno/piena adjective
  = full
  pieno di errori = full of mistakes

pietra noun, feminine
  una pietra = a stone

pigiama noun, masculine
  un pigiama = a pair of pyjamas

pigro/pigra adjective
  = lazy

pila noun, feminine
- **una pila** = a battery
- **una pila di giornali** = a pile of newspapers

pillola noun, feminine
  una pillola = a pill

pilota noun, masculine/feminine (plural **piloti/pilote**)
  un/una pilota
  (of a plane) = a pilot
  (of a racing car) = a driver

pino noun, masculine
  un pino = a pine tree

pioggia noun, feminine (plural **piogge**)
  la pioggia = the rain

piombo noun, masculine
  il piombo = lead

piovere verb [49] (**!** + essere or avere)
  = to rain
  piove = it's raining

piovve ▶ **piovere**

pipì✘ noun, feminine
  fare la pipì = to pee

piscina noun, feminine
  una piscina = a swimming pool

pisello noun, masculine
  i piselli = peas

pista noun, feminine
- **una pista** = a track
- **una pista** = a ski slope
- **la pista** = the runway

pistola noun, feminine
  una pistola = a gun

pittore/pittrice noun, masculine/feminine
  un pittore/una pittrice = a painter

pittura noun, feminine
- **la pittura** = painting
- **la pittura** = paint

più adverb
- • = more
  = most
  è più alto di me = he's taller than me
  è il più alto della classe = he's the tallest in the class
  mettici più zucchero = put more sugar in it
  chi ha fatto più errori? = who made the most mistakes?
- • = any more
  non esiste più = it doesn't exist any more
  non ci vado mai più = I'm never going there again
- • = plus
  cinque più cinque = five plus five

piuma noun, feminine
  una piuma = a feather

piumone® noun, masculine
  un piumone = a duvet

P

piuttosto *adverb*
= rather
sono piuttosto stanco = I'm rather tired

plastica *noun, feminine*
la plastica = plastic
una bottiglia di plastica = a plastic bottle

po'
1 *noun, masculine*
un po' di = a little
un po' di vino = a little wine
dura un po' di tempo = it lasts some time
2 un po' *adverb*
= a bit, a little
un po' stanco = a bit tired, a little tired
ho dormito un po' = I slept a little

poco/poca (*plural* **pochi/poche**)
1 *adjective*
poco tempo = not much time
pochi turisti = not many tourists
troppo poca pasta = not enough pasta
2 poco *adverb*
• (*with verbs*) = not much
ho dormito poco = I didn't sleep much
• (*with adjectives*) = not very
poco gentile = not very nice
poco profondo = shallow

poesia *noun, feminine*
• la poesia = poetry
• una poesia = a poem

poeta *noun, masculine* (*plural* **poeti**)
un poeta = a poet

poi *adverb*
• = then
= next
prima o poi = sooner or later
da lunedì in poi = from Monday onward(s)
• = besides

poiché *conjunction*
= since

polacco/polacca *adjective* (*plural* **polacchi/polacche**)
= Polish

polemica *noun, feminine*
una polemica = a controversy

politica *noun, feminine*
• la politica = politics
• una politica = a policy

politico/politica (*plural* **politici/politiche**)
1 *adjective*
= political
2 politico *noun, masculine*
un politico = a politician

polizia *noun, feminine*
la polizia = the police

poliziotto *noun, masculine*
un poliziotto = a policeman

pollice *noun, masculine*
• un pollice = a thumb
• un pollice = an inch

pollo *noun, masculine*
un pollo = a chicken
mi piace il pollo = I like chicken

polmone *noun, masculine*
un polmone = a lung

Polonia *noun, feminine*
la Polonia = Poland

polpo *noun, masculine*
un polpo = an octopus

polso *noun, masculine*
• il polso = the wrist
• il polso = the pulse

poltrona *noun, feminine*
una poltrona = an armchair

polvere *noun, feminine*
• la polvere = powder
• la polvere = dust

pomeriggio *noun, masculine* (*plural* **pomeriggi**)
un pomeriggio = an afternoon
nel pomeriggio = in the afternoon

pomodoro *noun, masculine*
un pomodoro = a tomato

pompelmo *noun, masculine*
un pompelmo = a grapefruit

pompiere *noun, masculine*
un pompiere = a firefighter
i pompieri = the fire brigade, the fire department

pone, pongo, etc ▶ porre

ponte *noun, masculine*
un ponte = a bridge

popolare *adjective*
= popular

popolazione *noun, feminine*
la popolazione = the population

popolo *noun, masculine*
un popolo = a people

porcellana *noun, feminine*
la porcellana = china

porco *noun, masculine* (*plural* **porci**)
un porco = a pig

porre *verb* 50
= to put

porta *noun, feminine*
una porta = a door

portacenere *noun, masculine* (**!** *never changes*)
un portacenere = an ashtray

portafoglio *noun, masculine* (*plural* **portafogli**)
un portafoglio = a wallet

portare *verb* 1
• = to carry
• = to bring
= to take
'da portar via' = 'to take away'

portata noun, feminine
• una portata = a course
• a portata di mano = within reach

portatile adjective
= portable

portato/portata adjective
essere portato/portata per le lingue = to be good at languages

portavoce noun, masculine/feminine
(! never changes)
un/una portavoce = a spokesperson

porto noun, masculine
un porto = a port

posate noun, feminine plural
le posate = cutlery

pose, posi, etc ▶ porre

positivo/positiva adjective
= positive

posizione noun, feminine
una posizione = a position

possa, possano ▶ potere

possedere verb 51
= to possess

possiamo ▶ potere

possibile adjective
= possible

possibilità noun, feminine (! never changes)
• una possibilità = a possibility
• una possibilità = a chance

possibilmente adverb
= if possible

possiede, possiedo, etc ▶
possedere

posso, possono ▶ potere

posta noun, feminine
la posta = the post, the mail

posta elettronica noun, feminine
una posta elettronica = an email

postino/postina noun,
masculine/feminine
un postino/una postina = a postman/a postwoman, a letter carrier

posto noun, masculine
• un posto = a place
• un posto = a seat
• a posto = tidy
mettere a posto = to tidy up

posto/posta ▶ porre

potabile adjective
acqua potabile = drinking water

potente adjective
= powerful

potenza noun, feminine
la potenza = power

potere
1 verb 52
= to be able
= can
non posso venire = I can't come
lo posso provare? = can I try it on?
non si può fare così = you can't do that
2 noun, masculine
il potere = power

potrà, potuto/potuta, etc ▶
potere

povero/povera adjective
= poor
povero Renato! = poor Renato!

pranzo noun, masculine
il pranzo = lunch

pratica noun, feminine
la pratica = practice
in pratica = practically

praticamente adverb
= practically

pratico/pratica adjective (plural
pratici/pratiche)
= practical

prato noun, masculine
• un prato = a meadow
• un prato = a lawn

precedente adjective
= previous

preciso/precisa adjective
= precise

preferenza noun, feminine
una preferenza = a preference

preferire verb 9
= to prefer

preferito/preferita adjective
= favo(u)rite

prefisso noun, masculine
• un prefisso = a prefix
• un prefisso telefonico = a dialling code, an area code

pregare verb 5
• = to pray
• pregare qualcuno di fare qualcosa = to ask someone to do something

preghiera noun, feminine
una preghiera = a prayer

pregiudizio noun, masculine (plural
pregiudizi)
un pregiudizio = a prejudice

prego exclamation
• 'grazie!'—'prego!' = 'thank you!'—'you're welcome!'
• 'posso fumare?'—'prego!' = 'can I smoke?'—'please do!'

P

premere verb 8
= to press

premio noun, masculine (plural **premi**)
un premio = a prize

prendere verb 53
• = to take
chi ha preso la mia borsa? = who took my bag?
ho preso l'autobus = I took the bus
• = to get
vai a prendere le posate! = go and get the cutlery!
• = to catch
prendere la palla = to catch the ball
prendere freddo = to catch cold
• (talking about food, drink) = to have
prendi un caffè? = would you like a coffee?
• (in a car) = to pick up
devo andare a prenderli alla stazione = I have to pick them up from the station

prenotare verb 1
= to book

prenotazione noun, feminine
una prenotazione = a booking

preoccupare verb 1
1 (! + avere)
= to worry
2 preoccuparsi (! + essere)
= to worry
= to be worried

preoccupato/preoccupata
adjective
= worried

preparare verb 1
= to prepare
preparare la colazione = to fix breakfast

presa noun, feminine
una presa = a socket

prese, presi ▶ prendere

presentare verb 1
• = to introduce
• = to present

presente
1 adjective
= present
2 noun, masculine
il presente = the present

preservativo noun, masculine
un preservativo = a condom

preside noun, masculine/feminine
il/la preside = the headteacher, the principal

presidente/presidentessa noun,
masculine/feminine
il presidente/la presidentessa = the president

preso/presa ▶ prendere

pressione noun, feminine
la pressione = the pressure

prestare verb 1
= to lend

prestito noun, masculine
un prestito = a loan
prendere in prestito qualcosa = to borrow something

presto adverb
• = early
• = soon
• fare presto = to be quick

prete noun, masculine
un prete = a priest

pretendere verb 53
• = to demand
• = to expect

pretese, preteso/pretesa, etc ▶
pretendere

prevenzione noun, feminine
la prevenzione = prevention

previsione noun, feminine
una previsione = a forecast
le previsioni del tempo = the weather forecast

previsto/prevista adjective
= expected

prezioso/preziosa adjective
= precious

prezzemolo noun, masculine
il prezzemolo = parsley

prezzo noun, masculine
un prezzo = a price

prigione noun, feminine
una prigione = a prison

prigioniero/prigioniera noun,
masculine/feminine
un prigioniero/una prigioniera = a prisoner

prima adverb
• = before
• prima di = before
prima della lezione = before the lesson
• prima che = before
prima che se ne accorga = before he realizes

primavera noun, feminine
la primavera = spring

primo/prima
1 adjective
= first
il primo maggio = the first of May
2 primo noun, masculine
il primo = the first course

principale adjective
= principal
= main

principe/principessa noun,
masculine/feminine
un principe/una principessa = a prince/a
princess

principiante noun, masculine/feminine
un/una principiante = a beginner

principio noun, masculine (plural
principi)
• un principio = a principle
• il principio = the beginning

privato/privata adjective
= private

privilegio noun, masculine (plural
privilegi)
un privilegio = a privilege

privo/priva adjective
privo di sintomi = without symptoms

probabile adjective
= probable

probabilmente adverb
= probably

problema noun, masculine (plural
problemi)
un problema = a problem
non c'è problema! = no problem!

processo noun, masculine
• un processo = a process
• un processo = a trial

prodotto/prodotta
1 ▶ produrre
2 prodotto noun, masculine
un prodotto = a product

produce, producono, etc ▶
produrre

produrre verb 54
= to produce

produsse, produssi, etc ▶
produrre

professionale adjective
= professional

professione noun, feminine
una professione = a profession

professionista noun, masculine/
feminine (plural professionisti/
professioniste)
un/una professionista = a professional

professore/professoressa noun,
masculine/feminine
un professore/una professoressa = a
teacher

profondità noun, feminine
la profondità = the depth

profondo/profonda adjective
= deep

profugo/profuga noun, masculine/
feminine (plural profughi/profughe)
un profugo/una profuga = a refugee

profumo noun, masculine
un profumo = a perfume

profumeria noun, feminine
una profumeria = a perfumery

progetto noun, masculine
un progetto = a plan
= a project

programma noun, masculine (plural
programmi)
• un programma = a program(me)
• un programma = a plan

progresso noun, masculine
il progresso = progress
fare progressi = to make progress

proibire verb 9
= to forbid
proibire a qualcuno di fare qualcosa = to
forbid someone to do something

promessa noun, feminine
una promessa = a promise

promesso/promessa ▶
promettere

promettere verb 40
= to promise

promise, promisi, etc ▶
promettere

**promosse, promosso/promossa,
etc** ▶ promuovere

promozione noun, feminine
una promozione = a promotion

promuovere verb 42
• = to promote
• essere promosso/promossa = to be
promoted
(at school) = to go up a year

pronto/pronta
1 adjective
= ready
2 pronto exclamation
pronto? = hello!

pronuncia noun, feminine (plural
pronunce)
la pronuncia = pronunciation

pronunciare verb 2
= to pronounce
come si pronuncia? = how do you
pronounce it?

propone, propongo, etc ▶
proporre

proporre verb 50
= to propose
= to suggest

propose, proposi, etc ▶ proporre

proposito noun, masculine
• un proposito = a purpose
• a proposito = by the way

proposta *noun, feminine*
una proposta = a proposal
= a suggestion

proposto/proposta ▶ **proporre**

proprietà *noun, feminine* (**!** *never changes*)
la proprietà = property

proprietario/proprietaria *noun, masculine/feminine* (*plural* **proprietari/proprietarie**)
il proprietario/la proprietaria = the owner

proprio/propria (*plural* **propri/proprie**)
1 *adjective*
la propria camera = one's own room
2 proprio *adverb*
• = just
proprio in quel momento = just at that moment
• = really
è proprio vero! = it's really true!

prosciutto *noun, masculine*
il prosciutto crudo = cured ham
il prosciutto cotto = cooked ham

prossimo/prossima *adjective*
= next
venerdì prossimo = next Friday

prostituto/prostituta *noun, masculine/feminine*
un prostituto/una prostituta = a prostitute

proteggere *verb* 39
= to protect

protesse, protessi, etc ▶ **proteggere**

protesta *noun, feminine*
una protesta = a protest

protestante *noun, masculine/feminine*
un/una protestante = a Protestant

protestare *verb* 1
= to protest

protetto/protetta ▶ **proteggere**

protezione *noun, feminine*
la protezione = protection

prova *noun, feminine*
• una prova = a trial
• le prove = the proof
• una prova = a rehearsal

provare *verb* 1
• = to try (on)
• provare a fare qualcosa = to try to do something
• = to rehearse

provincia *noun, feminine* (*plural* **province**)
una provincia = a province

provocare *verb* 4
= to cause

♦ may be considered offensive

provvisorio/provvisoria *adjective*
= temporary

prudente *adjective*
= careful

psichiatra *noun, masculine/feminine* (*plural* **psichiatri/psichiatre**)
uno/una psichiatra = a psychiatrist

psicologia *noun, feminine*
la psicologia = psychology

psicologo/psicologa *noun masculine/feminine* (*plural* **psicologi/psicologhe**)
uno psicologo/una psicologa = a psychologist

pubblicare *verb* 4
= to publish

pubblicità *noun, feminine* (**!** *never changes*)
la pubblicità = advertising
una pubblicità = an advertisement

pubblico/pubblica (*plural* **pubblici/pubbliche**)
1 *adjective*
= public
2 pubblico *noun, masculine*
• il pubblico = the public
• il pubblico = the audience

pugilato *noun, masculine*
il pugilato = boxing

pugile *noun, masculine*
un pugile = a boxer

Puglia *noun, feminine*
la Puglia = Apulia

pugliese *adjective*
= Apulian

pugno *noun, masculine*
un pugno = a fist
= a punch

pulire *verb* 9
= to clean

pulito/pulita *adjective*
= clean

pulizia *noun, feminine*
fare le pulizie = to do the cleaning

pullman *noun, masculine* (**!** *never changes*)
un pullman = a coach, a bus

pungere *verb* 48
= to sting

punire *verb* 9
= to punish

punizione *noun, feminine*
una punizione = a punishment

punse, punsero, etc ▶ **pungere**

punta *noun, feminine*
una punta = a point

puntare *verb* 1
= to point

puntata *noun, feminine*
una puntata = an episode

punteggiatura *noun, feminine*
la punteggiatura = punctuation

punteggio *noun, masculine* (*plural* **punteggi**)
il punteggio = the score

punto/punta
1 ▶ **pungere**
2 punto *noun, masculine*
• un punto = a point
• un punto = a stitch
• un punto = a full stop, a period
punto e virgola = semicolon
due punti = colon

puntuale *adjective*
= punctual
= on time

puntura *noun, feminine*
una puntura = an injection

può, puoi ▶ **potere**

purché *conjunction*
= as long as

pure *adverb*
• = as well
• fai pure! = go ahead!
si accomodi pure! = do sit down!

purè *noun, masculine*
il purè di patate = mashed potatoes

puro/pura *adjective*
= pure

purtroppo *adverb*
= unfortunately

puttana⚬ *noun, feminine*
una puttana = a whore

puzza *noun, feminine*
una puzza = a stink

puzzare *verb* [1]
= to stink

puzzo *noun, masculine* ▶ **puzza**

Qq

---

qua *adverb*
= here
vieni qua! = come here!

quaderno *noun, masculine*
un quaderno = an exercise book

quadrato/quadrata
1 *adjective*
= square
2 quadrato *noun, masculine*
un quadrato = a square

quadro/quadra
1 *adjective*
un metro quadro = a square metre, a square meter
2 quadro *noun, masculine*
un quadro = a painting

qualche *adjective*
= a few
qualche ostrica = a few oysters
> **!** Qualche *is always followed by a singular noun.*

qualcosa *pronoun*
= something
= anything
qualcosa di strano = something strange
c'è qualcosa che non va? = is there anything wrong?

qualcuno/qualcuna *pronoun*
1 = some
ne ho preso qualcuno = I took some
qualcuna è marcia = some of them are rotten
2 qualcuno
= someone
= anyone
qualcun altro = someone else
ha chiamato qualcuno? = did anyone call?

quale
1 *adjective*
= which
= what
quali scarpe mi metto? = which shoes shall I wear?
qual è il tuo numero di telefono? = what's your phone number?
2 *pronoun*
• = which (one)
= what
quale preferisci? = which one do you prefer?
qual è il mio? = which one is mine?
qual è il tuo colore preferito? = what's your favourite colour?
• il quale/la quale = who, whom
= which
del quale = whose

qualifica *noun, feminine* (*plural* **qualifiche**)
una qualifica = a qualification

qualità *noun, feminine* (**!** *never changes*)
una qualità = a quality

qualsiasi, qualunque *adjective*
= any
in qualsiasi momento = at any time
qualsiasi cosa = anything

quando
1 *adverb*
= when
quando sei arrivato? = when did you arrive?
                    ⋯▶

Q

2 *conjunction*
= when
quando lo leggerai, capirai tutto = you'll understand everything when you read it

quantità *noun, feminine* (**!** *never changes*)
una quantità = a quantity

quanto/quanta
1 *adjective*
• **quanto/quanta** = how much
quanti/quante = how many
quanto tempo hai? = how much time do you have?
quanti ne vuoi? = how many do you want?
quanti ne abbiamo oggi? = what's the date today?
• (*in exclamations*) = what a lot
quanta gente! = what a lot of people!
2 quanto *adverb*
• (*in questions*) = how much
quanto viene? = how much is it?
quanto ci hai messo? = how long did you take?
• (*in exclamations*)
quanto mi piace! = I like it so much!
quant'è bello! = it's so beautiful!
• (*with adjectives*) = how
quant'è lungo? = how long is it?

quaranta *number*
= forty

quarantesimo/quarantesima *adjective*
= fortieth

quarantina *noun, feminine*
una quarantina di scioperanti = about forty strikers

quaresima *noun, feminine*
quaresima = Lent

quartiere *noun, masculine*
un quartiere = a neighbo(u)rhood

quarto/quarta *adjective*
= fourth

quasi *adverb*
= almost
quasi mai = hardly ever

quattordicenne *adjective*
= fourteen-year-old

quattordicesimo/quattordicesima *adjective*
= fourteenth

quattordici *number*
= fourteen

quattrini *noun, masculine plural*
i quattrini = money

quattro *number*
= four

quattrocento
1 *number*
= four hundred

2 Quattrocento *noun, masculine*
il Quattrocento = the 15th century

quello/quella
1 *adjective*

> **!** *Before masculine nouns beginning with z, ps, gn, or s + another consonant,* **quello** *is used in the singular and* **quegli** *in the plural. Before masculine nouns beginning with other consonants,* **quel** *is used in the singular and* **quei** *in the plural. Before all nouns beginning with a vowel,* **quell'** *is used in the singular and* **quegli** *(masculine) or* **quelle** *(feminine) in the plural.*

quel/quella = that
quei/quelle = those
quell'informazione = that information
quegli uomini = those men
quel negozio lì = that shop
2 *pronoun*
• **quello/quella** = that (one)
quelli/quelle = those (ones)
voglio quello là = I want that one
• **quello rosso** = the red one
quelli verdi = the green ones
quello che ti piace = the one you like
• **quello che vorrei fare** = what I'd like to do

questione *noun, feminine*
una questione = an issue

questo/questa
1 *adjective* (*sometimes* **quest'** *before a vowel*)
questo/questa = this
questi/queste = these
quest'estate = this summer
2 *pronoun*
= this (one)
questo/questa = this (one)
questi/queste = these (ones)
voglio questi qui = I want these ones

questura *noun, feminine*
la questura = the police station

qui *adverb*
= here
voglio restare qui = I want to stay here

quindi
1 *conjunction*
= so
2 *adverb*
= then

quindicenne *adjective*
= fifteen-year-old

quindicesimo/quindicesima *adjective*
= fifteenth

quindici *number*
= fifteen

quindicina *noun, feminine*
• una quindicina di ragazzi = about fifteen
  boys
• una quindicina di giorni = a fortnight,
  two weeks

quinto/quinta *adjective*
= fifth

quotidiano/quotidiana
1 *adjective*
= daily
2 quotidiano *noun, masculine*
  un quotidiano = a daily newspaper

Rr

rabbia *noun, feminine*
• la rabbia = anger
• la rabbia = rabies

racchetta *noun, feminine*
  una racchetta = a racket

raccogliere *verb* 22
= to pick (up)

raccolgo, **raccolse**, **etc** ▶
raccogliere

raccolta *noun, feminine*
• la raccolta = the harvest
• una raccolta = a collection

raccolto/raccolta
1 ▶ **raccogliere**
2 raccolto *noun, masculine*
  il raccolto = the harvest

raccomandare *verb* 1
= to recommend

raccomandata *noun, feminine*
  una raccomandata = a recorded-delivery
  letter, a certified letter

raccontare *verb* 1
= to tell

racconto *noun, masculine*
  un racconto = a story

raddoppiare *verb* 6
= to double

radice *noun, feminine*
  una radice = a root

radio *noun, feminine* (**!** *never changes*)
  una radio = a radio
  alla radio = on the radio

radiografia *noun, feminine*
  una radiografia = an X-ray

raffinato/raffinata *adjective*
= refined

rafforzare *verb* 1
= to strengthen

raffreddarsi *verb* 1 (**!** + *essere*)
= to cool down
= to get cold

raffreddato/raffreddata *adjective*
  essere raffreddato/raffreddata = to have a
  cold

raffreddore *noun, masculine*
  un raffreddore = a cold

ragazzo/ragazza *noun, masculine/*
  feminine
  un ragazzo/una ragazza = a boy/a girl
  i ragazzi = the children

raggio *noun, masculine* (*plural* **raggi**)
  un raggio = a ray

raggiungere *verb* 48
= to reach

raggiunse, **raggiunto/raggiunta**,
etc ▶ **raggiungere**

ragione *noun, feminine*
• una ragione = a reason
• aver ragione = to be right

ragioneria *noun, feminine*
  la ragioneria = accountancy

ragionevole *adjective*
= reasonable

ragioniere/ragioniera *noun,*
  masculine/feminine
  un ragioniere/una ragioniera = an
  accountant

ragnatela *noun, feminine*
  una ragnatela = a spider's web
  = a cobweb

ragno *noun, masculine*
  un ragno = a spider

rallentare *verb* 1
= to slow down

ramo *noun, masculine*
  un ramo = a branch

rana *noun, feminine*
  una rana = a frog

rapido/rapida *adjective*
= quick

rapina *noun, feminine*
  una rapina = a robbery

rapinare *verb* 1
= to rob

rapinatore/rapinatrice *noun,*
  masculine/feminine
  un rapinatore/una rapinatrice = a robber

rapire *verb* 9
= to kidnap

rapporto *noun, masculine*
  un rapporto = a relationship

R

rappresentante *noun,*
masculine|feminine
un/una rappresentante = a representative

rappresentare *verb* [1]
= to represent

raro/rara *adjective*
= rare

rasoio *noun, masculine* (*plural* **rasoi**)
un rasoio = a razor

rassicurare *verb* [1]
= to reassure

rata *noun, feminine*
una rata = an instal(l)ment

razza *noun, feminine*
• una razza = a race
• una razza canina = a breed of dog

razzismo *noun, masculine*
il razzismo = racism

razzista *noun, masculine|feminine* (*plural*
razzisti/razziste)
un/una razzista = a racist

re *noun, masculine* (**!** *never changes*)
un re = a king

reagire *verb* [9]
= to react

reale *adjective*
• = real
• = royal

realista *noun, masculine|feminine* (*plural*
realisti/realiste)
un/una realista = a realist

realizzare *verb* [1]
• = to achieve
• = to realize

realmente *adverb*
= really

realtà *noun, feminine*
la realtà = reality
in realtà = really

reazione *noun, feminine*
una reazione = a reaction

recente *adjective*
= recent
di recente = recently

recitare *verb* [1]
= to act

réclame *noun, feminine* (**!** *never*
changes)
una réclame = an advert

reclamo *noun, masculine*
un reclamo = a complaint

recuperare *verb* [1]
= to get back

redattore/redattrice *noun,*
masculine|feminine
un redattore/una redattrice = an editor

referenza *noun, feminine*
una referenza = a reference

regalare *verb* [1]
= to give

regalo *noun, masculine*
un regalo = a present

reggere *verb* [39]
1 (**!** + *avere*)
= to hold (up)
2 **reggersi** (**!** + *essere*)
reggersi in piedi = to stand up

reggiseno *noun, masculine*
un reggiseno = a bra

regina *noun, feminine*
una regina = a queen

regionale *adjective*
= regional

regione *noun, feminine*
una regione = a region

regista *noun, masculine|feminine* (*plural*
registi/registe)
un/una regista = a director

registrare *verb* [1]
= to record

registratore *noun, masculine*
un registratore = a tape recorder

registrazione *noun, feminine*
una registrazione = a recording

registro *noun, masculine*
un registro = a register

regno *noun, masculine*
un regno = a kingdom

Regno Unito *noun, masculine*
il Regno Unito = the United Kingdom

regola *noun, feminine*
una regola = a rule

regolare
1 *adjective*
= regular
2 *verb* [1]
• = to regulate
• = to adjust
• = to settle

relativo/relativa *adjective*
= relative

relazione *noun, feminine*
• una relazione = a relationship
• una relazione = a report

religione *noun, feminine*
la religione = religion

religioso/religiosa *adjective*
= religious

rendere *verb* [53]
• = to give back
• = to make
rendere qualcuno felice = to make
someone happy

reparto noun, masculine
un reparto = a department
(in a hospital) = a ward

replica noun, feminine (plural **repliche**)
una replica = a repeat

repubblica noun, feminine (plural
repubbliche)
una repubblica = a republic

requisito noun, masculine
un requisito = a condition

residente noun, masculine/feminine
un/una residente = a resident

resistente adjective
= strong

resistere verb 16
resistere a qualcosa = to resist something

rese, **reso/resa**, etc ▶ **rendere**

respingere verb 48
= to reject
essere respinto/respinta = to fail

respinse, **respinto/respinta**, etc
▶ **respingere**

respirare verb 1
= to breathe

respiro noun, masculine
il respiro = breath

responsabile
1 adjective
• = responsible
• essere responsabile = to be in charge
2 noun, masculine/feminine
il/la responsabile = the person in charge

responsabilità noun, feminine (! never
changes)
una responsabilità = a responsibility

restare verb 1
• = to stay
me ne restano quattro = I have four left

restaurare verb 1
= to restore

restauro noun, masculine
un restauro = a restoration

restituire verb 9
= to give back

resto noun, masculine
• il resto del latte = the rest of the milk
• i resti = the leftovers
• il resto = the change

rete noun, feminine
• una rete = a net
• una rete = a network

retromarcia noun, feminine
la retromarcia = reverse gear

rettangolo noun, masculine
un rettangolo = a rectangle

retto/retta
1 ▶ **reggere**
2 adjective
= straight

riassumere verb 17
= to summarize

riassunto/riassunta
1 ▶ **riassumere**
2 riassunto noun, masculine
un riassunto = a summary

ribelle noun, masculine/feminine
un/una ribelle = a rebel

ribes noun, masculine (! never changes)
il ribes nero = blackcurrants
il ribes rosso = redcurrants

ricarica (telefonica) noun, feminine
una ricarica telefonica = a top-up card

ricaricare verb
= to recharge

ricattare verb 1
= to blackmail

riccio/riccia (plural **ricci/ricce**)
1 adjective
= curly
2 riccio noun, masculine
• un riccio = a curl
• un riccio = a hedgehog

ricco/ricca adjective (plural
ricchi/ricche)
= rich

ricerca noun, feminine (plural **ricerche**)
• la ricerca = research
• una ricerca = a project

ricetta noun, feminine
• una ricetta = a recipe
• una ricetta medica = a prescription

ricevere verb 8
= to receive

ricevuta noun, feminine
una ricevuta = a receipt

richiamare verb 1
• = to call back
• = to attract

richiedente asilo noun, masculine
/feminine
un/una richiedente asilo = an asylum-
seeker

richiedere verb 20
= to require

richiese, **richiesi**, etc ▶
richiedere

richiesta noun, feminine
una richiesta = a request

richiesto/richiesta ▶ **richiedere**

riciclare verb 1
= to recycle

R

ricominciare verb [2] (**!** + *essere* or *avere*)
= to start again

riconobbe, **riconobbi**, etc ▶ riconoscere

riconoscere verb [25]
= to recognize

ricordare verb [1]
1 (**!** + *avere*)
• = to remember
• = to remind
2 **ricordarsi** (**!** + *essere*)
ricordarsi = to remember
ricordarsi di fare qualcosa = to remember to do something
non mi ricordo = I can't remember

ricordo noun, masculine
• un ricordo = a memory
• un ricordo = a souvenir

ricoverare verb [1]
1 (**!** + *avere*)
ricoverare qualcuno = to take someone into hospital
essere ricoverato/ricoverata = to be taken into hospital
2 **ricoverarsi** (**!** + *essere*)
ricoverarsi = to go into hospital

ridere verb [30]
= to laugh

ridicolo/ridicola adjective
= ridiculous

ridotto/ridotta, **riduce**, etc ▶ ridurre

ridurre verb [54]
= to reduce

riduzione noun, feminine
una riduzione = a reduction

riempire verb [55]
= to fill

riesce, **riesco**, etc ▶ riuscire

rifà, **rifaccio**, etc ▶ rifare

rifare verb [38]
• = to do again
• rifare il letto = to make the bed

rifatto/rifatta ▶ rifare

riferire verb [9]
1 (**!** + *avere*)
essere riferito a qualcosa = to refer to something
2 **riferirsi** (**!** + *essere*)
riferirsi a qualcosa = to refer to something

rifiutare verb [1]
1 (**!** + *avere*)
= to refuse
2 **rifiutarsi** (**!** + *essere*)
rifiutarsi di fare qualcosa = to refuse to do something

rifiuto noun, masculine
• un rifiuto = a refusal
• i rifiuti = rubbish, garbage

riflesso noun, masculine
un riflesso = a reflection

riflettere verb [8]
= to reflect

riforma noun, feminine
una riforma = a reform

rifornire verb [9]
= to supply

riga noun, feminine (plural **righe**)
• una riga = a line
• una riga = a stripe
una camicia a righe = a striped shirt
• una riga = a parting, a part

rigido/rigida adjective
= rigid
= stiff

riguardare verb [1]
= to concern
non ti riguarda! = it has nothing to do with you!

riguardo noun, masculine
• con riguardo = with respect
• riguardo a
riguardo all'annuncio = concerning the ad

rilasciare verb [6]
• = to release
• = to issue

rilassarsi verb [1] (**!** + *essere*)
= to relax

rima noun, feminine
una rima = a rhyme

rimandare verb [1]
• = to send back
• = to postpone

rimanere verb [56] (**!** + *essere*)
• = to stay
• = to be left
me ne rimangono tre = I have three left
• = to be
sono rimasto deluso = I was disappointed
rimanere male = to be offended

rimango, **rimarrà**, **rimase**, etc ▶ rimanere

rimasto/rimasta
1 ▶ rimanere
2 adjective
= left over

rimborso noun, masculine
un rimborso = a refund

rimpiangere verb [48]
= to regret

Rinascimento noun, masculine
il Rinascimento = the Renaissance

rinchiudere verb [21]
  rinchiudere qualcuno = to shut someone up

rinfrescare verb [4]
  = to refresh

ringraziare verb [6]
  = to thank

rinnovare verb [1]
  = to renew

rintracciare verb [2]
  = to get in touch with

rinunciare verb [2]
  rinunciare a qualcosa = to give
    something up
  ci rinuncio! = I give up!

rinviare verb [7]
  = to postpone

riparare verb [1]
1 (! + *avere*)
  = to repair
2 **ripararsi** (! + *essere*)
  ripararsi = to shelter

ripassare verb [1]
  = to revise

ripetere verb [8]
  = to repeat

ripetizione noun, feminine
  la ripetizione = repetition

ripiano noun, masculine
  un ripiano = a shelf

ripido/ripida adjective
  = steep

ripieno noun, masculine
  il ripieno = the stuffing

riposarsi verb [1] (! + *essere*)
  = to rest

riposo noun, masculine
  il riposo = rest

riprendere verb [53]
• = to take back
  = to take again
• = to resume

riprese, **ripreso/ripresa**, etc ▶ riprendere

riprodurre verb [54]
  = to reproduce

risalga, **risalgono**, etc ▶ risalire

risalire verb [61]
• (! + *essere* or *avere*) = to go back up
• (! + *essere*) **risalire a** = to date back to
  risale al Medioevo = it dates back to the
    Middle Ages

risata noun, feminine
  una risata = a laugh

riscaldamento noun, masculine
  il riscaldamento = the heating

riscaldare verb [1]
  = to heat (up)
  = to warm (up)

rischiare verb [6]
  = to risk

rischio noun, masculine (plural **rischi**)
  un rischio = a risk

rise, **risi**, etc ▶ ridere

riservare verb [1]
  = to reserve

riso[1] ▶ ridere

riso[2] noun, masculine
  il riso = rice

risolse, **risolto/risolta**, etc ▶ risolvere

risolvere verb [57]
  = to solve

risorsa noun, feminine
  le risorse = resources

risparmiare verb [6]
  = to save

risparmio noun, masculine (plural **risparmi**)
  un risparmio = a saving

rispettare verb [1]
  = to respect

rispetto noun, masculine
  il rispetto = respect

rispondere verb [58]
  rispondere a qualcuno = to answer someone

rispose, **risposi**, etc ▶ rispondere

risposta noun feminine
  una risposta = an answer
  = a reply

risposto/risposta ▶ rispondere

ristorante noun, masculine
  un ristorante = a restaurant

risultato noun, masculine
  un risultato = a result

ritardare verb [1]
  = to delay
  = to be late

ritardo noun, masculine
  un ritardo = a delay
  arrivare in ritardo = to arrive late

ritenere verb [73]
• = to consider
• = to hold back

ritengo, **ritiene**, etc ▶ ritenere

ritirare verb [1]
• = to withdraw
• = to pick up

ritmo noun, masculine
  il ritmo = rhythm

R

ritorno *noun, masculine*
il ritorno = return

ritratto *noun, masculine*
un ritratto = a portrait

riunione *noun, feminine*
una riunione = a meeting

riunire *verb* [9]
1 (**!** + *avere*) = to gather together
2 **riunirsi** (**!** + *essere*)
riunirsi = to meet

riuscire *verb* [75] (**!** + *essere*)
riuscire a fare qualcosa = to manage to
do something
non mi riesce, non ci riesco = I can't
manage

riuscita *noun, feminine*
la riuscita = the success

riuscito/riuscita *adjective*
= successful

riva *noun, feminine*
la riva = the bank

rivale *noun, masculine|feminine*
un/una rivale = a rival

rivista *noun, feminine*
una rivista = a magazine

rivolgere *verb* [59]
1 (**!** + *avere*)
rivolgere la parola a qualcuno = to speak
to someone
2 **rivolgersi** (**!** + *essere*)
rivolgersi a qualcuno = to speak to
someone

rivolse, **rivolto/rivolta** ▶ **rivolgere**

rivoluzione *noun, feminine*
una rivoluzione = a revolution

roba *noun, feminine*
la roba = stuff

roccia *noun, feminine* (*plural* **rocce**)
una roccia = a rock

Roma *noun*
= Rome

romanico/romanica *adjective* (*plural*
romanici/romaniche)
= romanesque

romano/romana *adjective*
= Roman

romanzo *noun, masculine*
un romanzo = a novel

rompere *verb* [60]
1 (**!** + *avere*)
= to break
2 **rompersi** (**!** + *essere*)
rompersi = to break
si è rotta la sedia = the chair broke

rosa
1 *noun, feminine*
una rosa = a rose
2 *adjective* (**!** *never changes*)
= pink

rosmarino *noun, masculine*
il rosmarino = rosemary

rossetto *noun, masculine*
il rossetto = lipstick

rosso/rossa *adjective*
= red

rotolare *verb* [1]
= to roll

rotondo/rotonda *adjective*
= round

rotto/rotta
1 ▶ **rompere**
2 *adjective*
= broken

rottura *noun, feminine*
• una rottura = a break
• che rottura!✱ = what a pain!

roulotte *noun, feminine* (**!** *never*
changes)
una roulotte = a caravan, a trailer

rovescia *noun, feminine*, **rovescio**
noun, masculine
alla rovescia, a rovescio = the wrong way
round

rovesciare *verb* [6]
• = to overturn
• = to spill

rovinare *verb* [1]
= to ruin

rubare *verb* [1]
= to steal

rubinetto *noun, masculine*
un rubinetto = a tap, a faucet

ruga *noun, feminine* (*plural* **rughe**)
una ruga = a wrinkle

ruggine *noun, feminine*
la ruggine = rust

ruggire *verb* [9]
= to roar

rullino *noun, masculine*
un rullino = a film

rumore *noun, masculine*
un rumore = a noise

rumoroso/rumorosa *adjective*
= noisy

ruolo *noun, masculine*
un ruolo = a role

ruota *noun, feminine*
una ruota = a wheel

ruppe, **ruppi**, etc ▶ **rompere**

ruscello *noun, masculine*
un ruscello = a stream

russo/russa *adjective*
= Russian

ruvido/ruvida *adjective*
= rough

sabato *noun, masculine*
= Saturday
arrivo sabato = I'm arriving on Saturday
il sabato = on Saturdays

sabbia *noun, feminine*
la sabbia = sand

sacchetto *noun, masculine*
un sacchetto = a bag

sacco *noun, masculine (plural* **sacchi**)
• un sacco = a bag
• un sacco di soldi = loads of money

sacro/sacra *adjective*
= sacred

saggio/saggia (*plural* **saggi/sagge**)
1 *adjective*
= wise
2 *noun, masculine*
• un saggio = a sage
• un saggio = an essay

Sagittario *noun, masculine*
= Sagittarius

sai ▶ **sapere**

sala *noun, feminine*
una sala = a living room
una sala da pranzo = a dining room

salame *noun, masculine*
il salame = salami

salario *noun, masculine (plural* **salari**)
un salario = a salary

salato/salata *adjective*
• (*when it's food*)
(*having a lot of salt*) = salty
(*not sweet*) = savo(u)ry
• (*when it's a price*) = high

saldo/salda
1 *adjective*
= steady
2 **saldo** *noun, masculine*
• il saldo = the balance
• i saldi = the sales

sale *noun, masculine*
il sale = salt

salgo, salgono, etc ▶ **salire**

salire *verb* [61] (**!** + *essere* or *avere*)
• = to go up
salire le scale = to go up the stairs
• (*with vehicles*)
salire [sul treno | sull'autobus | sulla bici] = to
get on [the train | the bus | the bike]
salire in macchina = to get in the car

salita *noun, feminine*
• una salita = a climb
• una salita = a slope
in salita = uphill

salmone *noun, masculine*
il salmone = salmon

salotto *noun, masculine*
il salotto = the living room

salsa *noun, feminine*
una salsa = a sauce

salsiccia *noun, feminine (plural*
salsicce)
una salsiccia = a sausage

saltare *verb* [1] (**!** + *essere* or *avere*)
• = to jump
• far saltare un edificio = to blow up a
building

salto *noun, masculine*
• un salto = a jump
• fare un salto da qualcuno = to drop in on
someone

salumeria *noun, feminine*
una salumeria = a delicatessen

salumi *noun, masculine plural*
i salumi = cured meats

salutare *verb* [1]
= to say hello/goodbye
salutami Gabriele = say hello to Gabriele
for me
ti saluta Iacopo = Iacopo says hello

salute *noun, feminine*
• la salute = health
• salute! = cheers!

saluto *noun, masculine*
• un saluto = a greeting
• (*in a letter*)
tanti saluti, Elena = lots of love, Elena
cordiali saluti = (yours) sincerely

salvare *verb* [1]
= to save
= to rescue

salve *exclamation*
salve! = hi!

salvo *preposition*
= except

salvo/salva *adjective*
= safe

sammarinese *adjective*
= San Marinese

san ▶ **santo**

S

sandalo *noun, masculine*
un sandalo = a sandal

sangue *noun, masculine*
il sangue = blood
una bistecca al sangue = a rare steak

sanguinare *verb* 1
= to bleed
mi sanguina il naso = my nose is
bleeding

sanno ▶ **sapere**

sano/sana *adjective*
= healthy
sano e salvo/sana e salva = safe and
sound

santo/santa
1 *adjective*
= holy
2 *noun, masculine/feminine*
• un santo/una santa = a saint
San Francesco/Santa Chiara = Saint
Francis/Saint Clare
• San Valentino = Valentine's Day
Santo Stefano = Boxing Day, December
26

sapere *verb* 62
• = to know
so che verrà = I know he'll come
• = can
so nuotare = I can swim
• = to find out
= to hear
ho saputo che ti sposi = I heard you're
getting married
• sapere di qualcosa = to smell of
something
= to taste of something
sa di pesce = it smells of fish

sapone *noun, masculine*
il sapone = soap

sapore *noun, masculine*
un sapore = a taste

sappiamo, saprà, etc ▶ **sapere**

sarà, sarai, etc ▶ **essere**

Sardegna *noun, feminine*
la Sardegna = Sardinia

sardo/sarda *adjective*
= Sardinian

saremo, sarò, etc ▶ **essere**

sasso *noun, masculine*
un sasso = a stone

sazio/sazia *adjective* (*plural* **sazi/sazie**)
= full
sono sazio = I'm full

sbagliare *verb* 6
1 (**!** + *avere*)
ho sbagliato numero = I got the wrong
number

2 **sbagliarsi** (**!** + *essere*)
sbagliarsi = to make a mistake
mi sono sbagliato = I made a mistake

sbagliato/sbagliata *adjective*
= wrong

sbaglio *noun, masculine* (*plural* **sbagli**)
fare uno sbaglio = to make a mistake
per sbaglio = by mistake

sbattere *verb* 8
• = to beat
• = to bang
la porta sbatteva = the door was banging

sbrigarsi *verb* 5 (**!** + *essere*)
= to hurry up
sbrigati! = hurry up!

sbucciare *verb* 2
= to peel

scacchi *noun, masculine plural*
gli scacchi = chess

scadenza *noun, feminine*
una scadenza = a deadline

scadere *verb* 19 (**!** + *essere*)
= to expire
il tempo è scaduto = time is up

scaduto/scaduta *adjective*
= out-of-date

scaffale *noun, masculine*
uno scaffale = shelves

scala *noun, feminine*
• una scala = a ladder
• le scale = the stairs
• una scala = a scale

scaldare *verb* 1
= to heat up
= to warm up

scalzo/scalza *adjective*
= barefoot

scambiare *verb* 6
• = to exchange
• scambiare A per B = to mistake A for B

scambio *noun, masculine* (*plural*
scambi)
uno scambio = an exchange

scandalo *noun, masculine*
uno scandalo = a scandal

scappare *verb* 1 (**!** + *essere*)
• = to run away
• = to dash

scaricare *verb*
= to unload

scarico/scarica *adjective* (*plural*
scarichi/scariche)
(*when it's a battery*) = flat

scarpa *noun, feminine*
una scarpa = a shoe
= a boot
una scarpa da ginnastica = a trainer, a
sneaker

✱ in informal situations

scarso/scarsa *adjective*
= poor

scartare *verb* 1
• = to discard
= to reject
• = to unwrap

scatenare *verb* 1
= to unleash

scatola *noun, feminine*
• una scatola = a box
• una scatola = a tin, a can

scatoletta *noun, feminine*
una scatoletta = a tin, a can

scattare *verb* 1
= to go off
scattare una foto = to take a picture

scatto *noun, masculine*
• uno scatto = a click
• uno scatto = a jerk
• di scatto = suddenly

scavare *verb* 1
= to dig

scegliere *verb* 22
= to choose

scelgo, **scelse**, etc ▶ **scegliere**

scelta *noun, feminine*
una scelta = a choice

scelto/scelta ▶ **scegliere**

scemo/scema✻ *adjective*
= stupid

scena *noun, feminine*
una scena = a scene

scendere *verb* 53 (**!** + *essere* or *avere*)
= to come down
= to go down

scese, **sceso/scesa** ▶ **scendere**

scheda di memoria *noun, feminine*
una scheda di memoria = a memory stick

schedina *noun, feminine*
fare la schedina = to do the pools

scheletro *noun, masculine*
lo scheletro = the skeleton

schermo *noun, masculine*
uno schermo = a screen

scherzare *verb* 1
= to joke

scherzo *noun, masculine*
uno scherzo = a joke
fare uno scherzo a qualcuno = to play a
joke on someone

schiacciare *verb* 2
• = to squash
= to crush
• schiacciare una noce = to crack a walnut

schiaffo *noun, masculine*
uno schiaffo = a slap

schiavo/schiava *noun,*
masculine/feminine
uno schiavo/una schiava = a slave

schiena *noun, feminine*
la schiena = the back

schifo✻ *noun, masculine*
che schifo! = yuck!
fare schifo = to be disgusting
= to be awful

schifoso/schifosa✻ *adjective*
= disgusting
= horrible

schiuma *noun, feminine*
la schiuma = foam
= froth

schizzare *verb* 1
= to splash

sci *noun, masculine* (**!** *never changes*)
• lo sci = skiing
fare dello sci = to ski
lo sci acquatico/d'acqua/nautico = water-
skiing
• uno sci = a ski

sciare *verb* 7
= to ski

sciarpa *noun, feminine*
una sciarpa = a scarf

scientifico/scientifica *adjective*
(*plural* **scientifici/scientifiche**)
= scientific

scienza *noun, feminine*
la scienza = science

scienziato/scienziata *noun,*
masculine/feminine
uno scienziato/una scienziata = a
scientist

scimmia *noun, feminine*
una scimmia = a monkey

sciocchezza *noun, feminine*
• una sciocchezza = a silly thing
dire sciocchezze = to say something
stupid
• costa una sciocchezza = it costs next to
nothing

sciocco/sciocca *adjective* (*plural*
sciocchi/sciocche)
= silly

sciogliere *verb* 22
1 (**!** + *avere*)
• = to dissolve
• = to loosen
2 **sciogliersi** (**!** + *essere*)
• sciogliersi = to melt
• sciogliersi = to dissolve

sciolgo, **sciolto/sciolta**, etc ▶
sciogliere

sciopero *noun, masculine*
uno sciopero = a strike

S

sciroppo *noun, masculine*
uno sciroppo = a syrup

sciupare *verb* [1]
= to spoil

scivolare *verb* [1] (**!** + *essere*)
= to slip
= to slide

scocciare * *verb* [2]
= to annoy

scocciatura * *noun, feminine*
una scocciatura = a nuisance

scoglio *noun, masculine* (*plural* **scogli**)
uno scoglio = a rock

scolastico/scolastica *adjective*
(*plural* **scolastici/scolastiche**)
= school
l'anno scolastico = the school year

scommessa *noun, feminine*
una scommessa = a bet
fare una scommessa = to place a bet

scommettere *verb* [40]
= to bet

scomodo/scomoda *adjective*
• = uncomfortable
• = inconvenient

scomparire *verb* [14] (**!** + *essere*)
= to disappear

scomparsa *noun, feminine*
la scomparsa = the disappearance

**scomparso/scomparsa,
scomparve, etc** ▶ **scomparire**

scompartimento *noun, masculine*
uno scompartimento = a compartment

sconcertare *verb* [1]
= to disconcert

sconfitta *noun, feminine*
una sconfitta = a defeat

sconosciuto/sconosciuta
1 *adjective*
= unknown
2 *noun, masculine/feminine*
uno sconosciuto/una sconosciuta = a
stranger

sconsigliare *verb* [6]
= to advise against

scontato/scontata *adjective*
• = reduced
• è scontato che = it goes without saying
that
dare per scontato qualcosa = to take
something for granted

sconto *noun, masculine*
uno sconto = a discount
sconti = reductions

scontrino *noun, masculine*
uno scontrino = a receipt

scontro *noun, masculine*
uno scontro = a crash

sconvolgente *adjective*
= upsetting

sconvolto/sconvolta *adjective*
= distraught

scopa *noun, feminine*
una scopa = a broom

scoperta *noun, feminine*
una scoperta = a discovery

scoperto/scoperta ▶ **scoprire**

scopo *noun, masculine*
uno scopo = a purpose

scoppiare *verb* [6] (**!** + *essere*)
• (*when it's a bomb*) = to explode
• (*when it's a tyre*) = to burst
• scoppiare dal caldo = to be boiling

scoppio *noun, masculine* (*plural* **scoppi**)
• uno scoppio = an explosion

scoprire *verb* [15]
= to discover

scoraggiare *verb* [3]
= to discourage

scordare *verb* [1]
1 (**!** + *avere*)
= to forget
2 **scordarsi** (**!** + *essere*)
mi sono scordato di spegnerlo = I forgot
to switch it off

scorpione *noun, masculine*
1 uno scorpione = a scorpion
2 Scorpione
Scorpione = Scorpio

scorrere *verb* [26]
• (**!** + *essere*) = to flow
• (**!** + *avere*) = to glance through
• (*on a computer*) = to scroll
scorrere verso l'alto/il basso
= to scroll up/down

scorretto/scorretta *adjective*
= improper

scorso/scorsa
1 ▶ **scorrere**
2 *adjective*
= last
l'anno scorso = last year

scortese *adjective*
= rude

scossa *noun, feminine*
• prendere la scossa = to get a shock
• una scossa = a tremor

scosse, scossi, etc ▶ **scuotere**

scosso/scossa
1 ▶ **scuotere**
2 *adjective*
= shocked

scotch ® *noun, masculine*
lo scotch = Sellotape®, Scotch tape®

scottare *verb* 1
1 = to burn
2 scottarsi (**!** + *essere*)
  scottarsi = to burn oneself
  = to get burnt

Scozia *noun, feminine*
  la Scozia = Scotland

scozzese *adjective*
  = Scottish

scrisse, **scritto/scritta**, etc ▶
  scrivere

scrittore/scrittrice *noun, masculine/feminine*
  uno scrittore/una scrittrice = a writer

scrittura *noun, feminine*
  la scrittura = the writing

scrivania *noun, feminine*
  una scrivania = a desk

scrivere *verb* 65
  = to write
  c'è scritto 'privato' = it says 'private'

scultura *noun, feminine*
  una scultura = a sculpture

scuola *noun, feminine*
  una scuola = a school
una scuola guida = a driving school
una scuola materna = a nursery school
una scuola media = a middle school

scuotere *verb* 66
  = to shake

scuro/scura *adjective*
  = dark

scusa *noun, feminine*
• **una scusa** = an excuse
• **le scuse** = an apology

scusarsi *verb* 1 (**!** + *essere*)
  = to apologize

sdraio *noun, feminine* (**!** *never changes*)
  una sdraio = a deckchair

sdraiarsi *verb* 6 (**!** + *essere*)
  = to lie down

sdraiato/sdraiata *adjective*
  stare sdraiato/sdraiata = to be lying (down)

se
1 ▶ **si**
2 ▶ **sé**
3 *conjunction*
  = if
  se lo vedrò, glielo dirò = If I see him I'll tell him

sé *pronoun*
  = himself/herself
  = itself
  = themselves
  = yourself

vuole tenere tutto per sé = he wants to keep everything for himself
  ! *When* **sé** *comes before* **stesso/stessa**, *it is usually spelled* **se**.

Francesca pensa solo a se stessa
  = Francesca thinks only of herself

sebbene *conjunction*
  = although

seccato/seccata *adjective*
  = annoyed

secchio *noun, masculine* (*plural* **secchi**)
  un secchio = a bucket

secco/secca *adjective* (*plural* **secchi/secche**)
  = dry

secolo *noun, masculine*
  un secolo = a century
  da secoli = for ages

secondo/seconda
1 *adjective*
  = second
2 secondo *noun, masculine*
• **un secondo** = a second
• **il secondo** = the main course
3 *preposition*
  secondo me = in my opinion
  secondo il dizionario = according to the dictionary

sedersi *verb* 51 (**!** + *essere*)
  = to sit down
  siediti! = sit down!

sedia *noun, feminine*
  una sedia = a chair
una sedia a rotelle = a wheelchair
una sedia a sdraio = a deckchair

sedicenne *adjective*
  = sixteen-year-old

sedicesimo/sedicesima *adjective*
  = sixteenth

sedici *number*
  = sixteen

sedile *noun, masculine*
  un sedile = a seat

seduto/seduta
1 ▶ **sedersi**
2 *adjective*
  = sitting
  era seduto per terra = he was sitting on the ground

segnalare *verb* 1
  = to report

segnale *noun, masculine*
  un segnale = a signal
  = a sign

segnare *verb* 1
• = to mark
• = to write down

S

segno noun, masculine
• un segno = a sign
• un segno = a mark

segretario/segretaria noun,
masculine/feminine (plural
segretari/segretarie)
un segretario/una segretaria = a secretary

segreteria noun, feminine
una segreteria = an office
una segreteria telefonica = an
answering machine

segreto/segreta
1 adjective
= secret
2 segreto noun, masculine
un segreto = a secret

seguente adjective
= following

seguire verb 10
= to follow

sei
1 ▶ essere
2 number
= six

seicento
1 number
= six hundred
2 Seicento noun
il Seicento = the 17th century

sella noun, feminine
una sella = a saddle

sellino noun, masculine
un sellino = a saddle

selvaggina noun, feminine
la selvaggina = game

selvaggio/selvaggia adjective (plural
selvaggi/selvagge)
= wild

selvatico/selvatica adjective (plural
selvatici/selvatiche)
= wild

semaforo noun, masculine
il semaforo = the traffic lights

sembrare verb 1 (! + essere)
= to seem
= to look (like)
sembra impossibile = it seems impossible
sembri un pagliaccio = you look like a
clown
mi sembra che abbia ragione tu = I think
you're right
mi sembra di sì = I think so
mi sembrava di volare = I felt as I were
flying

seme noun, masculine
un seme = a seed

seminare verb 1
= to sow

semplice adjective
• = simple
• = plain

sempre adverb
• = always
come sempre = as usual
per sempre = for ever
• = still
lavora sempre qui = he still works here

senato noun, masculine
il senato = the senate

senatore/senatrice noun,
masculine/feminine
un senatore/una senatrice = a senator

senese adjective
= Sienese

seno noun, masculine
un seno = a breast
il seno = the bust

sensato/sensata adjective
= sensible

sensazione noun, feminine
una sensazione = a sensation
ho la sensazione che... = I have a
feeling that...

sensibile adjective
= sensitive

senso noun, masculine
• un senso = a sense
• un senso = a direction
'senso unico' = 'one way'

sentiero noun, masculine
un sentiero = a path

sentimentale adjective
= sentimental

sentire verb 10
1 (! + avere)
• = to feel
• = to hear
non ti sento = I can't hear you
• = to smell
• = to taste
2 sentirsi (! + essere)
sentirsi = to feel
mi sento male = I don't feel well

senz'altro adverb
= definitely

senza preposition, conjunction
= without
senza pensarci = without thinking about
it

separare verb 1
= to separate

separato/separata adjective
• = separate
• (when it's a couple) = separated

seppe, seppi, etc ▶ sapere

sequestrare verb [1]
 = to seize
 = to kidnap

sera noun, feminine
 una sera = an evening

serale adjective
 = evening

serata noun, feminine
 una serata = an evening

sereno/serena adjective
 • = peaceful
 • = happy
 • (talking about the weather) = clear

serie noun, feminine (! never changes)
 una serie = a series

serio/seria adjective (plural seri/serie)
 = serious
 sul serio = seriously

serpente noun, masculine
 un serpente = a snake

serra noun, feminine
 una serra = a greenhouse

serratura noun, feminine
 una serratura = a lock

servire verb [10]
1 (! + avere)
 • = to serve
 • = to be useful
  ti serve il coltello? = do you need the
   knife?
  non mi serve più = I don't need it any
   more
2 servirsi (! + essere)
  servirsi = to help oneself
  serviti! = help yourself!

servizio noun, masculine (plural servizi)
 il servizio = the service

sessanta number
 = sixty

sessantesimo/sessantesima
 adjective
 = sixtieth

sesso noun, masculine
 il sesso = sex

sessuale adjective
 = sexual

sesto/sesta adjective
 = sixth

seta noun, feminine
 la seta = silk

sete noun, feminine
 la sete = thirst
 aver sete = to be thirsty

settanta number
 = seventy

settantesimo/settantesima
 adjective
 = seventieth

sette number
 = seven

settecento
1 number
 = seven hundred
2 Settecento noun, masculine
 il Settecento = the 18th century

settembre noun, masculine
 = September

settentrionale adjective
 = northern

settimana noun, feminine
 una settimana = a week
 una settimana bianca = a skiing holiday

settimanale adjective
 = weekly

settimo/settima adjective
 = seventh

severo/severa adjective
 = strict

sezione noun, feminine
 una sezione = a section

sfacciato/sfacciata adjective
 = cheeky

sfidare verb [1]
 = to challenge

sfilata noun, feminine
 una sfilata = a parade
 una sfilata di moda = a fashion show

sfocato/sfocata adjective
 = blurred

sfogliare verb [6]
 = to flick through

sfondo noun, masculine
 uno sfondo = a background

sfortuna noun, feminine
 la sfortuna = bad luck
 avere sfortuna = to be unlucky

sfortunato/sfortunata adjective
 = unlucky

sforzarsi verb [1] (! + essere)
 = to make an effort

sforzo noun, masculine
 uno sforzo = an effort
 fare uno sforzo = to make an effort

sfruttare verb [1]
 = to take advantage of

sfuggire verb [10] (! + essere)
 = to escape
 mi sfugge il nome = the name escapes me

sgombrare verb [1]
 = to clear

S

si

Si is the reflexive pronoun of the third person singular and plural. It is also used with **lei** meaning 'you':

si sono divertiti	= *they enjoyed themselves*
si è divertita, signora Giusti?	= *did you enjoy yourself, Mrs Giusti?*

Si is the reciprocal pronoun for the third person plural, and can be translated as 'each other' or 'one another':

non si capiscono	= *they don't understand each other*

Si is also used with a verb as a less formal alternative to the passive:

l'olio si fa con le olive	= *oil is made from olives*
non si accettano carte di credito	= *credit cards are not accepted*

and to form impersonal constructions:

in campagna si dorme bene	= *you sleep well in the country*

It sometimes also replaces the first person plural ('we'):

si prende un taxi?	= *shall we take a taxi?*

---

sgomento/sgomenta
1 *adjective*
  = dismayed
2 **sgomento** *noun, masculine*
  lo sgomento = dismay

sgradevole *adjective*
  = unpleasant

sgridare *verb* 1.
  = to tell off

sguardo *noun, masculine*
  uno sguardo = a look

si (**se** *before* lo/la, li/le, *and* ne)
pronoun
  ▶ **102** *See the boxed note.*
  = (to) himself/herself
  = (to) itself
  = (to) themselves
  = (to) yourself

sì *adverb*
  = yes
  dire di sì = to say yes
  sì che mi piace = I do like it
  Laura non è sposata ma Elena sì = Laura
    isn't married but Elena is

sia
1 ▶ **essere**
2 *conjunction*
  sia Paolo che Luca = both Paolo and
    Luca
  sia oggi che domani = either today or
    tomorrow

siamo, **siano** ▶ **essere**

sicché *conjunction*
  = so

siccome *conjunction*
  = since

Sicilia *noun, feminine*
  la Sicilia = Sicily

siciliano/siciliana *adjective*
  = Sicilian

sicuramente *adverb*
  = certainly

sicurezza *noun, feminine*
  la sicurezza = safety

sicuro/sicura *adjective*
  • = sure
    di sicuro = definitely
  • = safe
  • **sicuro/sicura di sé** = self-confident

siede, **siedo**, etc ▶ **sedersi**

siete ▶ **essere**

sigaretta *noun, feminine*
  una sigaretta = a cigarette

sigaro *noun, masculine*
  un sigaro = a cigar

significare *verb* 4
  = to mean
  che significa questa parola? = what does
    this word mean?

significato *noun, masculine*
  il significato = the meaning

signora *noun, feminine*
  • **una signora** = a lady
  • **buongiorno, signora!** = good morning,
    madam!
  • **la signora Martini** = Mrs Martini

signore *noun, masculine*
  • **un signore** = a gentleman
  • **buongiorno, signore!** = good morning, sir!
    buonasera, signori! = good evening,
    ladies and gentlemen!
  • **il signor Martini** = Mr Martini
    i signori Martini = Mr and Mrs Martini

signorina *noun, feminine*
  • **una signorina** = a young lady   ····▶

- **buongiorno, signorina!** = good morning, miss!
- **la signorina Martini** = Miss Martini

sii ▶ **essere**

silenzio *noun, masculine*
il silenzio = silence

silenzioso/silenziosa *adjective*
= silent
= quiet

simile *adjective*
= similar
è simile a quello di Monica = it's similar to Monica's

simpatia *noun, feminine*
la simpatia = friendliness

simpatico/simpatica *adjective*
(*plural* simpatici/simpatiche)
= nice
mi è simpatica = I like her

sinceramente *adverb*
= honestly

sincero/sincera *adjective*
= sincere
a essere sincero/sincera = to be honest

sindacato *noun, masculine*
un sindacato = a union

sindaco *noun, masculine* (*plural* sindaci)
il sindaco = the mayor

singhiozzo *noun, masculine*
avere il singhiozzo = to have hiccups

singolare *adjective*
= singular

singolo/singola *adjective*
= single

sinistro/sinistra
1 *adjective*
= left
la mano sinistra = the left hand
2 **sinistra** *noun, feminine*
la sinistra = the left
girare a sinistra = to turn left

sino ▶ **fino**

sintomo *noun, masculine*
un sintomo = a symptom

sistema *noun, masculine* (*plural* sistemi)
un sistema = a system

sistemare *verb* ⓵
= to sort out

sito web *noun, masculine*
un sito web = a website

situazione *noun, feminine*
una situazione = a situation

slip *noun, masculine* (**!** *never changes*)
uno slip = a pair of underpants

slogare *verb* ⑤
= to sprain
mi sono slogato la caviglia = I sprained my ankle

smalto *noun, masculine*
lo smalto per le unghie = nail polish

smarrire *verb* ⑨
1 = to lose
2 **smarrirsi** (**!** + *essere*)
smarrirsi = to get lost

smentire *verb* ⑨
= to deny

smesso/smessa ▶ **smettere**

smettere *verb* ㊵
= to stop
ha smesso di piovere = it's stopped raining
smettila! = stop it!

smise, smisi, etc ▶ **smettere**

smontare *verb* ⓵
= to take apart

sms *noun, masculine*
uno sms = a text message

snello/snella *adjective*
= slim

so ▶ **sapere**

soccorso *noun, masculine*
il soccorso = help

sociale *adjective*
= social

società *noun, feminine* (**!** *never changes*)
- la società = society
- una società = a company

socievole *adjective*
= sociable

socio/socia *noun, masculine/feminine*
(*plural* soci/socie)
un socio/una socia = a member
= a partner

soddisfare *verb* ㊳
= to satisfy

soddisfatto/soddisfatta
1 ▶ **soddisfare**
2 *adjective*
= satisfied

sodo/soda
1 *adjective*
= solid
un uovo sodo = a hard-boiled egg
2 **sodo** *adverb*
dormire sodo = to sleep soundly
lavorare sodo = to work hard

sofà *noun, masculine* (**!** *never changes*)
un sofà = a sofa

sofferto/sofferta ▶ **soffrire**

soffiare *verb* ⑥
= to blow

S

soffitta noun, feminine
la soffitta = the attic

soffitto noun, masculine
il soffitto = the ceiling

soffocare verb 4
= to suffocate
= to choke

soffrire verb 10
= to suffer
= to be in pain
soffre di cuore = he has heart problems

soggetto noun, masculine
un soggetto = a subject

soggiorno noun, masculine
• un soggiorno = a stay
• un soggiorno = a living room

sognare verb 1
= to dream

sogno noun, masculine
un sogno = a dream

soldato noun, masculine
un soldato = a soldier

soldi noun, masculine plural
i soldi = money
quanti soldi hai? = how much money do
you have?

sole noun, masculine
il sole = the sun
c'è il sole = it's sunny

solido/solida adjective
= solid

solito/solita adjective
= usual
di solito = usually
come al solito = as usual

sollevare verb 1
= to lift

sollievo noun, masculine
il sollievo = relief

solo/sola
1 adjective
= alone
da solo/sola = on one's own
sentirsi solo/sola = to feel lonely
2 solo adverb
= only

soltanto adverb
= only

soluzione noun, feminine
una soluzione = a solution

sommare verb 1
• = to add up
• tutto sommato = all things considered

sondaggio noun, masculine (plural
sondaggi)
un sondaggio = a survey

sonno noun, masculine
il sonno = sleep
aver sonno = to be sleepy

sono ▶ essere

sopportare verb 1
= to put up with
non la sopporto = I can't stand her

sopra
1 preposition
= over
= on top of
= above
2 adverb
= on top
di sopra = upstairs

soprattutto adverb
= especially

sopravvissuto/sopravvissuta ▶
sopravvivere

sopravvivere verb 80 (! + essere)
= to survive

sordo/sorda adjective
= deaf

sorella noun, feminine
una sorella = a sister

sorellastra noun, feminine
una sorellastra = a step-sister

sorgente noun, feminine
una sorgente = a spring

sorgere verb 64 (! + essere)
• = to rise
• = to arise

sorpassare verb 1
= to overtake

sorprendente adjective
= surprising

sorprendere verb 53
= to surprise

sorpresa noun, feminine
una sorpresa = a surprise

sorprese, sorpresi ▶ sorprendere

sorpreso/sorpresa
1 ▶ sorprendere
2 adjective
= surprised

sorridere verb 30
= to smile

sorrise, sorrisi ▶ sorridere

sorriso
1 ▶ sorridere
2 noun, masculine
un sorriso = a smile

sorte noun, feminine
la sorte = fate

sorto/sorta ▶ sorgere

sospettare verb 1
= to suspect

sospetto/sospetta
1 adjective
= suspicious
2 sospetto noun, masculine
• un sospetto = a suspicion
• un sospetto = a suspect

sospiro noun, masculine
un sospiro = a sigh

sosta noun, feminine
una sosta = a stop
= a break

sostanza noun, feminine
una sostanza = a substance

sostenere verb 73
• = to support
• = to maintain

sostengo, sostengono, etc ►
sostenere

sostenitore/sostenitrice noun,
masculine/feminine
un sostenitore/una sostenitrice = a
supporter

**sostenuto/sostenuta, sostiene,
etc** ► sostenere

sostituire verb 9
= to substitute
= to change

sottile adjective
• = subtle
• = thin

sotto
1 preposition
= under
= below
2 adverb
= underneath
di sotto = downstairs

sottofondo noun, masculine
un sottofondo = a background

sottolineare verb 1
= to underline

sottotitolo noun, masculine
i sottotitoli = subtitles

spaccare verb 4
= to break

spada noun, feminine
una spada = a sword

Spagna noun, feminine
la Spagna = Spain

spagnolo/spagnola adjective
= Spanish

spago noun, masculine
lo spago = string

spalla noun, feminine
la spalla = the shoulder

sparare verb 1
sparare a qualcuno = to shoot someone

spargere verb 68
• = to scatter
• spargere la voce = to spread the word

sparire verb 9 (! + essere)
= to disappear

sparse, sparso/sparsa ► spargere

spaventare verb 1
= to scare

spavento noun, masculine
prendere uno spavento = to get a fright

spaventoso/spaventosa adjective
= terrifying

spazio noun, masculine (plural spazi)
lo spazio = space

spazzare verb 1
= to sweep

spazzatura noun, feminine
la spazzatura = rubbish, garbage

spazzola noun, feminine
una spazzola = a brush

spazzolare verb 1
= to brush
spazzolarsi i capelli = to brush one's hair

spazzolino noun, masculine
uno spazzolino = a toothbrush

specchio noun, masculine (plural
specchi)
uno specchio = a mirror

speciale adjective
= special

specialità noun, feminine (! never
changes)
una specialità = a speciality, a specialty

specializzato/specializzata
adjective
= specialized

specialmente adverb
= especially

specie noun, feminine (! never changes)
• una specie = a species
• una specie di = a kind of

specifico/specifica adjective (plural
specifici/specifiche)
= specific

spedire verb 9
= to send

spegnere verb 69
1 = to switch off
= to blow out
2 spegnersi (! + essere)
spegnersi = to go out

spendere verb 53
= to spend

S

spense, spensi ▶ spegnere

spento/spenta
1 ▶ spegnere
2 adjective
= off
= out

speranza noun, feminine
la speranza = hope

sperare verb 1
= to hope
spero di vederti presto = I hope to see
you soon

spesa noun, feminine
• una spesa = an expense
• fare la spesa = to do the shopping

spese, speso/spesa, etc ▶
spendere

spesso/spessa
1 adjective
= thick
2 **spesso** adverb
= often

spettacolo noun, masculine
uno spettacolo = a show

spettatore/spettatrice noun,
masculine/feminine
uno spettatore/una spettatrice = a
spectator
gli spettatori = the audience

spezia noun, feminine
una spezia = a spice

spia noun, feminine
una spia = a spy

spiacevole adjective
= unpleasant

spiaggia noun, feminine (plural **spiagge**)
una spiaggia = a beach

spiccioli noun, masculine plural
gli spiccioli = small change

spiegare verb 5
= to explain

spiegazione noun, feminine
una spiegazione = an explanation

spilla noun, feminine
una spilla = a brooch

spillo noun, masculine
uno spillo = a pin

spina noun, feminine
• una spina = a thorn
• una spina di pesce = a fish bone
• una spina = a plug

spinaci noun, masculine plural
gli spinaci = spinach

spingere verb 48
= to push

spinse, spinsi, etc ▶ spingere

spinto/spinta
1 ▶ spingere
2 adjective
= risqué

spirito noun, masculine
lo spirito = the spirit

spiritoso/spiritosa adjective
= witty

splendido/splendida adjective
= splendid
= beautiful

spogliarsi verb 6 (! + essere)
= to strip

spogliatoio noun, masculine (plural
spogliatoi)
uno spogliatoio = a changing room

spolverare verb 1
= to dust

sporcare verb 4
1 = to dirty
2 sporcarsi (! + essere)
sporcarsi = to get dirty

sporco/sporca adjective (plural
sporchi/sporche)
= dirty

sport noun, masculine (! never changes)
lo sport = sport, sports

sportello noun, masculine
• (of a car)
uno sportello = a door
• (in a bank)
uno sportello = a counter

sportivo/sportiva adjective
= sporty

sposare verb 1
1 = to marry
2 sposarsi (! + essere) = to get married

sposato/sposata adjective
= married
è sposato con una pittrice = he's married
to a painter

sposo/sposa noun, masculine/feminine
lo sposo/la sposa = the bridegroom/the
bride
gli sposi = the bride and groom

spostare verb 1
1 = to move
2 spostarsi (! + essere) = to move

spot noun, masculine (! never changes)
uno spot pubblicitario = an advert

sprecare verb 4
= to waste

spreco noun, masculine (plural **sprechi**)
uno spreco = a waste

spremuta noun, feminine
una spremuta d'arancia = a fresh orange
juice

spruzzare *verb* 1
= to spray

spugna *noun, feminine*
una spugna = a sponge

spumante *noun, masculine*
lo spumante = sparkling wine

spuntino *noun, masculine*
uno spuntino = a snack

sputare *verb* 1
= to spit (out)

squadra *noun, feminine*
una squadra = a team

squalo *noun, masculine*
uno squalo = a shark

squillare *verb* 1
= to ring

sta, **sta'** ▶ **stare**

stabilire *verb* 9
1 = to establish
2 **stabilirsi** (! + *essere*)
stabilirsi = to settle (down)

staccare *verb* 4
1 (! + *avere*)
• = to remove
• = to unplug
2 **staccarsi** (! + *essere*)
staccarsi = to come off

stadio *noun, masculine* (*plural* **stadi**)
• uno stadio = a stage
• uno stadio = a stadium

stagione *noun, feminine*
una stagione = a season

stai ▶ **stare**

stalla *noun, feminine*
una stalla = a stable

stamani, **stamattina** *adverb*
= this morning

stampa *noun, feminine*
la stampa = the press

stampante *noun, feminine*
una stampante = a printer

stampare *verb* 1
= to print

stampatello *noun, masculine*
scrivere in stampatello = to print

stanchezza *noun, feminine*
la stanchezza = tiredness

stanco/stanca *adjective* (*plural* **stanchi/stanche**)
= tired

stanno ▶ **stare**

stanotte *adverb*
• = tonight
• = last night

stanza *noun, feminine*
una stanza = a room

stappare *verb* 1
= to open

stare *verb* 70 (! + *essere*)
• = to stay
voglio stare a casa = I want to stay at home
• = to be
come stai? = how are you?
sto benissimo = I'm very well
• = to suit
ti sta benissimo! = it really suits you!
• = to fit
le scarpe non mi stanno più = my shoes don't fit me any more
• (*with the gerund*)
sto lavorando = I'm working
stavano mangiando = they were eating
• stare per fare qualcosa = to be about to do something
stavo per dirtelo = I was just about to tell you

starnutire *verb* 9
= to sneeze

stasera *adverb*
= this evening

statale *adjective*
= state

state ▶ **stare**

statistica *noun, feminine* (*plural* **statistiche**)
la statistica = statistics
una statistica = a statistic

Stati Uniti *noun, masculine plural*
gli Stati Uniti = the United States

stato *noun, masculine*
uno stato = a state

stato/stata
1 ▶ **essere**
2 ▶ **stare**

statua *noun, feminine*
una statua = a statue

stazione *noun, feminine*
una stazione = a station
una stazione di servizio = a service area

stella *noun, feminine*
una stella = a star
un albergo a tre stelle = a three-star hotel

stendere *verb* 53
• = to spread out
• stendere il bucato = to hang out the washing

sterlina *noun, feminine*
una sterlina = a pound

sterzare *verb* 1
• = to steer
• = to swerve

S

steso/stesa
1 ▶ **stendere**
2 *adjective*
= lying

stesso/stessa
1 *adjective*
• = same
  lo stesso giorno = the same day
• **il presidente stesso** = the president himself
  se stesso/se stessa = himself/herself
  se stessi = themselves
2 *pronoun*
  = the same one
3 **lo stesso**
• = anyway
  ha continuato lo stesso = he carried on anyway
• **per me è lo stesso** = it's all the same to me

stette, stia, etc ▶ **stare**

stile *noun, masculine*
uno **stile** = a style

stilista *noun, masculine/feminine (plural stilisti/stiliste)*
uno/una stilista = a designer

stimare *verb* [1]
= to respect

stipendio *noun, masculine (plural stipendi)*
uno stipendio = a salary

stirare *verb* [1]
= to iron

stivale *noun, masculine*
uno stivale = a boot

sto ▶ **stare**

stoffa *noun, feminine*
la stoffa = material

stomaco *noun, masculine (plural stomachi)*
lo stomaco = the stomach

storia *noun, feminine*
• **una storia** = a story
• **la storia** = history

storico/storica *adjective (plural storici/storiche)*
= historic
= historical

storto/storta *adjective*
= crooked

straccio *noun, masculine (plural stracci)*
• **uno straccio** = a rag
• **uno straccio** = a cloth

strada *noun, feminine*
una strada = a road

strage *noun, feminine*
una strage = a massacre

straniero/straniera
1 *adjective*
= foreign
2 *noun, masculine/feminine*
uno straniero/una straniera = a foreigner

strano/strana *adjective*
= strange

straordinario/straordinaria *adjective (plural straordinari/straordinarie)*
= extraordinary

strappare *verb* [1]
= to tear

strategia *noun, feminine*
una strategia = a strategy

strato *noun, masculine*
uno strato = a layer

strega *noun, feminine (plural streghe)*
una strega = a witch

stressante *adjective*
= stressful

stressato/stressata *adjective*
essere stressato/stressata = to be under stress

stretto/stretta
1 ▶ **stringere**
2 *adjective*
• = narrow
• = tight

strillare *verb* [1]
= to scream

stringa *noun, feminine (plural stringhe)*
una stringa = a lace

stringere *verb* [71]
= to squeeze
stringere la mano a qualcuno = to shake someone's hand

strinse, strinsi, etc ▶ **stringere**

striscia *noun, feminine (plural strisce)*
una striscia = a strip
= a stripe

strofinare *verb* [1]
= to rub

stronzo/stronza❖ *noun, masculine/feminine*
uno stronza/una stronza = a bastard

stronzata❖ *noun, feminine*
una stronzata = bullshit

strozzare *verb* [1]
= to strangle

strumento *noun, masculine*
uno strumento = an instrument

struttura *noun, feminine*
una struttura = a structure

studente/studentessa *noun, masculine/feminine*
uno studente/una studentessa = a student

studiare *verb* 6
= to study

studio *noun, masculine (plural* **studi***)*
• lo studio = study
• uno studio = a studio
= a study

stufa *noun, feminine*
una stufa = a stove
una stufa elettrica = an electric fire

stufarsi *verb* 1 *(! + essere)*
= to get fed up

stufo/stufa *adjective*
essere stufo/stufa di qualcosa = to be fed up of something

stupendo/stupenda *adjective*
= fantastic

stupido/stupida *adjective*
= stupid

stupire *verb* 9
= to amaze

su
1 *preposition*

> **!** *Note that* **su** *combines with* **il**, **la**, *etc.*
> Su + il = sul; su + l' = sull'; su + lo
> = sullo; su + i = sui; su + gli = sugli;
> su + la = sulla; su + le = sulle.

• = on
su un aereo per New York = on a plane for New York
sulla destra = on the right
• sul giornale = in the newspaper
• nove su dieci = nine out of ten
• un libro sulla Toscana = a book about Tuscany
2 *adverb*
• = up
• = upstairs

subire *verb* 9
= to undergo

subito *adverb*
= immediately

succedere *verb* 23 *(! + essere)*
= to happen
non succede niente = nothing's happening
cos'è successo? = what's happened?

successe, successero, etc ▶ **succedere**

successo/successa
1 ▶ **succedere**
2 successo *noun, masculine*
il successo = success

succhiare *verb* 6
= to suck

succo *noun, masculine (plural* **succhi***)*
il succo = juice

sud *noun, masculine*
il sud = the south

Sudafrica *noun, masculine*
il Sudafrica = South Africa

sudare *verb* 1
= to sweat

sudest *noun, masculine*
il sudest = the south-east

sudicio/sudicia *adjective (plural* **sudici/sudice***)*
= dirty

sudore *noun, masculine*
il sudore = sweat

sudovest *noun, masculine*
il sudovest = the south-west

sufficiente *adjective*
= sufficient

suggerimento *noun, masculine*
un suggerimento = a suggestion

suggerire *verb* 9
= to suggest

sugli ▶ **su**

sugo *noun, masculine (plural* **sughi***)*
il sugo = sauce
= gravy

sui ▶ **su**

suicidarsi *verb* 1 *(! + essere)*
= to commit suicide

suicidio *noun, masculine (plural* **suicidi***)*
il suicidio = suicide

sul, sulla, sullo, etc ▶ **su**

suo/sua
1 *adjective (plural* **suoi/sue***)*
= his/her
= its
2 *pronoun*
= his/hers
il suo/la sua = his one
= her one

suocero/suocera *noun, masculine/feminine*
il suocero/la suocera = the father-in-law/the mother-in-law
i suoceri = the in-laws

suoi ▶ **suo**

suola *noun, feminine*
una suola = a sole

suonare *verb* 1
• = to sound
suonare il clacson = to sound one's horn
• = to ring
il telefono suona = the telephone is ringing   ····▶

S

• = to play
suono il violino = I play the violin

suoneria *noun, feminine*
una suoneria = a ringtone

suono *noun, masculine*
un suono = a sound

suora *noun, feminine*
una suora = a nun

superare *verb* 1
• = to overcome
• = to overtake

superficiale *adjective*
= superficial

superficie *noun, feminine* (! *never changes*)
una superficie = a surface

superiore *adjective*
= superior
= upper

supermercato *noun, masculine*
un supermercato = a supermarket

supplemento *noun, masculine*
un supplemento = a supplement

suppone, suppongo, etc ▶ supporre

supporre *verb* 50
= to suppose, to guess

suppose, supposto/supposta, etc ▶ supporre

surgelato *adjective*
= frozen

susina *noun, feminine*
una susina = a plum

sussurrare *verb* 1
= to whisper

svantaggio *noun, masculine* (*plural* svantaggi)
uno svantaggio = a disadvantage

sveglia *noun, feminine*
una sveglia = an alarm clock

svegliarsi *verb* 6 (! + *essere*)
= to wake up

sveglio/sveglia *adjective* (*plural* svegli/svegli e)
= awake

svelto/svelta *adjective*
= quick

svenga, svengo, etc ▶ svenire

svenire *verb* 78 (! + *essere*)
= to faint

svenne, svenuto/svenuta, etc ▶ svenire

svestirsi *verb* 10 (! + *essere*)
= to undress

---

sviluppare *verb* 1
= to develop

sviluppo *noun, masculine*
uno sviluppo = a development

Svizzera *noun, feminine*
la Svizzera = Switzerland

svizzero/svizzera *adjective*
= Swiss

svolgere *verb* 59
= to carry out

svolta *noun, feminine*
• una svolta = a turning
• una svolta = a turning point

svolto/svolta ▶ svolgere

svuotare *verb* 1
= to empty

Tt

---

tabaccaio/tabaccaia *noun, masculine/feminine* (*plural* tabaccai/tabaccaie)
un tabaccaio/una tabaccaia = a tobacconist

tabaccheria *noun, feminine*
una tabaccheria = a tobacconist's, a smoke shop

tabacco *noun, masculine*
il tabacco = tobacco

tacchino *noun, masculine*
un tacchino = a turkey

taccio, tacciono, etc ▶ tacere

tacco *noun, masculine* (*plural* tacchi)
un tacco = a heel

tacere *verb* 72
= to be silent

taciuto/taciuta ▶ tacere

taglia *noun, feminine*
una taglia = a size

tagliare *verb* 6
= to cut
mi sono tagliato un dito = I've cut my finger

tagliente *adjective*
= sharp

taglio *noun, masculine* (*plural* tagli)
un taglio = a cut

tailleur *noun, masculine* (! *never changes*)
un tailleur = a suit

---

tale
1 *adjective*
= such
un tale successo = such as success
2 *pronoun*
un tale = someone
quel tale = that person

talento *noun, masculine*
il talento = talent

tallone *noun, masculine*
un tallone = a heel

talmente *adverb*
= so
talmente stupido = so stupid

tamburo *noun, masculine*
un tamburo = a drum

Tamigi *noun, masculine*
il Tamigi = the Thames

tangente *noun, feminine*
una tangente = a bribe

tanto/tanta
1 *adjective, pronoun*
tanto/tanta = so much
tanti/tante = so many
è successo tante volte = it's happened
    lots of times
tanto tempo fa = a long time ago
2 **tanto** *adverb*
= so (much)
= a lot
tanto caldo = so hot
mi piace tanto = I really like it

tappeto *noun, masculine*
un tappeto = a carpet
= a rug

tappo *noun, masculine*
un tappo = a top
= a cork

tardi *adverb*
= late
fare tardi = to be late

targa *noun, feminine (plural* **targhe**)
una targa = a number plate, a license
    plate

tartaruga *noun, feminine (plural*
tartarughe)
una tartaruga = a tortoise
= a turtle

tasca *noun, feminine (plural* **tasche**)
una tasca = a pocket

tassa *noun, feminine*
una tassa = a tax

tassista *noun, masculine/feminine (plural*
tassisti/tassiste)
un/una tassista = a taxi driver

tasso *noun, masculine*
il tasso = the rate

tasto *noun, masculine*
un tasto = key

tavola *noun, feminine*
• **una tavola** = a table
• **una tavola** = a plank

tavolo *noun, masculine*
un tavolo = a table

tazza *noun, feminine*
una tazza = a cup

tazzina *noun, feminine*
una tazzina = a coffee cup

te *pronoun*
1 ▶ **ti**
2 = you
= to you
= yourself
è per te = it's for you

tè *noun, masculine* (! *never changes*)
il tè = tea

teatro *noun, masculine*
un teatro = a theatre, a theater

tecnico/tecnica *adjective* (*plural*
tecnici/tecniche)
= technical

tecnologia *noun, feminine*
la tecnologia = technology

tedesco/tedesca *adjective* (*plural*
tedeschi/tedesche)
= German

tela *noun, feminine*
la tela = canvas

telecomando *noun, masculine*
il telecomando = the remote control

telefonare *verb* 1
telefonare a = to phone

telefonata *noun, feminine*
una telefonata = a phone call

telefonino✶ *noun, masculine*
un telefonino = a mobile phone, a
    cell phone

telefono *noun, masculine*
un telefono = a telephone
un telefono cellulare = a mobile phone,
a cell phone

telegiornale *noun, masculine*
il telegiornale = the news

televisione *noun, feminine*
la televisione = television

televisore *noun, masculine*
un televisore = a TV

tema *noun, masculine (plural* **temi**)
• **il tema** = the theme
• **un tema** = an essay

temere *verb* 8
= to be afraid

temperatura *noun, feminine*
la temperatura = the temperature

T

tempio *noun, masculine* (*plural* **templi**)
un tempio = a temple

tempo *noun, masculine*
• il tempo = time
tanto tempo fa = a long time ago
il tempo libero = spare time
• il tempo = the weather
che tempo fa? = what's the weather like?

temporale *noun, masculine*
un temporale = a storm

tenda *noun, feminine*
• una tenda = a tent
• le tende = curtains, drapes

tendenza *noun, feminine*
una tendenza = a tendency

tendere *verb* 53
• = to hold out
• tende a parlare troppo = he tends to
speak too much

tenere *verb* 73
• = to hold
• = to keep
• tieni! = here you are!

tenero/tenera *adjective*
= tender

tengo, **tengono** ▶ **tenere**

tennista *noun, masculine/feminine* (*plural*
tennisti/tenniste)
un/una tennista = a tennis player

tensione *noun, feminine*
la tensione = tension

tentare *verb* 1
• = to tempt
• tentare di fare qualcosa = to attempt to
do something

tentativo *noun, masculine*
un tentativo = an attempt

tenuto/tenuta ▶ **tenere**

teoria *noun, feminine*
una teoria = a theory

teppista *noun, masculine/feminine* (*plural*
teppisti/teppiste)
un/una teppista = a hooligan

terapia *noun, feminine*
la terapia = therapy

terme *noun, feminine plural*
le terme = the baths

terminare *verb* 1
= to end

termine *noun, masculine*
• un termine = a term
• il termine = the end

terra *noun, feminine*
la terra = the earth
= the land
per terra = on the ground

terrazza *noun, feminine*, **terrazzo**
noun, masculine
un terrazzo = a balcony

terremoto *noun, masculine*
un terremoto = an earthquake

terreno *noun, masculine*
il terreno = land
un terreno = a piece of land

terribile *adjective*
= terrible

territorio *noun, masculine* (*plural*
territori)
un territorio = a territory

terrore *noun, masculine*
il terrore = terror

terrorismo *noun, masculine*
il terrorismo = terrorism

terrorista *noun, masculine/feminine*
(*plural* **terroristi/terroriste**)
un/una terrorista = a terrorist

terzo/terza *adjective*
= third

teso/tesa *adjective*
= tense

tesoro *noun, masculine*
• il tesoro = treasure
• ciao, tesoro = hi, darling

tessera *noun, feminine*
una tessera = a membership card

tessuto *noun, masculine*
un tessuto = a fabric

testa *noun, feminine*
• la testa = the head
• sei sterline a testa = six pounds each

testamento *noun, masculine*
un testamento = a will

testardo/testarda *adjective*
= stubborn

testimone *noun, masculine/feminine*
un/una testimone = a witness

testo *noun, masculine*
un testo = a text

tetto *noun, masculine*
un tetto = a roof

Tevere *noun, masculine*
il Tevere = the Tiber

ti (**te** *before* **lo/la**, **li/le**, *and* **ne**) *pronoun*
= you
= to you
= yourself
non ti credo! = I don't believe you!
ti spiego come funziona = I'll explain to
you how it works
ti sei fatto male? = did you hurt yourself?
te lo apro = I'll open it for you

ticket *noun, masculine* (**!** *never changes*)
il ticket = the prescription charge

✱ in informal situations

tiene, **tieni** ▶ tenere

tifare verb [1]
  tifare per la Juve = to support Juventus

tifoso/tifosa noun, masculine/feminine
  un tifoso/una tifosa = a supporter

tigre noun, feminine
  una tigre = a tiger

timbrare verb [1]
  = to stamp

timbro noun, masculine
  un timbro = a stamp

timido/timida adjective
  = shy

tinello noun, masculine
  il tinello = the dining room

tingere verb [48]
  = to dye

tinse, **tinsi**, **etc** ▶ tingere

tinta noun, feminine
  la tinta = dye
  = paint

tinto/tinta ▶ tingere

tintoria noun, feminine
  una tintoria = a dry-cleaner's

tipico/tipica adjective (plural
  tipici/tipiche)
  = typical

tipo noun, masculine
• un tipo di = a kind of
• quel tipo✱ = that guy

tirare verb [1]
• = to pull
• = to throw

tiro noun, masculine
  un tiro = a throw

titolare noun, masculine/feminine
  il/la titolare = the owner

titolo noun, masculine
  un titolo = a title
  un titolo di studio = a qualification

tivù noun, feminine (**!** never changes)
  la tivù = the TV

tizio/tizia✱ noun, masculine/feminine
  (plural **tizi/tizie**)
  un tizio/una tizia = a guy/a girl

toccare verb [4]
  = to touch

togliere verb [22]
  = to remove
  mi sono tolto le scarpe = I took off my
    shoes

toilette noun, feminine (**!** never changes)
  una toilette = a toilet, a bathroom

tolgo, **tolgono**, **etc** ▶ togliere

tollerare verb [1]
  = to tolerate

tolse, **tolto/tolta**, **etc** ▶ togliere

tomba noun, feminine
  una tomba = a grave

tondo/tonda adjective
  = round

tonnellata noun, feminine
  una tonnellata = a tonne

tonno noun, masculine
  il tonno = tuna

tono noun, masculine
  un tono = a tone

topo noun, masculine
  un topo = a mouse

torinese adjective
  = Turinese

Torino noun
  = Turin

tornare verb [1] (**!** + essere)
• = to come back
  = to go back
• non torna = it doesn't add up

toro noun, masculine
  1 un toro = a bull
  2 Toro = Taurus

torre noun, feminine
  una torre = a tower

torta noun. feminine
  una torta = a cake

Toscana noun, feminine
  la Toscana = Tuscany

toscano/toscana adjective
  = Tuscan

tossicodipendente noun,
  masculine/feminine
  un/una tossicodipendente = a drug addict

tosse noun, feminine
  la tosse = a cough

tossire verb [9]
  = to cough

totale
  1 adjective
  = total
  2 noun, masculine
  il totale = the total

totocalcio noun, masculine
  il totocalcio = the football pools

tournée noun, feminine (**!** never
  changes)
  una tournée = a tour

tovaglia noun, feminine
  una tovaglia = a tablecloth

tovagliolo noun, masculine
  un tovagliolo = a napkin

tra ▶ fra

T

traccia *noun, feminine (plural* **tracce**)
una traccia = a trace
le tracce = the trail

tradire *verb* 9
= to betray

tradizionale *adjective*
= traditional

tradizione *noun, feminine*
una tradizione = a tradition

tradotto/**tradotta** ▶ tradurre

tradurre *verb* 54
= to translate

tradusse, **tradussi**, etc ▶ tradurre

traduttore/**traduttrice** *noun,*
masculine/feminine
un traduttore/una traduttrice = a
translator

traduzione *noun, feminine*
una traduzione = a translation

trae, **traete**, etc ▶ trarre

traffico *noun, masculine*
il traffico = the traffic

tragedia *noun, feminine*
una tragedia = a tragedy

traggo, **traggono**, etc ▶ trarre

traghetto *noun, masculine*
un traghetto = a ferry

tragico/**tragica** *adjective (plural*
tragici/**tragiche**)
= tragic

trai, **traiamo**, etc ▶ trarre

trama *noun, feminine*
la trama = the plot

tramite *preposition*
= by means of
= through

tramonto *noun, masculine*
il tramonto = sunset

tranello *noun, masculine*
un tranello = a trap

tranne *preposition*
= except

tranquillo/**tranquilla** *adjective*
• = peaceful
• = happy

trapano *noun, masculine*
un trapano = a drill

trapianto *noun, masculine*
un trapianto = a transplant

trappola *noun, feminine*
una trappola = a trap

trapunta *noun, feminine*
una trapunta = a quilt

trarre *verb* 74
= to draw
trarre una conclusione = to draw a
conclusion
il film è stato tratto da un romanzo = the
film was taken from a novel

trascinare *verb* 1
= to drag

trascorrere *verb* 26
= to spend

trascorse, **trascorso**/**trascorsa**
▶ trascorrere

trascurare *verb* 1
= to neglect

trasferire *verb* 9
1 = to transfer
2 **trasferirsi** (**!** + *essere*)
trasferirsi = to move

trasformare *verb* 1
1 = to transform
2 **trasformarsi** (**!** + *essere*)
trasformarsi in qualcosa = to change into
something

trasloco *noun, masculine (plural*
traslochi)
un trasloco = a removal

trasmesso/**trasmessa** ▶
trasmettere

trasmettere *verb* 40
= to broadcast

trasmise, **trasmisi**, etc ▶
trasmettere

trasmissione *noun, feminine*
una trasmissione = a program(me)

trasparente *adjective*
= transparent

trasporto *noun, masculine*
il trasporto = transport, transportation

trasse, **trassi**, etc ▶ trarre

trattamento *noun, masculine*
un trattamento = a treatment

trattare *verb* 1
1 (**!** + *avere*)
• = to treat
• trattare con qualcuno = to deal with
someone
2 **trattarsi** (**!** + *essere*)
si tratta di = it's about

trattenere *verb* 73
= to hold (back)
trattenere il respiro = to hold one's breath

trattengo, **trattiene** ▶ trattenere

tratto/**tratta** ▶ trarre

traversa *noun, feminine*
una traversa = a side street

tre *number*
= three

trecento
1 *number*
= three hundred
2 **Trecento** *noun, masculine*
il Trecento = the 14th century

tredicenne *adjective*
= thirteen-year-old

tredicesimo/tredicesima *adjective*
= thirteenth

tredici *number*
= thirteen

tremare *verb* 1
= to shake

tremendo/tremenda *adjective*
= awful

treno *noun, masculine*
un treno = a train

trenta *number*
= thirty

trentesimo/trentesima *adjective*
= thirtieth

trentina *noun, feminine*
una trentina di macchine = about thirty
cars

triangolo *noun, masculine*
un triangolo = a triangle

tribù *noun, feminine* (**!** *never changes*)
una tribù = a tribe

tribunale *noun, masculine*
un tribunale = a court

trimestre *noun, masculine*
un trimestre = a term

triste *adjective*
= sad

tristezza *noun, feminine*
la tristezza = sadness

tritare *verb* 1
= to chop

trofeo *noun, masculine*
un trofeo = a trophy

tromba *noun, feminine*
una tromba = a trumpet

tronco *noun, masculine* (*plural* **tronchi**)
un tronco = a trunk

troppo/troppa
1 *adjective, pronoun*
troppo/troppa = too much
troppi/troppe = too many
troppo zucchero = too much sugar
troppe mosche = too many flies

2 **troppo** *adverb*
• = too much
parli troppo = you talk too much
• (*with adjectives and adverbs*) = too
è troppo caldo = it's too hot

trovare *verb* 1
1 = to find
non trovo i miei occhiali = I can't find my
glasses
2 **trovarsi** (**!** + *essere*)
• dove si trova il cinema? = where is the
cinema?
• trovarsi = to meet
dove ci troviamo? = where shall we meet?

truccare *verb* 4
1 = to rig
2 **truccarsi** (**!** + *essere*) = to put on one's
make-up

trucco *noun, masculine* (*plural* **trucchi**)
• un trucco = a trick
• il trucco = make-up

truffare *verb* 1
= to swindle

truppe *noun, feminine plural*
le truppe = troops

tu *pronoun*
= you
tu dove vuoi andare? = where do you
want to go?

tubo *noun, masculine*
• un tubo = a tube
• un tubo = a pipe

tuffare *verb* 1
1 = to dip
2 **tuffarsi** (**!** + *essere*)
tuffarsi = to dive

tuffo *noun, masculine*
fare un tuffo = to go for a dip

tuo/tua
1 *adjective* (*plural* **tuoi/tue**)
= your
2 *pronoun*
= yours
il tuo/la tua = your one

tuono *noun, masculine*
un tuono = a clap of thunder
i tuoni = thunder

turismo *noun, masculine*
il turismo = tourism

turista *noun, masculine/feminine* (*plural*
turisti/turiste)
un/una turista = a tourist

turistico/turistica *adjective* (*plural*
turistici/turistiche)
= tourist

T

turno *noun, masculine*
un turno = a turn
= a shift

tuta *noun, feminine*
• una tuta = a suit
• una tuta = overalls, coveralls
una tuta da ginnastica = a tracksuit

tuttavia *conjunction*
= but

tutto/tutta
1 *adjective*
= all
tutto il tempo = all the time
tutti i ragazzi/tutte le ragazze = all the boys/all the girls
tutto il giorno = all day
tutti i giorni = every day
2 **tutto** *pronoun*
= everything
non è tutto = that's not all
3 **tutti** *pronoun*
= everyone
tutti vogliono la stessa cosa = everyone wants the same thing

Uu

ubbidire, etc ▶ **obbedire**, etc

ubriaco/ubriaca *adjective (plural ubriachi/ubriache)*
= drunk

uccello *noun, masculine*
un uccello = a bird

uccidere *verb* 30
= to kill

uccise, **ucciso/uccisa**, etc ▶ **uccidere**

UE *noun, feminine*
l'UE = the EU

ufficiale
1 *adjective*
= official
2 *noun, masculine*
un ufficiale = an officer

ufficio *noun, masculine (plural uffici)*
un ufficio = an office
in ufficio = in the office

uguale *adjective*
= the same
è uguale a quello vecchio = it's the same as the old one
per me è uguale = it's all the same to me

ulteriore *adjective*
= further

ultimamente *adverb*
= recently

ultimo/ultima *adjective*
= last
= latest
l'ultimo dell'anno = New Year's Eve

umano/umana *adjective*
= human

umbro/umbra *adjective*
= Umbrian

umidità *noun, feminine*
l'umidità = dampness

umido/umida *adjective*
= damp
= humid

umore *noun, masculine*
un umore = a mood
di buon umore = in a good mood

umorismo *noun, masculine*
l'umorismo = humo(u)r

un, **un'** ▶ **uno/una**

undicenne *adjective*
= eleven-year-old

undicesimo/undicesima *adjective*
= eleventh

undici *number*
= eleven

unghia *noun, feminine (plural unghie)*
un'unghia = a nail

unico/unica *adjective (plural unici/uniche)*
• = only
l'unico problema = the only problem
figlio unico = an only child
• = unique

unione *noun, feminine*
un'unione = a union

unire *verb* 9
= to unite

unità *noun, feminine (! never changes)*
• l'unità = unity
• un'unità = a unit

università *noun, feminine (! never changes)*
un'università = a university

universitario/universitaria *adjective (plural universitari/universitarie)*
= university

universo *noun, masculine*
l'universo = the universe

uno/una
1 *number*

> **!** *Before masculine singular nouns beginning with z, ps, gn, or s + another consonant,* **uno** *is used. Before masculine singular nouns beginning with another consonant or a vowel,* **un** *is used. Before feminine singular nouns beginning with a vowel,* **un'** *is used.*

....➤

= one
ne voglio uno solo = I just want one
un giorno = one day
un'altra volta = another time
2 *determiner*
= a, an
vuoi un gelato? = do you want an ice cream?

unto/unta *adjective*
= oily
= greasy

uomo *noun, masculine* (*plural* **uomini**)
un uomo = a man

uovo *noun, masculine* (*plural* **uova**)

> **!** *Note that* **uova** *is feminine.*

un uovo = an egg

uragano *noun, masculine*
un uragano = a hurricane

urgente *adjective*
= urgent

urlare *verb* [1]
= to shout
= to scream

urlo *noun, masculine* (*plural* **urli** *and* **urla**)

> **!** *Note that* **urla** *is feminine. It is used when talking about the shouts of a crowd.*

un urlo = a shout
= a scream

urtare *verb* [1]
• = to bump into
• **urtare contro qualcosa** = to crash into something

usanza *noun, feminine*
un'usanza = a custom

usare *verb* [1]
= to use

usato/usata *adjective*
= used

uscire *verb* [75] (**!** + *essere*)
= to go out
= to come out
= to get out

uscita *noun, feminine*
l'uscita = the exit

uso *noun, masculine*
un uso = a use

utile *adjective*
= useful

utilizzare *verb* [1]
= to use

uva *noun, feminine*
l'uva = grapes
un chicco d'uva = a grape

va, **va'** ▶ **andare**

vacanza *noun, feminine*
una vacanza = a holiday, a vacation
in vacanza = on holiday, on vacation

vada, **vado**, **etc** ▶ **andare**

vago/vaga *adjective*
= vague

vagone *noun, masculine*
un vagone = a carriage, a car

vai ▶ **andare**

valanga *noun, feminine* (*plural* **valanghe**)
• **una valanga** = an avalanche
• **una valanga di lettere** = a flood of letters

valere *verb* [76] (**!** + *essere*)
• = to be worth
quanto vale? = how much is it worth?
non vale la pena = it's not worth it
• **non vale!** = it's not fair!

valgo, **valgono**, **etc** ▶ **valere**

valido/valida *adjective*
= valid

valigia *noun, feminine* (*plural* **valigie** *or* **valige**)
una valigia = a suitcase
fare le valigie = to pack
disfare le valigie = to unpack

valle *noun, feminine*
una valle = a valley

valore *noun, masculine*
il valore = the value

valse, **valso/valsa**, **etc** ▶ **valere**

valuta *noun, feminine*
la valuta = currency

vanga *noun, feminine* (*plural* **vanghe**)
una vanga = a spade

vanitoso/vanitosa *adjective*
= vain

vanno ▶ **andare**

vantaggio *noun, masculine* (*plural* **vantaggi**)
un vantaggio = an advantage

vantarsi *verb* [1] (**!** + *essere*)
= to boast

vapore *noun, masculine*
il vapore = steam

variabile *adjective*
= variable
= changeable

varietà *noun, feminine* (**!** *never changes*)
la varietà = variety

vario/varia *adjective* (*plural* **vari/varie**)
• = various
• = several

varrà, varranno, etc ▶ **valere**

vasca *noun, feminine* (*plural* **vasche**)
una vasca da bagno = a bath, a bathtub

vaso *noun, masculine*
un vaso = a vase

vassoio *noun, masculine* (*plural* **vassoi**)
un vassoio = a tray

ve ▶ **vi**

vecchiaia *noun, feminine*
la vecchiaia = old age

vecchio/vecchia *adjective* (*plural* **vecchi/vecchie**)
= old

vedere *verb* [77]
= to see
non vedo niente = I can't see anything
non ci vedo = I can't see

vedovo/vedova *noun, masculine/feminine*
un vedovo/una vedova = a widower/a widow

vedrà, vedremo, etc ▶ **vedere**

veicolo *noun, masculine*
un veicolo = a vehicle

vela *noun, feminine*
• una vela = a sail
• la vela = sailing

veleno *noun, masculine*
il veleno = poison

velenoso/velenosa *adjective*
= poisonous

veloce *adjective, adverb*
= fast

velocemente *adverb*
= fast

velocità *noun, feminine*
la velocità = speed

vendemmia *noun, feminine*
la vendemmia = the grape harvest

vendere *verb* [8]
= to sell
'vendesi' = 'for sale'

vendicarsi *verb* [4] (**!** + *essere*)
= to take revenge

vendita *noun, feminine*
una vendita = a sale

venerdì *noun, masculine* (**!** *never changes*)
= Friday

arrivo venerdì = I'm arriving on Friday
il venerdì = on Fridays

Venezia *noun*
= Venice

veneziano/veneziana *adjective*
= Venetian

venga, vengo, etc ▶ **venire**

venire *verb* [78] (**!** + *essere*)
• = to come
da dove viene? = where does he come from?
• = to cost
viene cinquantamila euro = it's fifty thousand euros
• (*with the past participle*) = to be
le bottiglie vengono riciclate = the bottles are recycled

venne, venni, etc ▶ **venire**

ventenne *adjective*
= twenty-year-old

ventesimo/ventesima *adjective*
= twentieth

venti *number*
= twenty

ventina *noun, feminine*
una ventina di studenti = about twenty students

vento *noun, masculine*
il vento = the wind
c'è vento = it's windy

venuto/venuta ▶ **venire**

veramente *adverb*
= really

verde *adjective*
= green

verdura *noun, feminine*
la verdura = vegetables

Vergine *noun, feminine*
Vergine = Virgo

vergogna *noun, feminine*
la vergogna = shame
che vergogna! = how embarrassing!

vergognarsi *verb* [1] (**!** + *essere*)
• = to be ashamed
• = to be embarrassed

verifica *noun, feminine* (*plural* **verifiche**)
una verifica = a check
= a test

verità *noun, feminine* (**!** *never changes*)
la verità = the truth

vernice *noun, feminine*
la vernice = paint

vero/vera *adjective*
• = true
• = real

....▶

- **(non è) vero?**
  è tuo, (non è) vero? = it's yours, isn't it?
  verrai, (non è) vero? = you'll come, won't
  you?

verrà, verremo, etc ▶ **venire**

versare verb ①
- = to pour
- = to spill

verso preposition
- = toward(s)
- **verso le nove** = at about nine o'clock

verticale adjective
= vertical

vescovo noun, masculine
un vescovo = a bishop

vespa noun, feminine
- **una vespa** = a wasp
- **una vespa®** = a scooter

vestire verb ⑩
1 = to dress
2 vestirsi (**!** + essere)
  vestirsi = to get dressed

vestito noun, masculine
- **un vestito**
  (when it's a woman's) = a dress
  (when it's a man's) = a suit
- **i vestiti** = clothes

vetrina noun, feminine
  una vetrina = a shop window, a store
  window

vetro noun, masculine
  il vetro = glass
  un vetro = a pane of glass

vi (**ve** before **lo/la, li/le,** and **ne**)
1 pronoun
  = you
  = to you
  = yourselves
  vi aspetto là = I'll be waiting for you
  there
  divertitevi! = enjoy yourselves!
2 adverb
  = there

via
1 noun, feminine
  una via = a street
2 adverb
  = away
  va' via! = go away!

viaggiare verb ③
  = to travel

viaggio noun, masculine (plural **viaggi**)
  un viaggio = a journey
  = a trip
un viaggio di nozze = a honeymoon

vicino/vicina
1 adjective
  = near
  la primavera è vicina = spring is near

un paese vicino al mare = a village near
  the sea
2 vicino adverb
  = near
  = nearby
3 noun, masculine/feminine
  un vicino/una vicina = a neighbo(u)r

vide, vidi, etc ▶ **vedere**

videoregistratore noun, masculine
  un videoregistratore = a video recorder

viene, vieni ▶ **venire**

vietare verb ①
  = to forbid
  vietato fumare = no smoking

vigile noun, masculine
  un vigile (urbano) = a traffic warden
  i vigili del fuoco = the fire brigade, the
    fire department

vigilia noun, feminine
  la vigilia = the day before
  la Vigilia di Natale = Christmas Eve

vincere verb ⑦⑨
- = to win
- = to beat

vincitore/vincitrice noun,
  masculine/feminine
  il vincitore/la vincitrice = the winner

vino noun, masculine
  il vino = wine

vinse, vinto/vinta, etc ▶ **vincere**

viola adjective (**!** never changes)
  = purple

violentare verb ①
  = to rape

violento/violenta adjective
  = violent

violenza noun, feminine
  la violenza = violence

violino noun, masculine
  un violino = a violin

virgola noun, feminine
- **una virgola** = a comma
- **due virgola cinque** = two point five

virgolette noun, feminine plural
  le virgolette = quotation marks
  fra virgolette = in quotation marks

visibile adjective
  = visible

visita noun, feminine
- **una visita** = a visit
- **una visita medica** = a medical
    examination

visitare verb ①
  = to visit

viso noun, masculine
  il viso = the face

V

volere

1 volere functions as an ordinary verb:

= to want

vuole un cagnolino	= he wants a puppy
voglio dormire	= I want to sleep
voglio che tu mi dica la verità	= I want you to tell me the truth

! Note that the subjunctive is used after **volere che**.

2 volere is used with **ci** to form **ci vuole**, **ci vogliono**, etc:

volerci (**!** + essere)	= to be necessary
ci vuole pazienza	= you need patience
mi ci vogliono delle olive	= I need some olives
c'è voluto un po' di tempo	= it took some time

3 volere is used in the *conditional tense* to form polite requests and offers. The forms of this tense are:

vorrei
vorresti
vorrebbe
vorremmo
vorreste
vorrebbero

vorrei un caffè	= I'd like a coffee
vorremmo prenotare due posti	= we'd like to book two seats

---

visse, **vissuto/vissuta**, etc ▶
vivere

vista noun, feminine
• **la vista** = eyesight
  farsi controllare la vista = to have one's
  eyes tested
• **la vista** = the view

visto/vista
1 ▶ **vedere**
2 **visto** noun, masculine
  un visto = a visa

vita noun, feminine
• **la vita** = life
• **la vita** = the waist

vite noun, feminine
• **una vite** = a screw
• **una vite** = a vine

vitello noun, masculine
  un vitello = a calf
  il vitello = veal

vittima noun, feminine
  una vittima = a victim

vittoria noun, feminine
  una vittoria = a victory

vivace adjective
  = lively

vivere verb 80 (**!** + essere)
  = to live

vivo/viva adjective
  = alive
  = living

vizio noun, masculine (plural **vizi**)
  un vizio = a vice

vocabolario noun, masculine (plural
  vocabolari)
  un vocabolario = a dictionary

voce noun, feminine
  una voce = a voice
  leggere ad alta voce = to read aloud

voglia noun, feminine
  una voglia = a desire
  aver voglia di fare qualcosa = to feel like
    doing something
  non ho voglia = I don't feel like it

vogliamo, **voglio**, etc ▶ **volere**

voi pronoun
  = you
  voi altri = you lot, you guys

volante noun, masculine
  il volante = the steering wheel

volare verb 1 (**!** + essere or avere)
  = to fly

volentieri adverb
  = willingly
  vengo volentieri = I'd love to come

volere verb 81
  ▶ 120 See the boxed note.
  voler dire = to mean
  voglio dire = I mean
  che vuol dire? = what does it mean?

volle, **volli**, etc ▶ **volere**

volo *noun, masculine*
  un volo = a flight
  un volo di linea = a scheduled flight

volpe *noun, feminine*
  una volpe = a fox

volta *noun, feminine*
  la volta = the time
  la prima volta = the first time
  una volta = once
  due volte = twice
  ancora una volta = once again

voltare *verb* [1]
1 (**!** + *avere*)
  = to turn
2 **voltarsi** (**!** + *essere*)
  voltarsi = to turn round

volto *noun, masculine*
  il volto = the face

volume *noun, masculine*
  il volume = the volume

vongola *noun, feminine*
  una vongola = a clam

vorrà, **vorrebbe**, **vorrei**, etc ▶
  volere

vostro/vostra
1 *adjective*
  = your
  i vostri cugini = your cousins
  a casa vostra = at your house
2 *pronoun*
  = yours
  il vostro/la vostra = your one

votare *verb* [1]
  = to vote

voto *noun, masculine*
• un voto = a vote
• (*at school*)
  un voto = a mark, a grade

vulcano *noun, masculine*
  un vulcano = a volcano

vuoi, **vuole** ▶ **volere**

vuotare *verb* [1]
  = to empty

vuoto/vuota *adjective*
  = empty

Web *noun, masculine*
  il Web = the Web

würstel *noun, masculine* (**!** *never changes*)
  un würstel = a frankfurter, a wiener

zaino *noun, masculine*
  uno zaino = a backpack

zampa *noun, feminine*
  una zampa = a paw

zanzara *noun, feminine*
  una zanzara = a mosquito

zero *number*
  = zero
  = nought
  abbiamo vinto tre a zero = we won three-nil

zingaro/zingara *noun, masculine/feminine*
  uno zingaro/una zingara = a gypsy

zio/zia *noun, masculine/feminine* (*plural zii/zie*)
  uno zio/una zia = an aunt/an uncle
  gli zii = uncle and aunt
  tutti gli zii = all my aunts and uncles

zitto/zitta *adjective*
  stare zitto/zitta = to be quiet
  stai zitto! = shut up!

zona *noun, feminine*
  una zona = an area

zucchero *noun, masculine*
  lo zucchero = sugar

zucchino *noun, masculine*
  uno zucchino = a courgette, a zucchini

zuppa *noun, feminine*
  la zuppa = soup
  la zuppa inglese = trifle

W
Z

Dictionary know-how

This section contains a number of short exercises which will help you to use your dictionary more effectively. You will find answers to all of these exercises at the end of the section.

1 Identifying Italian nouns and adjectives

Here is an Italian advertisement for a German restaurant. See if you can find ten different nouns and underline them. Then look for eight different adjectives and underline them. Make a list of each type of word. If you are not sure of some of the words, look them up in the Italian-English half of the dictionary and see if the term 'noun' or 'adjective' is used to describe them.

> ### RISTORANTE TEDESCO
>
> Il più moderno ristorante nel centro della città. Venite ad assaggiare le tradizionali specialità della cucina tedesca e a bere le migliori birre mondiali. Trascorrerete una serata straordinaria. Musica tutte le sere. Ampio parcheggio.

2 Checking the gender of Italian nouns

Here are some English nouns that appear in the English-Italian half of the dictionary. Find out what their Italian equivalents are and make two separate lists, masculine nouns and feminine nouns.

answer	hotel	magazine	salt
calendar	island	oyster	tiger
doorbell	jumper	pencil case	wallpaper
fever	library	raincoat	water-skiing

3 Identifying Italian and English pronouns

Each of the following phrases appears in the Italian-English half of this dictionary in entries where a pronoun is the headword. In each one, underline the pronoun(s) and give the English equivalent(s).

sono io

quello rosso

voglio questi qui

vieni con me?

mi ha spiegato come funziona

vado con loro

ne ho tanti

ci hanno visto

divertitevi!

4 **Recognizing Italian verbs**

Underline the verb in each sentence.

I ragazzi vanno a scuola in bicicletta.

Sofia non sa nuotare.

I pompieri arrivarono dopo cinque minuti.

Ogni anno passiamo le vacanze in Italia.

Mia sorella ha avuto in regalo un orologio.

5 **Identifying subjects and objects**

We have left out the subjects and objects from this Italian message. Choose suitable words from the list below in order to complete it. When you have finished, list the subjects and objects separately.

Luciana ha appena telefonato. Oggi è .... di suo fratello.
..............ha adesso .... e ....vuole preparargli
.... Naturalmente di questo .... non sa niente e
.... dobbiamo tenere .... lontano da casa per fargli ....

Così ho mandato questo .... a Marco: " Ci troviamo alla gelateria del Corso alle 5 per mangiare .... insieme a te". Goloso com'è, ha risposto che usciva subito! Poi ho chiamato .... e quasi.................. vengono! Ci sarai anche............, vero?

Ciao,

Gemma

14 anni	Marco	messaggio	tutti
il ragazzo	una festa	noi	tu
lei	la sorpresa	lui	
il compleanno	un po' di amici	un gelato	

6 Word search

Here is a grid in which are hidden twelve Italian words: 3 masculine nouns,
3 feminine nouns, 2 adjectives, 2 verbs, 1 pronoun, and 1 adverb. They may
appear horizontally, vertically or diagonally, and in either direction (backwards
or forwards). When you have found them, circle them. If you are not sure of any
of them, look them up in the Italian-English section of the dictionary.

f	i	o	p	s	t	b	k	l	a	**augurare**
t	o	p	z	t	r	f	g	a	t	**mio**
e	x	g	i	a	l	l	o	g	m	**difetto**
m	u	m	f	r	i	e	d	o	e	**erba**
p	q	e	n	e	n	f	r	b	n	**giallo**
o	i	m	a	i	e	v	r	b	t	**lago**
n	u	d	s	t	a	s	e	r	a	**linea**
d	i	f	e	t	t	o	z	h	l	**macchina**
t	p	a	u	g	u	r	a	r	e	**mentale**
a	n	i	h	c	c	a	m	a	r	**stare**

(extra words: **stasera**, **tempo**)

7 Masculine or feminine?

Many Italian nouns also have a feminine form. This is particularly true of words
denoting an occupation – *un commesso, una commessa*. Some simply change from
-o to -a for the feminine form, but not all do. Use your dictionary to find the
feminine form of the following nouns:

un alunno   **un dentista**   **un residente**   **uno zio**

un attore   **un invitato**   **uno scrittore**

un chimico   **un passeggero**   **un traduttore**

8 Find the preposition

Use your dictionary to find the English for the following Italian sentences and
underline the English and Italian prepositions.

L'aereo parte da Milano alle 8.

A Paolo non piace il tè.

Scusi, c'è un autobus per andare al Colosseo?

Vorrei un po' di formaggio.

Gli occhiali sono sul tavolo.

9 **Choosing the right word**

Very often you cannot use a word exactly as it is given in the dictionary. In the case of adjectives, you have to make sure that you select the form which is appropriate to the noun you are using. Use your dictionary and your own knowledge to find the correct form of the adjective to match the nouns in the following sentences.

Questi libri mi sembrano .... (*interesting*)

Le fragole che abbiamo mangiato erano molto .... (*sweet*)

Mio padre è ...., ma mia madre è .... (*Italian*) (*German*)

Le mie scarpe non sono ...., sono ....! (*clean*) (*dirty*)

Anna ha dei .... occhi e dei ....capelli. (*beautiful*)

Stasera ti metti i pantaloni ....o quelli ....? (*white*) (*grey*)

10 **Translating phrasal verbs**

Use your dictionary to find the correct translation for the following English sentences containing phrasal verbs.

The button's come off.

He has given up smoking.

She took off her shoes.

To get off the train.

He walked out of the room.

11 **Forming the subjunctive**

It's important not to be afraid of the subjunctive, because it is so common in Italian. Using the English-Italian side of the dictionary and the verb tables on pages 293–313, translate these sentences into Italian.

I think the plane from Rome has already arrived.

I thought the plane from Rome had already arrived.

I hope you didn't give it to your brother..

I think that the show finishes at 9.00.

I expect you to phone me at least once a week.

12 Which meaning?

Some words have more than one meaning and it is important to check that you have chosen the right one. In this dictionary the different meanings of a word are marked by a bullet point • .

We have given you one meaning of the Italian words below. Use your dictionary to find another one.

muto	• dumb	• ....
un soggiorno	• a living room	• ....
allora	• then	• ....
il capo	• the head	• ....
emozionato	• excited	• ....
un motivo	• a reason	• ....
un casino	• a mess	• ....
frequentare	• to go to	• ....
una fuga	• an escape	• ....
la fotografia	• photography	• ....

13 Italian reflexive verbs

Use your dictionary to translate the following sentences.

He is called James.

We met in France. (got to know each other)

They got up early.

Go and get dressed.

Please sit down. (to several people)

They got married on Saturday.

14 **False friends**

Some Italian words look the same as, or very similar to English words, but in fact have a different meaning. Use your dictionary to find the meaning of the following Italian words.

agenda	firma
ape	libreria
caldo	mobile
casino	romanzo
fabbrica	rumore
fingere	sensibile

15 **Crossword**

Across

1 to avoid
4 opposite (adjective)
6 uncle
8 from
9 to the (before a singular masculine noun)

Down

1 heroines
2 business, company
3 absence
5 I
7 a masculine article

Answers

1

Nouns: ristorante, centro, città, specialità, cucina, birra, serata, musica, sera, parcheggio

Adjectives: moderno, tradizionale, tedesco, migliore, mondiale, straordinario, tutto, ampio

2

Masculine nouns: calendario, campanello, albergo, maglione, portamatite, impermeabile, sale, sci nautico

Feminine nouns: risposta, febbre, isola, biblioteca, rivista, ostrica, tigre, carta da parati

3

sono <u>io</u> (it's <u>me</u>)

<u>quello</u> rosso (the red <u>one</u>)

voglio <u>questi</u> qui (I want these <u>ones</u>)

vieni con <u>me</u>? (are <u>you</u> coming with <u>me</u>?)

<u>mi</u> ha spiegato come funziona (<u>he</u> explained to <u>me</u> how <u>it</u> works)

vado con <u>loro</u> (<u>I</u>'m going with <u>them</u>)

<u>ne</u> ho tanti (<u>I</u>'ve got lots of <u>them</u>)

<u>ci</u> hanno visto (<u>they</u>'ve seen <u>us</u>)

divertite<u>vi</u>! (enjoy <u>yourselves</u>!)

4

I ragazzi <u>vanno</u> a scuola in bicicletta.

Sofia non <u>sa nuotare</u>.

I pompieri <u>arrivarono</u> dopo cinque minuti.

Ogni anno <u>passiamo</u> le vacanze in Italia.

Mia sorella <u>ha avuto</u> in regalo un orologio.

5

Luciana ha appena telefonato. Oggi è il compleanno di suo fratello. Marco ha adesso 14 anni e lei vuole preparargli una festa. Naturalmente di questo lui non sa niente e noi dobbiamo tenere il ragazzo lontano da casa per fargli la sorpresa.

Così ho mandato questo messaggio a Marco: "Ci troviamo alla gelateria del Corso alle 5 per mangiare un gelato insieme a te". Goloso com'è, ha detto che usciva subito! Poi ho chiamato un po' di amici e quasi tutti vengono! Ci sarai anche tu, vero?

Ciao

Gemma

subjects	objects
il compleanno	14 anni
Marco	una festa
lei	il ragazzo
lui	la sorpresa
noi	messaggio
tutti	un gelato
tu	un po' di amici

6

7

un'alunna

un'attrice

una chimica

una dentista

un'invitata

una passeggera

una residente

una scrittrice

una traduttrice

una zia

8

L'aereo parte <u>da</u> Milano <u>alle</u> 8.
The plane leaves Milan <u>at</u> eight.

<u>A</u> Paolo non piace il tè.
Paolo doesn't like tea.

Scusi, c'è un autobus <u>per</u> andare <u>al</u> Colosseo?
Excuse me, is there a bus that goes <u>to</u> the Colosseum?

Vorrei un po' <u>di</u> formaggio.
I would like some cheese.

Gli occhiali sono <u>sul</u> tavolo.
The spectacles are <u>on</u> the table.

9

Questi libri mi sembrano <u>interessanti</u>.

Le fragole che abbiamo mangiato erano molto <u>dolci</u>.

Mio padre è <u>italiano</u>, ma mia madre è <u>tedesca</u>.

Le mie scarpe non sono <u>pulite</u>, sono <u>sporche</u>!

Anna ha dei <u>begli</u> occhi e dei <u>bei</u> capelli.

Stasera ti metti i pantaloni <u>bianchi</u> o quelli <u>grigi</u>?

10

Il bottone si è staccato.

Ha smesso di fumare.

Si è tolta le scarpe.

Scendere dal treno.

È uscito dalla stanza.

Dictionary know-how

11

Penso che l'aereo da Roma sia già arrivato.

Pensavo che l'aereo da Roma fosse già arrivato.

Spero che tu non l'abbia dato a tuo fratello.

Penso che lo spettacolo finisca alle 9.00.

Mi aspetto che tu mi telefoni almeno una volta la settimana.

12

muto: silent

un soggiorno: a stay

allora: well

il capo: the boss

emozionato: nervous

un motivo: a pattern

un casino: a racket

frequentare: to hang around with

una fuga: a leak

la fotografia: the photograph

13

Si chiama James.

Ci siamo conosciuti in Francia.

Si sono alzati presto.

Vai a vestirti.

Accomodatevi, prego.

Si sono sposati sabato.

14

diary

bee

hot

mess; racket

factory

to pretend

signature

bookshop

piece of furniture

novel

noise

sensitive

15

Aa

a, an *determiner*
  a, an = un/una (**!** uno *before a masculine noun beginning with z, ps, gn, or s + another consonant;* un' *before a feminine noun beginning with a vowel*)
  a boy/a girl = un ragazzo/una ragazza
  a Scotsman/a Scotswoman = uno scozzese/una scozzese
  an Englishman/an Englishwoman = un inglese/un'inglese
  my mother's a doctor = mia madre fa il dottore

able *adjective*
  • (*having the possibility*)
  he's able to walk now = ora può camminare
  • (*having the skill or knowledge*)
  to be able to [drive | read | type] = saper [guidare | leggere | battere a macchina]
  • (*failure*)
  I wasn't able to do it = non ho potuto farlo

aboard *adverb*
  to go aboard = salire a bordo (**!** + *essere*)

about

> **!** Often **about** occurs in combinations with verbs, for example: **bring about, run about,** etc. To find the correct translations for this type of verb, look up the separate dictionary entries at **bring, run,** etc.

1 *preposition*
  it's a book about Italy = è un libro sull'Italia
  to talk about something = parlare di qualcosa
2 *adverb*
  = circa
  I have about 20 euros left = mi sono rimaste circa 20 euro
  we arrived at about midnight = siamo arrivati verso mezzanotte
3 to be about to = stare per
  to be about to [leave | cry | fall asleep] = stare per [partire | piangere | addormentarsi]

above
1 *preposition*
  = sopra
  their apartment is above the shop = il loro appartamento è sopra il negozio
2 above all = soprattutto

abroad *adverb*
  = all'estero
  we're going abroad = andiamo all'estero

absent *adjective*
  = assente

accent *noun*
  an accent = un accento

accept *verb*
  = accettare

accident *noun*
  • (*causing injury or damage*)
  an accident = un incidente
  • **I heard about it by accident** = l'ho saputo per caso

accommodation *noun*
  I'm looking for accommodation = devo trovare un alloggio

accompany *verb*
  = accompagnare

account *noun*
  • (*in a bank or post office*)
  an account = un conto
  there's no money in my account = non ho soldi sul conto
  • **to take travelling expenses into account** = tenere conto delle spese di viaggio

accountant *noun* ▶ 281│
  an accountant = un ragioniere/una ragioniera

accuse *verb*
  to accuse someone of cheating = accusare qualcuno di imbrogliare

across *preposition*
  • **to walk across the street** = attraversare la strada
  to run across the street = attraversare la strada di corsa
  to swim across the Channel = attraversare la Manica a nuoto
  a journey across Africa = un viaggio attraverso l'Africa
  • (*on the other side of*) = dall'altra parte di
  he lives across the road = abita dall'altra parte della strada

act *verb*
  • (*to do something*) = agire
  • (*to play a role*) = recitare

activity *noun*
  an activity = un'attività

actor *noun* ▶ 281│
  an actor = un attore

actress *noun* ▶ 281│
  an actress = un'attrice

actually *adverb*

> **!** Note that **actually** is not translated by **attualmente**.

did she actually say that? = ha veramente detto così?
actually, I'm rather tired = veramente sono piuttosto stanco

adapt *verb*

to adapt something = adattare qualcosa
to adapt to something = adattarsi a qualcosa (**!** + *essere*)

add *verb*

• (*to put in*) = aggiungere
• (*in arithmetic*) = sommare

address *noun*

an address = un indirizzo

admire *verb*

= ammirare

admit *verb*

• (*to recognize as being true*) = riconoscere
• (*to own up*) = confessare
• **to be admitted to (the) hospital** = essere ricoverato/ricoverata in ospedale

adolescent *noun*

an adolescent = un adolescente/un'adolescente

adopt *verb*

= adottare

adult *noun*

an adult = un adulto/un'adulta

advantage *noun*

• (*a positive point*)
an advantage = un vantaggio
• **to take advantage of a situation** = approfittare di una situazione

adventure *noun*

an adventure = un'avventura

advertisement *noun*

• (*on TV, in the cinema*)
an advertisement = una pubblicità
• (*in a newspaper*)
an advertisement = un annuncio

advertising *noun*

advertising = la pubblicità

advice *noun*

a piece of advice = un consiglio
advice = dei consigli (*plural*)

advise *verb*

to advise someone to rest = consigliare a qualcuno di riposare
I've been advised not to go there = mi hanno consigliato di non andarci

aerial *noun*

an aerial = un'antenna

aerobics *noun* ▶ 178 |

aerobics = l'aerobica (*singular*)

affect *verb*

the farmers have been affected by the drought = gli agricoltori sono stati colpiti dalla siccità
the war will affect tourism = la guerra avrà un effetto negativo sul turismo

afford *verb*

I can't afford a car = non posso permettermi la macchina

afraid *adjective*

to be afraid of spiders = avere paura dei ragni

Africa *noun* ▶ 151 |

Africa = l'Africa

African ▶ 199 |

1 *adjective*
= africano/africana
2 *noun*
the Africans = gli africani

after

1 *preposition*
= dopo
we'll leave after breakfast = partiamo dopo colazione
the day after tomorrow = dopodomani
2 *conjunction*
after I had ironed my shirts, I put them away = dopo aver stirato le camicie le ho messe via
after we had eaten, we went out = dopo mangiato siamo usciti
3 after all = dopotutto

afternoon *noun* ▶ 146 |, ▶ 267 |

an afternoon = un pomeriggio

afterwards, afterward (*US English*) *adverb*

= dopo

again *adverb*

= di nuovo
are you going camping again this year? = vai di nuovo in campeggio quest'anno?

> **!** Note that there will very often be a specific Italian verb to translate the idea of doing something again - **to start again** = *ricominciare*, **to do the work again** = *rifare il lavoro*, **to see someone again** = *rivedere qualcuno*.

against *preposition*

= contro

age *noun* ▶ 125 |

age = l'età (*feminine*)
he's my age, he's the same age as me = ha la mia età

aged *adjective*

a boy aged 13 = un ragazzo di 13 anni

ago *adverb*

two weeks ago = due settimane fa
a long time ago = molto tempo fa

Age

Note that, where English says **to be X years old**, Italian says **avere X anni**.

How old?

*how old **are you**?* = quanti anni **hai**?
*what age **is he**?* = quanti anni **ha**?

The word **anni** is not dropped:

*he is forty-two **(years old)*** = ha quarantadue **anni**
*the house is a hundred **years** old* = la casa ha cent'**anni**

To say **twenty-year-old**, **thirty-year old**, etc Italian uses the ending –**enne** added to the number. Note that not all numbers can take this ending: those which commonly take it are given in this dictionary.

*an **eighteen-year-old** girl* = una ragazza **diciottenne**
twelve-year-olds = i **dodicenni**

Comparing ages

I'm older than you = sono più vecchia di te
she's younger than him = è più giovane di lui
Anne's two years younger = Anne ha due anni di meno
Tom's five years older than Jo = Tom ha cinque anni più di Jo

Approximate ages

he is about fifty = è sulla cinquantina
she's just over sixty = ha appena superato i sessanta

---

agree *verb*
• *(to have the same opinion)* = essere d'accordo
  I don't agree with you = non sono d'accordo con te
• *(to be prepared to do something)*
  to agree to come a week later = accettare di venire una settimana dopo
• *(to reach a decision)* = rimanere d'accordo (**!** + *essere*)
  we agreed to meet = siamo rimasti d'accordo di vederci

agriculture *noun*
  agriculture = l'agricoltura

ahead *adverb*
  to go ahead = andare avanti (**!** + *essere*)

Aids *noun* ▶ 193 |
  Aids = l'Aids (*masculine*)

aim
1 *noun*
  an aim = uno scopo
2 *verb*
• *(to be directed at)*
  it's aimed at young people = è rivolto ai giovani
• *(when using a weapon)*
  to aim a rifle at someone = puntare un fucile contro qualcuno

air *noun*
  air = l'aria
  to throw a ball up in the air = lanciare una palla in aria

air force *noun*
  the air force = l'aeronautica militare

air hostess *noun* ▶ 281 | (*British English*)
  an air hostess = un'assistente di volo

airmail *noun*
  to send a letter by airmail = spedire una lettera per posta aerea

airport *noun*
  an airport = un aeroporto

alarm clock *noun*
  an alarm clock = una sveglia

alcohol *noun*
  alcohol = l'alcol (*masculine*)

alive *adjective*
  = vivo/viva

all
1 *determiner*
  = tutto/tutta (+ *singular*)
  = tutti/tutte (+ *plural*)
  I worked all week = ho lavorato tutta la settimana
  all the guests have left = tutti gli invitati sono andati via
2 *pronoun*
  = tutto
  that's all = è tutto
3 *adverb*
  all alone = tutto solo/tutta sola

allow verb
to allow someone to [watch TV | play | go out] = permettere a qualcuno di [guardare la TV | giocare | uscire]
I'm not allowed to smoke at home = non mi fanno fumare in casa
smoking is not allowed = non è permesso fumare

all right adjective
• (when giving your opinion)
the film was all right = il film non era male
• (when talking about health)
are you all right? = tutto bene?
• (when making arrangements)
is it all right if I come later? = va bene se vengo più tardi?
all right! = va bene!

almost adverb
= quasi
I've almost finished = ho quasi finito

alone
1 adjective
= solo/sola
to be all alone = essere tutto solo/tutta sola
leave me alone! = lasciami in pace!
2 adverb
[to work | to live | to travel] alone = [lavorare | abitare | viaggiare] da solo/da sola

along preposition
= lungo
there are seats all along the canal = ci sono panchine lungo tutto il canale

aloud adverb
to read aloud = leggere ad alta voce

already adverb
= già
it's ten o'clock already = sono già le dieci
have you finished already? = hai già finito?

also adverb
= anche

although conjunction
= anche se
although she's strict, she's fair = anche se è severa, è giusta

always adverb
= sempre
I always go to Italy in (the) summer = vado sempre in Italia d'estate

amazed adjective
to be amazed = rimanere stupito/stupita (**!** + essere)

amazing adjective
= incredibile

ambition noun
an ambition = un'aspirazione

ambitious adjective
= ambizioso/ambiziosa

ambulance noun
an ambulance = un'ambulanza

America noun ▶ 151 |
America = l'America

American ▶ 199 |
1 adjective
= americano/americana
2 noun
the Americans = gli americani

among, amongst preposition
= fra, tra
unemployment among young people = la disoccupazione tra i giovani

amount noun
an amount = una quantità

amusement arcade noun
an amusement arcade = una sala giochi

amusement park noun
an amusement park = un parco dei divertimenti

an ▶ a

ancestor noun
an ancestor = un antenato/un'antenata

and conjunction
• and = e

> **!** Note that before a vowel, especially before e, **ed** is also possible.

a red and white sweater = un maglione rosso e bianco
she stood up and went out = si è alzata ed è uscita
faster and faster = sempre più veloce
• (in numbers and is not translated)
three hundred and sixty-five = trecentosessantacinque

anger noun
anger = la rabbia

angry adjective
= arrabbiato/arrabbiata
to be angry with someone = essere arrabbiato con qualcuno
to get angry = arrabbiarsi (**!** + essere)

animal noun
an animal = un animale

ankle noun ▶ 137 |
the ankle = la caviglia

announcement noun
an announcement = un annuncio

annoy verb
to annoy someone = dare fastidio a qualcuno

annoyed adjective
to be annoyed with someone = essere seccato/seccata con qualcuno

another
1 determiner
another = un altro/un'altra ····▶

another cup of coffee? = un altro caffè?
2 *pronoun*
  **there are some pears left—would you
  like another?** = sono rimaste delle
  pere—ne vuoi un'altra?

> **!** *Note that it is necessary to use* **ne,**
> *which might be translated as* **'of it'** *or*
> **'of them',** *with pronouns like* **another.**
> *See also* **any, a few, a lot,** *etc for this
> use of* **ne.**

answer
1 *noun*
  an answer = una risposta
  there's no answer (*at the door*) = non c'è
  nessuno
  (*on the phone*) = non risponde nessuno
2 *verb*
  = rispondere
  to answer a question = rispondere a una
  domanda
  to answer the phone = rispondere al
  telefono

answering machine *noun*
  an answering machine = una segreteria
  telefonica

ant *noun*
  an ant = una formica

antique *noun*
  an antique = un pezzo d'antiquariato
  an antique shop = un negozio
  d'antiquariato

anxious *adjective*
  = preoccupato/preoccupata
  to get anxious = preoccuparsi (**!** +
  essere)

any
1 *determiner*
• (*in questions*) = del/della (+ *singular*)
  = dei/delle (+ *plural*)

> **!** *Before masculine nouns beginning
> with* z, ps, gn, *or* s + *another
> consonant,* **dello** *is used in the singular
> and* **degli** *in the plural. Before
> masculine and feminine singular nouns
> beginning with a vowel,* **dell'** *is used.*
> **Degli** *is used before masculine plural
> nouns beginning with a vowel.*

  is there any tea? = c'è del tè?
  have you got any money? = hai soldi?
• (*with the negative*)
  I didn't find any mistakes = non ho
  trovato nessun errore
  we don't have any bread = non abbiamo
  pane
  I didn't have any friends = non avevo
  amici
• (*whatever*) = qualsiasi
  you can take any bus to go into town
  = per andare in città puoi prendere
  qualsiasi autobus

2 *pronoun*
  do you have any? = ne hai?
  he doesn't have any = non ne ha

> **!** *Note that it is necessary to use* **ne,**
> *which might be translated as* **'of it'** *or*
> **'of them',** *with pronouns like* **any.** *See
> also* **another, a few, a lot,** *etc for this
> use of* **ne.**

anyone *pronoun* (*also* **anybody**)
• (*in questions*) = qualcuno
  does anyone have an umbrella? =
  qualcuno ha un ombrello?
• (*with the negative*) = nessuno
  there isn't anyone at home = non c'è
  nessuno in casa
• (*everyone*)
  anyone can go = chiunque può andarci

anything *pronoun*
• (*in questions*) = qualcosa
  do you need anything? = ha bisogno di
  qualcosa?
• (*with the negative*) = niente
  she didn't say anything = non ha detto
  niente
• (*everything*) = tutto
  I like anything to do with sports = mi
  piace tutto quello che ha a che fare con
  lo sport

anyway *adverb*
  = in ogni modo

anywhere *adverb*
• (*in questions*) = da qualche parte
  can you see a phone booth anywhere?
  = vedi una cabina telefonica da qualche
  parte?
• (*with the negative*) = da nessuna parte
  you're not going anywhere = non vai da
  nessuna parte
• (*any place*)
  we can meet anywhere you like = ci
  possiamo incontrare dovunque vuoi

apart
1 *adjective*
  they don't like being apart = a loro non
  piace stare lontani
2 apart from = a parte

apartment *noun*
  an apartment = un appartamento
  an apartment block = un palazzo

apologize *verb*
  = scusarsi (**!** + *essere*)

apology *noun*
  an apology = delle scuse (*plural*)
  to make an apology = scusarsi (**!** +
  essere)

appear *verb*
• (*to seem*)
  = sembrare (**!** + *essere*)
• (*to come into view*) = apparire (**!** +
  essere)

appetite *noun*
the appetite = l'appetito
to have a good appetite = avere un
ottimo appetito

apple *noun*
an apple = una mela
apple juice = il succo di mela

application *noun*
a job application = una domanda di
lavoro

apply *verb*
to apply for a job = fare una domanda di
lavoro

appointment *noun*
an appointment = un appuntamento
to make an appointment = prendere un
appuntamento

appreciate *verb*
he appreciates good food = gli piace la
buona tavola
I'd appreciate it = te ne sarei grato

approach *verb*
= avvicinarsi a (**!** + *essere*)

approve *verb*
to approve of someone = vedere
qualcuno di buon occhio

apricot *noun*
an apricot = un'albicocca

April *noun* ▶ 155 |
April = aprile (*masculine*)

Aquarius *noun*
Aquarius = Acquario

architect *noun* ▶ 281 |
an architect = un architetto

area *noun*
an area = una zona

area code *noun* (*US English*)
the area code = il prefisso telefonico

argue *verb*
= litigare
to argue about money = litigare per una
questione di soldi

argument *noun*
an argument = una discussione
to have an argument with someone
= litigare con qualcuno

Aries *noun*
Aries = Ariete (*masculine*)

arm *noun* ▶ 137 |
the arm = il braccio

> **!** *Note that the plural of* **braccio** *is*
> **braccia**. *It is masculine in the singular*
> *and feminine in the plural.*

she's hurt her arm = si è fatta male al
braccio
my arms hurt = mi fanno male le braccia

armchair *noun*
an armchair = una poltrona

armed *adjective*
= armato/armata

arms *noun*
arms = le armi

army *noun*
the army = l'esercito

around

> **!** *Often* **around** *occurs in combinations*
> *with verbs, for example:* run around,
> turn around, *etc. To find the correct*
> *translations for this type of verb, look*
> *up the separate dictionary entries at*
> run, turn, *etc.*

1 *preposition*
= intorno a
the people around me were speaking
Italian = la gente intorno a me parlava
italiano
to walk around the room = camminare
per la stanza
to go around the world = fare il giro del
mondo
2 *adverb*
• (*with numbers*) = circa
it costs around £200 = costa circa 200
sterline
• (*with times*) = verso
we'll be there at around four o'clock
= saremo lì verso le quattro

arrange *verb*
to arrange a break in Italy = organizzare
una vacanza in Italia
we arranged to have lunch together = ci
siamo accordati per pranzare insieme

arrest *verb*
= arrestare

arrive *verb*
= arrivare (**!** + *essere*)
we arrived at the station at noon = siamo
arrivati alla stazione a mezzogiorno

arrow *noun*
an arrow = una freccia

art *noun*
• art = l'arte (*feminine*)
• (*as a school subject*)
art = l'educazione artistica

art gallery *noun*
an art gallery = un museo

artificial *adjective*
= artificiale

artist *noun* ▶ 281 |
an artist = un artista/un'artista

as
1 *conjunction*
• as = come
as you know, we're leaving = come sai, ce
ne andiamo
• (*at the time when*)
the phone rang as I was getting out of
the bath = il telefono ha squillato
mentre uscivo dalla vasca   ····▶

I used to live there as a child = da
bambino abitavo là
- (*British English*) (*because, since*)
= siccome
  as you were out, I left a message
  = siccome eri fuori, ho lasciato un
  messaggio
2 *preposition*
  she's got a job as a teacher = lavora
  come insegnante
  he was dressed as a sailor = era vestito
  da marinaio
3 *adverb*
  as [intelligent | rich | strong] **as** = tanto
  [intelligente | ricco | forte] quanto
  I have as much work as you = ho tanto
  lavoro quanto te
  he plays as well as his sister = suona
  bene quanto la sorella
4 as usual = come al solito

ashamed *adjective*
  to be ashamed = vergognarsi (**!** + *essere*)

ashtray *noun*
  an ashtray = un portacenere

Asia *noun* ▶ 151 |
  Asia = l'Asia

Asian *adjective* ▶ 199 |
  = asiatico/asiatica

ask *verb*
- **to ask** = chiedere
  she asked him his name = gli ha chiesto
  come si chiamava
  to ask someone to [phone | leave a message
  | do the shopping] = chiedere a qualcuno
  di [telefonare | lasciare un messaggio | fare la
  spesa]
  I asked for a coffee = ho chiesto un caffè
  to ask to speak to someone = chiedere di
  parlare con qualcuno
  to ask someone a question = fare una
  domanda a qualcuno
- (*to invite*) = invitare
  to ask some friends to dinner = invitare
  degli amici a cena
  he asked her out = le ha chiesto di uscire
  con lui

asleep *adjective*
  to be asleep = dormire
  to fall asleep = addormentarsi (**!** + *essere*)

assistant *noun*
  an assistant = un assistente/un'assistente

asylum-seeker *noun*
  an asylum-seeker = un richiedente asilo
  /una richiedente asilo

at *preposition*

> **!** There are many verbs which involve
> the use of **at**, like **look at**, **laugh at**,
> **point at**, etc. For translations, look up
> the entries at **look**, **laugh**, **point**, etc.

- (*when talking about a position or place*)
= a

> **!** Note that before a vowel, especially
> before a, **ad** is also possible.

she's at an exhibition = è a una mostra
at the = al/alla (**!** + *singular*)
= ai/alle (+ *plural*)

> **!** Before masculine nouns beginning
> with z, ps, gn, or s + another
> consonant, **allo** is used in the singular
> and **agli** in the plural. Before masculine
> and feminine singular nouns beginning
> with a vowel, **all'** is used.

they're at the station = sono alla stazione
to be [at home | at school | at work] = essere
  [a casa | a scuola | al lavoro]
- (*at the house, shop, practice of*) = da
  we'll be at Francesca's = saremo da
  Francesca
  he's got an appointment at the dentist's
  = ha un appuntamento dal dentista
  at the office = in ufficio
- (*when talking about time*) = a
  the film starts at nine o'clock = il film
  comincia alle nove
- (*when talking about age*) = a
  she was able to read at four years of age
  = sapeva leggere a quattro anni

athlete *noun* ▶ 281 |
  an athlete = un atleta/un'atleta

athletics *noun* ▶ 178 |
  athletics (*in Britain*) = l'atletica
  (*in the US*) = lo sport

Atlantic *noun*
  the Atlantic = l'Atlantico

atmosphere *noun*
  the atmosphere = l'atmosfera

at sign *noun*
  an at sign = una chiocciola

attach *verb*
  = attaccare

attachment *noun*
  (*in an email*)
  an attachment = un allegato

attack *verb*
  to attack someone in the street
  = aggredire qualcuno per strada

attempt
1 *verb*
  to attempt to break the record = tentare
  di battere il record
2 *noun*
  an attempt = un tentativo

attend *verb*
  to attend the village school = frequentare
  la scuola del paese
  to attend evening classes = seguire corsi
  serali

attention *noun*
  attention = l'attenzione (*feminine*)   ····▶

to get someone's attention = attrarre
l'attenzione di qualcuno
to pay attention to the teacher = ascoltare
l'insegnante
pay attention to what you're doing! = fai
attenzione a quello che stai facendo!

attic *noun*
an attic = una soffitta

attitude *noun*
an attitude = un atteggiamento
**he has a strange attitude toward(s)
people** = ha un atteggiamento strano
con la gente

attract *verb*
(*a person*) = attrarre
(*insects*) = attirare

attractive *adjective*
= attraente

auburn *adjective* ▶ 147 |
= ramato/ramata

audience *noun*
the audience = il pubblico

August *noun* ▶ 155 |
August = agosto

aunt *noun*
an aunt = una zia

au pair *noun*
an au pair = una ragazza alla pari

Australia *noun* ▶ 151 |
Australia = l'Australia

Australian ▶ 199 |
1 *adjective*
= australiano/australiana
2 *noun*
the Australians = gli australiani

Austria *noun* ▶ 151 |
Austria = l'Austria

Austrian ▶ 199 |
1 *adjective*
= austriaco/austriaca
2 *noun*
the Austrians = gli austriaci

author *noun* ▶ 281 |
an author = un autore/un'autrice

automatic *adjective*
= automatico/automatica

autumn *noun*
autumn = l'autunno
in (the) autumn = d'autunno

available *adjective*
• (*on sale*) = disponibile
tickets for the concert are still available
= ci sono ancora biglietti per il concerto
• (*free*) = libero/libera
are you available? = sei libero?

average *adjective*
= medio/media
the average teenager = il tipico teenager

avoid *verb*
= evitare
to avoid spending money = evitare di
spendere

awake *adjective*
to be awake = essere sveglio/sveglia
to keep someone awake = tenere sveglio
qualcuno

award *noun*
an award = un premio

aware *adjective*
to be aware of the [problem | danger | risk]
= essere consapevole del [problema |
pericolo | rischio]

away *adverb*
• (*absent*)
to be away = essere via
she's away on business = è via per
lavoro
• (*in its place*)
= via
to put something away = mettere via
qualcosa
• (*when talking about distances*)
to be far away = essere lontano/lontana
London is 40 km away = Londra è a 40
km

awful *adjective*
• (*no good*) = brutto/brutta
the film was awful = il film era brutto
• (*causing shock*) = terribile
• **I feel awful** = non mi sento affatto bene

awkward *adjective*
(*describing a situation, a problem*)
= difficile
I feel awkward about telling him = mi
imbarazza dirglielo

axe, ax (*US English*) *noun*
an axe = un'ascia

Bb

baby *noun*
a baby = un bambino/una bambina

babysitter *noun*
= un/una babysitter

back

> **!** *Often* **back** *occurs in combinations
> with verbs, for example:* **come back,
> get back, give back,** *etc. To find the
> correct translations for this type of
> verb, look up the separate dictionary
> entries at* **come, get, give,** *etc.*

1 *noun*
• (*part of the body*) ▶ 137 | ····▶

the back = la schiena
I've hurt my back = mi sono fatto male
  alla schiena
• (*the rear*)
  at the back of the classroom = in fondo
    all'aula
  to sit in the back of the car = sedere
    dietro
2 *adverb*
• **to be back** = tornare (**!** + *essere*)
  I'll be back in five minutes = torno tra
    cinque minuti
• (*before in time*)
  back in January = a gennaio

background *noun*
• (*of a person*)
  he's from a comfortable background = è
    di famiglia piuttosto benestante
• (*of a picture*)
  the background = lo sfondo
  in the background = sullo sfondo

backpack *noun*
  a backpack = uno zaino

back to front *adverb*
  = al contrario
  he put his sweater on back to front = si è
    messo il maglione al contrario

backwards, backward (*US English*)
  adverb
  = all'indietro

bacon *noun*
  bacon = la pancetta

bad *adjective*
• (*unpleasant, serious*) = brutto/brutta
  a bad film = un brutto film
  I have some bad news = ho brutte
    notizie
  a bad accident = un brutto incidente
  to have a bad cold = avere un brutto
    raffreddore
  smoking is bad for you = fumare fa male
• (*incompetent*)
  to be bad [at maths | at tennis | at chess]
    = non essere bravo/brava [in matematica |
    a tennis | con gli scacchi]
• (*naughty, wicked*) = cattivo/cattiva
  a bad boy = un bambino cattivo
• (*talking about quality*)
  a bad idea = una cattiva idea
  'how was the film?'—'not bad' = 'com'era
    il film?'—'non era male'
• (*when talking about food*) = guasto/guasta

badly *adverb*
• (*not well*) = male
  she slept badly = ha dormito male
• (*seriously*) = gravemente
  he was badly injured = era ferito
    gravemente

badminton *noun* ▶ 178 |
  badminton = il badminton

bad-tempered *adjective*
  = irascibile

bag *noun*
• **a bag** = una borsa
• (*made of paper, plastic*)
  a bag = un sacchetto

baggage *noun*
  baggage = i bagagli (*plural*)

bake *verb*
  to bake bread = fare il pane
  to bake a cake = fare un dolce

baker *noun* ▶ 281 |
  a baker = un fornaio/una fornaia

bakery *noun* ▶ 281 |
  a bakery = un panificio

balance *noun*
  balance = l'equilibrio
  to lose one's balance = perdere
    l'equilibrio

balcony *noun*
  a balcony = un terrazzo

bald *adjective*
  = calvo/calva

ball *noun*
  a ball (*in football, rugby, or basketball*)
    = un pallone
  (*in tennis, golf, or cricket*) = una pallina
  (*in billiards*) = una palla
  to play ball = giocare a pallone

ballet *noun*
  ballet = la danza

balloon *noun*
• **a balloon** = un palloncino
• **a hot air balloon** = un pallone aerostatico

ban *verb*
  = proibire

banana *noun*
  a banana = una banana

band *noun*
  a band = un gruppo
  a rock band = un gruppo rock

bandage *noun*
  a bandage = una fascia

bang
1 *noun*
• (*a loud noise*)
  a bang = un colpo
• (*US English*) (*a fringe*)
  bangs = la frangia (*singular*)
2 *verb*
• (*to close with a bang*) = sbattere
• (*to hit*)
  to bang one's fist on the table = battere il
    pugno sul tavolo
  to bang one's head on the wall = battere
    la testa contro il muro

bank *noun*
  a bank = una banca
  a bank account = un conto in banca
  a bank manager = un direttore/una
    direttrice di banca

bank holiday noun (British English)
a bank holiday = un giorno festivo

bar noun
• (a place)
a bar = un bar
• (made of metal)
a bar = una sbarra
• (other uses)
a bar of soap = una saponetta
a bar of chocolate = una tavoletta di
cioccolata

barbecue noun
a barbecue = una grigliata

barely adverb
= a malapena
he was barely able to walk = riusciva a
malapena a camminare

bargain noun
a bargain = un affare

bark verb
= abbaiare

barrel noun
a barrel = un barile

base verb
to be based on a true story = essere
basato/basata su una storia vera

baseball noun ▶ 178|
baseball = il baseball

basement noun
a basement = un seminterrato

basically adverb
= fondamentalmente

basket noun
a basket = un cesto

basketball noun ▶ 178|
basketball = la pallacanestro

bat noun
• (in cricket or baseball)
a bat = una mazza
• (an animal)
a bat = un pipistrello

bath noun
• to have a bath = fare il bagno
he's in the bath = sta facendo il bagno
• (a bathtub)
a bath = una vasca

bathroom noun
a bathroom = un bagno
to go to the bathroom = andare in bagno
(**!** + essere)

battery noun
a battery (for a torch) = una pila
(for a car) = una batteria

battle noun
a battle = una battaglia

bay noun
a bay = un'insenatura

be verb
▶ See the boxed note on **be** for more
information and examples.
• to be = essere
to be intelligent = essere intelligente
he is tall = è alto
be polite! = sii gentile!
it's Monday = è lunedì
it's past midnight = è mezzanotte passata
I've never been to Spain = non sono mai
stato in Spagna
the house has been sold = la casa è stata
venduta
• (when talking about jobs) ▶ 281|
she is a lawyer = fa l'avvocato
• (when describing a physical or mental
state)
to be [cold | hungry | afraid] = avere [freddo |
fame | paura]
my feet are cold = ho i piedi freddi
I am 18 = ho diciotto anni
• (when describing the weather)
the weather is [fine | awful | cold] = fa [bello
| brutto | freddo]
it's raining = piove
• (when talking about health)
how are you? = come stai?
I'm very well = sto benissimo
• (when talking about prices)
how much is that umbrella? = quant'è
quell'ombrello?
how much is it all together? = quanto fa
in tutto?
that's 9 euros = fa 9 euro
• (in continuous tenses)
he is reading = sta leggendo
it was snowing = stava nevicando
I'm coming = arrivo
• (in questions and short answers)
it's a lovely house, isn't it? = è una bella
casa, non è vero?
'he's not here'—'yes he is' = 'non
c'è'—'sì, c'è'

beach noun
a beach = una spiaggia

beak noun
a beak = un becco

bean noun
a bean = un fagiolo

bear
1 noun
a bear = un orso
2 verb
= sopportare
I can't bear him = non lo sopporto

beard noun
a beard = una barba

beat verb
• (to hit hard) = picchiare
• (in cooking) = sbattere   ....➤

be

As an ordinary verb

When **be** is used as a simple verb in *subject* + *verb* sentences, it is usually translated by **essere** (**!** + *essere*):

I'm tired	= **sono** stanco
*the kids **have been** very good*	= i bambini **sono stati** proprio bravi

But note some expressions where italian uses **avere**:

she's twenty	= **ha** vent'anni
I'm hungry	= **ho** fame

As an auxiliary verb in progressive tenses

In English, **be** can be used in combination with another verb to form a progressive tense which allows us to express an idea of duration, of something happening over a period of time. To express the same idea in Italian there are also progressive forms using **stare** + **-ando/-endo**:

I'm looking for my glasses	= **sto cercando** gli occhiali
they were waiting for me	= mi **stavano aspettando**

However, these forms are only used to emphasize the fact that the action is continuing. Often the simple present and imperfect tenses are used to translate the progressive in English:

*where **are** you **going**?*	= dove vai?
*it **was snowing***	= nevicava

As part of the passive

In Italian the passive is formed using the verb **essere**, in a similar way to English:

*wine **is made** from grapes*	= il vino **è fatto** con l'uva
*she **was arrested***	= **è stata arrestata**

However, in spoken Italian the construction with **si** is more often used to express the same idea:

*oil **is made** from olives*	= l'olio **si fa** con le olive

---

- (*to win against*) = battere
  Scotland beat England two nil = la Scozia ha battuto l'Inghilterra due a zero
beat up = picchiare

beautiful *adjective*
= bello/bella

> **!** *Note that before masculine nouns beginning with z, ps, gn or s + another consonant, **bello** is used in the singular and **begli** in the plural. Before masculine nouns beginning with other consonants, **bel** is used in the singular and **bei** in the plural. Before all nouns beginning with a vowel, **bell'** is used in the singular and **begli** (masculine) or **belle** (feminine) in the plural.*

a beautiful girl = una bella ragazza
a beautiful place = un bel posto
they are beautiful cities = sono belle città

beauty *noun*
beauty = la bellezza

because
1 *conjunction*
= perché
he did it because he had to = lo ha fatto perché era necessario
2 **because of** = a causa di

we didn't go out because of the rain = non siamo usciti a causa della pioggia

become *verb*
= diventare (**!** + *essere*)

bed *noun*
a bed = un letto
to go to bed = andare a letto (**!** + *essere*)

bedroom *noun*
a bedroom = una camera

bee *noun*
a bee = un'ape

beef *noun*
beef = il manzo

beer *noun*
beer = la birra
a beer = una birra

before
1 *preposition*
= prima di
before the holidays = prima delle vacanze
the day before yesterday = ieri l'altro
2 *adverb*
= prima
two months before = due mesi prima
the day before = il giorno prima
have you been to Venice before? = sei già stato a Venezia?   ....➤

3 *conjunction*
  I'd like to see him before I go = vorrei
    vederlo prima di andare via
  I'd like to see him before he goes
    = vorrei vederlo prima che vada via

   ! *Note that the subjunctive is used after*
   prima che.

beggar *noun*
  a beggar = un/una mendicante

begin *verb*
  = cominciare
  to begin to [laugh | cry | rain] = cominciare
    a [ridere | piangere | piovere]

beginner *noun*
  a beginner = un/una principiante

beginning *noun*
  the beginning = l'inizio
  at the beginning of May = all'inizio di
    maggio

behave *verb*
  = comportarsi (! + *essere*)
  he behaved badly = si è comportato male
  to be well behaved = essere
    beneducato/beneducata
  behave yourself! = comportati bene!

behaviour (*British English*), **behavior**
(*US English*) *noun*
  behaviour = il comportamento

behind *preposition*
  = dietro
  behind the chair = dietro la sedia
  behind me = dietro di me

Belgian ▶ 199 |
1 *adjective*
  = belga
2 *noun*
  the Belgians = i belgi

Belgium *noun* ▶ 151 |
  Belgium = il Belgio

believe *verb*
  = credere
  to believe someone = credere a qualcuno

bell *noun*
  • (*in a church*)
  a bell = una campana
  • (*on a door or bicycle*)
  a bell = un campanello

belong *verb*
  • (*to be the property of*)
  to belong to someone = appartenere a
    qualcuno
  that book belongs to me = quel libro è
    mio
  • (*to be a member of*)
  to belong to a club = fare parte di un
    club

below *preposition*
  = sotto

belt *noun*
  a belt = una cintura

bench *noun*
  a bench = una panca
  (*in a park*) = una panchina

bend
1 *verb* = piegare
  to bend one's knees = piegare le
    ginocchia
2 *noun*
  a bend = una curva
  bend down = piegarsi (! + *essere*)

beneath *preposition*
  = sotto

beside *preposition*
  • (*next to*) = accanto a
  he is sitting beside me = è seduto
    accanto a me
  • (*near*) = vicino a
  I live beside the harbour = abito vicino al
    porto

best
1 *noun*
  the best = il/la migliore
  to be the best at Italian = essere il/la
    migliore in italiano
  who is the best at drawing? = chi disegna
    meglio?
  I'm doing my best = faccio del mio
    meglio
2 *adjective*
  = migliore
  the best hotel in town = il migliore
    albergo della città
  my best friend = il mio migliore amico/la
    mia migliore amica
  the best book I've ever read = il miglior
    libro che abbia mai letto

   ! *Note that the subjunctive is used after*
   il migliore . . . che.

3 *adverb*
  = meglio
  the best-dressed man = l'uomo meglio
    vestito
  I like tennis best = preferisco il tennis

bet *verb*
  = scommettere

better
1 *adjective*
  = migliore
  her new film is better than the others = il
    suo nuovo film è migliore degli altri
  he is better at sports than me = nelle
    attività sportive è più bravo di me
  the weather is going to get better = il
    tempo migliorerà
  he was ill but now he's better = era
    malato ma ora sta meglio
2 *adverb*
  = meglio
  he speaks French better than I do
    = parla francese meglio di me   ····▶

we'd better go = sarà meglio andare
it's better to [phone | write | check] = è
meglio [telefonare | scrivere | controllare]

between
1 *preposition*
= fra
there is a wall between the two gardens
= c'è un muro tra i due giardini
2 in **between** = in mezzo

beyond *preposition*
= oltre
beyond the mountains = oltre le
montagne

bicycle *noun*
a bicycle = una bicicletta

big *adjective*
• (*large*) = grande
a big garden = un giardino grande
a big party = una grande festa
• (*heavy, thick, serious*) = grosso/grossa
a big parcel = un grosso pacco
a big book = un libro grosso
to make a big mistake = fare un grosso
sbaglio

bill *noun*
• (*for gas, electricity, telephone*)
a bill = una bolletta
• (*in a restaurant, hotel*)
a bill = un conto
could we have the bill please? = il conto,
per favore
• (*US English*) (*money*)
a bill = una banconota

billiards *noun* ▶ 178 |
billiards = il biliardo

bin *noun* (*British English*)
a bin = una pattumiera

biology *noun*
biology = la biologia

bird *noun*
a bird = un uccello

birth *noun*
a birth = una nascita
place of birth = luogo di nascita

birthday *noun*
a birthday = un compleanno
happy birthday! = buon compleanno!

biscuit *noun* (*British English*)
a biscuit = un biscotto

bit
1 *noun*
(*of cheese, bread, wood*) = un pezzo
2 a **bit** (*British English*)
a bit [early | hot | odd] = un po' [presto | caldo
| strano]

bite *verb*
= mordere

bitter *adjective*
= amaro/amara

black *adjective* ▶ 147 |
= nero/nera

blackberry *noun*
a blackberry = una mora

blackboard *noun*
the blackboard = la lavagna

blackcurrant *noun*
blackcurrants = il ribes nero (*singular*)

blade *noun*
• (*of a knife, a sword*)
a blade = una lama
• a razor blade = una lametta
• a blade of grass = un filo d'erba

blame *verb*
to blame someone = dare la colpa a
qualcuno

blank *adjective*
(*describing a page*) = bianco/bianca
(*describing a cassette*) = vuoto/vuota

blanket *noun*
a blanket = una coperta

bleed *verb*
= sanguinare
my nose is bleeding = mi sanguina il
naso

blind
1 *adjective*
= cieco/cieca
2 *noun*
a roller blind = un avvolgibile
a venetian blind = una veneziana

blister *noun*
a blister = una vescica

block
1 *noun*
• (*a building*)
a block of apartments = un palazzo
• (*a group of houses*) = un isolato
• (*a large piece*)
a block = un blocco
2 *verb*
= bloccare
to block a road = bloccare una strada

blond, blonde *adjective* ▶ 147 |
= biondo/bionda
he has blond hair = ha i capelli biondi
my sister's blonde = mia sorella è bionda

blood *noun*
blood = il sangue

blouse *noun*
a blouse = una camicetta

blow
1 *verb*
• (*if it's the wind*) = soffiare
the wind blew the door shut = un colpo
di vento ha chiuso la porta
• (*if it's a person*)
to blow a whistle = fischiare
to blow one's nose = soffiarsi il naso
(**!** + *essere*)   ····▶

- (*if it's a light bulb*) = saltare (**!** + *essere*)
2 *noun*
 a blow = un colpo
blow away
 to be blown away = essere portato/portata
 via dal vento
blow down
 to be blown down = essere
 abbattuto/abbattuta dal vento
blow out = spegnere
 to blow out a candle = spegnere una
 candela
blow up
- (*to destroy*) = far saltare
 to blow up a car = far saltare una
 macchina
- (*to be destroyed*) = esplodere (**!** + *essere*)
- (*to put air into*) = gonfiare

blue *adjective* ▶ **147** |
- = blu (**!** *never changes*)
- (*when it's eyes, the sky*) = azzurro/azzurra

blush *verb*
 = arrossire (**!** + *essere*)

board
1 *noun*
- (*a piece of wood*)
 a board = una tavola
- (*for games*)
 a board = una scacchiera
- (*a blackboard*)
 a board = una lavagna
2 *verb*
 to board a ship = salire a bordo di una
 nave (**!** + *essere*)
3 **on board** = a bordo

boast *verb*
 = vantarsi (**!** + *essere*)

boat *noun*
 a boat = una barca

body *noun*
 the body = il corpo
 a dead body = un cadavere

boil *verb*
- (*if it's a person*)
 to boil water = far bollire l'acqua
 to boil an egg = far bollire un uovo
 a boiled egg
 (*soft*) = un uovo alla coque
 (*hard*) = un uovo sodo
- (*if it's water, milk*) = bollire

boiler *noun*
 a boiler = una caldaia

boiling *adjective*
 = bollente

bomb *noun*
 a bomb = una bomba

bone *noun* ▶ **137** |
 a bone (*in the body, in meat*) = un osso
 > **!** Look at the note at **osso**.
 (*in fish*) = una lisca

bonnet *noun* (*British English*)
 the bonnet (*in a car*) = il cofano

book
1 *noun*
 a book = un libro
2 *verb*
 = prenotare
 to book a room = prenotare una stanza
 the flight is fully booked = il volo è
 completo

booking *noun*
 a booking = una prenotazione

bookshop, bookstore *noun* ▶ **281** |
 a bookshop, a bookstore = una libreria

boot *noun*
- (*worn on the feet*)
 a boot = uno stivale
- (*British English*) (*of a car*)
 the boot = il bagagliaio

border *noun*
 a border = una frontiera
 to cross the border = passare la frontiera

bore *verb*
 = annoiare

bored *adjective*
 to be bored, to get bored = annoiarsi (**!** +
 essere)

boring *adjective*
 = noioso/noiosa

born *adjective*
 to be born = nascere (**!** + *essere*)
 he was born in 1988 = è nato nel 1988
 she was born in Italy = è nata in Italia

borrow *verb*
 = prendere in prestito
 to borrow some money from someone
 = prendere in prestito dei soldi da
 qualcuno

boss *noun*
 the boss = il capo

both
1 *determiner*
 both girls are blonde = entrambe le
 ragazze sono bionde
 both my sons = i miei due figli
 both Anne and Brian came = sono venuti
 sia Anne che Brian
2 *pronoun*
 = entrambi/entrambe
 you are both wrong, both of you are
 wrong = avete torto entrambi

bother *verb*
- (*to take the trouble*)
 don't bother to call back = non importa
 che tu richiami
- (*to annoy, to upset*) = dare fastidio a
- (*in polite apologies*) = disturbare
 I'm sorry to bother you = scusi se la
 disturbo

The human body

Note the use of **il/la**, etc in Italian where English uses **my**, **your**, etc.

*he raised **his** hand*	= ha alzato **la** mano
*she closed **her** eyes*	= ha chiuso **gli** occhi
***my** eye hurts*	= mi fa male **l'**occhio

For expressions which involve more than the simple movement of a body part, use a reflexive verb in Italian:

*she has broken **her** leg*	= **si** è rotta **la** gamba
*he was washing **his** hands*	= **si** lavava **le** mani

Note also the following:

*she broke **his** nose*	= **gli** ha rotto **il** naso

Describing people

Here are some ways of describing people in Italian:

his hair is long/he has long hair	= ha i capelli lunghi
a boy with long hair	= un ragazzo con i capelli lunghi
her eyes are blue/she has blue eyes	= ha gli occhi azzurri
the girl with blue eyes	= la ragazza con gli occhi azzurri

▶ For further expressions with terms referring to the body, look at the note on **illnesses, aches, and pains**.

---

bottle *noun*
a bottle = una bottiglia

bottle-opener *noun*
a bottle-opener = un apribottiglie

bottom
1 *noun*
• (*the lowest part*)
at the bottom of [the page | the stairs | the sea] = in fondo [alla pagina | alle scale | al mare]
• (*at the lowest level*)
to be bottom of the class = essere l'ultimo/l'ultima della classe
• (*part of the body*) ▶ **137**
the bottom = il sedere
2 *adjective*
the bottom [shelf | drawer | cupboard] = [lo scaffale | il cassetto | l'armadietto] in basso

bound: **to be bound to** *verb*
she's bound to complain = si lamenterà di sicuro
it was bound to happen = doveva succedere

bow[1] *noun*
• (*a knot*)
a bow = un fiocco
• (*a weapon*)
a bow = un arco

bow[2] *verb*
= fare un inchino

bowl *noun*
a bowl = una ciotola

bowling *noun* ▶ **178**
bowling = il bowling

box *noun*
a box = una scatola

boxing *noun* ▶ **178**
boxing = il pugilato

boy *noun*
a boy = un bambino
(*a teenager*) = un ragazzo

boyfriend *noun*
a boyfriend = un ragazzo

bra *noun*
a bra = un reggiseno

bracelet *noun*
a bracelet = un braccialetto

brain *noun* ▶ **137**
the brain = il cervello

brake
1 *noun*
a brake = un freno
2 *verb*
= frenare

branch *noun*
a branch = un ramo

brand-new *adjective*
= nuovo/nuova di zecca

brandy *noun*
brandy = il cognac

brave *adjective*
= coraggioso/coraggiosa

Brazil *noun* ▶ **151**
Brazil = il Brasile

bread *noun*
bread = il pane

break
1 *verb*
• (*to be damaged*) = rompersi (**!** + *essere*)
the chair broke = la sedia si è rotta   ••••▶

- (*to smash or damage*) = rompere
  to break an egg = rompere un uovo
- (*to injure*)
  to break one's leg = rompersi la gamba
  (**!** + *essere*)
  she broke her arm = si è rotta un braccio
- (*not to keep*)
  to break a promise = non mantenere una
  promessa
  to break the rules = non rispettare le
  regole
- **2** *noun*
- (*a short rest*)
  a break = una pausa
  to take a break = fare una pausa
- (*at school*)
  the break = l'intervallo
  break down
- (*if it's a TV, a car*) = rompersi (**!** + *essere*)
- (*to get upset*) = crollare (**!** + *essere*)
  break out
  = scoppiare (**!** + *essere*)
  break up
- (*if it's a crowd*) = sciogliersi (**!** + *essere*)
- (*if it's a couple*) = lasciarsi (**!** + *essere*)
  to break up with someone = lasciarsi da
  qualcuno
- (*to put an end to*) = mettere fine a

breakfast *noun*
breakfast = la colazione
to have breakfast = fare colazione

breast *noun* ▶ 137|
a breast = un seno

breath *noun*
breath = il respiro
to be out of breath = essere senza fiato
to hold one's breath = trattenere il
respiro

breathe *verb*
= respirare

breeze *noun*
a breeze = una brezza

brick *noun*
a brick = un mattone

bride *noun*
a bride = una sposa

bridegroom *noun*
a bridegroom = uno sposo

bridge *noun*
a bridge = un ponte

brief *adjective*
= breve

bright *adjective*
- (*describing colours*) = vivace
- (*having plenty of light*)
  = luminoso/luminosa
  a bright spell = una schiarita
  to get brighter = schiarire (**!** + *essere*)
- (*intelligent*) = sveglio/sveglia

✶ in informal situations

brilliant *adjective*
- (*very intelligent*) = brillante
- (*British English*) (*used for emphasis*)
  = fantastico/fantastica

bring *verb*
= portare
he brought his sister to the party = ha
portato sua sorella alla festa
bring about
to bring about a change = portare un
cambiamento
bring back = riportare
he brought me back my book = mi ha
riportato il libro
bring up = allevare
to bring up a child = allevare un bambino

Britain *noun* ▶ 151|
Britain = la Gran Bretagna

British ▶ 199| *adjective*
= britannico/britannica
a British passport = un passaporto
britannico

> **!** *Note that* **britannico/britannica** *is not
> very common in Italian. For most
> purposes it is more natural to use*
> **inglese, scozzese, gallese,** *or*
> **irlandese** *to describe oneself. Look at
> the entries for* **English, Scot, Welsh,**
> *and* **Irish** *to see how to refer to the
> people.*

broad *adjective*
= ampio/ampia

broadband *noun*
broadband = la banda larga

broadcast *verb*
= trasmettere

brochure *noun*
a brochure = un depliant

broke *adjective*
= al verde✶

broken *adjective*
= rotto/rotta

bronze *noun*
bronze = il bronzo

brother *noun*
a brother = un fratello

brother-in-law *noun*
a brother-in-law = un cognato

brown *adjective* ▶ 147|
- (*in colour*) = marrone
  to have brown eyes = avere gli occhi
  marroni
- (*describing hair*) = castano/castana
- (*tanned*) = abbronzato/abbronzata

bruise *noun* ▶ 193|
a bruise = un livido

brush
1 *noun*
• *(for hair, clothes or shoes)*
  a brush = una spazzola
• *(for sweeping up)*
  a brush = una scopa
• *(for painting)*
  a brush = un pennello
2 *verb*
  to brush one's hair = spazzolarsi i capelli
    (**!** + *essere*)
  to brush one's teeth = lavarsi i denti (**!** +
    essere)

Brussels *noun* ▶ 151 |
  Brussels = Bruxelles

bubble *noun*
  a bubble = una bolla

bucket *noun*
  a bucket = un secchio

budgerigar, budgie *noun*
  a budgerigar = un pappagallino

build *verb*
  = costruire

building *noun*
  a building = un edificio

bull *noun*
  a bull = un toro

bullet *noun*
  a bullet = una pallottola

bully *noun*
  a bully = un/una prepotente

bump *verb*
  to bump one's head = sbattere la testa
bump into
• *(to hit)* = sbattere contro
• *(to meet)* = imbattersi in (**!** + *essere*)

bunch *noun*
  a bunch of flowers = un mazzo di fiori
  a bunch of grapes = un grappolo d'uva

burger *noun*
  a burger = un hamburger

burglar *noun*
  a burglar = un ladro/una ladra

burn
1 *verb*
• = bruciare
• *(to injure)*
  to burn oneself = bruciarsi (**!** + *essere*)
  to burn one's finger = bruciarsi un dito
• *(in the sun)*
  to burn easily = bruciare facilmente
2 *noun*
  a burn = una bruciatura
burn down = incendiare

burner *noun*
  (for CDs, DVDs)
  a burner = un masterizzatore

burst *verb*
  = scoppiare (**!** + *essere*)

burst into
  to burst into tears = scoppiare a piangere
burst out
  to burst out laughing = scoppiare a ridere

bury *verb*
  = seppellire

bus *noun*
  a bus = un autobus

bus driver *noun* ▶ 281 |
  a bus driver = un autista/un'autista

bush *noun*
  a bush = un cespuglio

business *noun*
• *(commercial activities)*
  business = gli affari
  I'm going to London on business = vado
    a Londra per affari
• *(a company)*
  a business = un'impresa
• *(when protecting one's privacy)*
  it's none of your business = non sono
    affari tuoi

businessman *noun* ▶ 281 |
  a businessman = un imprenditore

businesswoman *noun* ▶ 281 |
  a businesswoman = un'imprenditrice

bus station *noun*
  a bus station = un deposito degli autobus

bus stop *noun*
  a bus stop = una fermata dell'autobus

busy *adjective*
  = impegnato/impegnata
  to be busy packing = essere impegnato a
    fare i bagagli
  to have a busy day = avere una giornata
    piena
  to lead a busy life = fare una vita attiva

but *conjunction*
  = ma
  **he understands Italian but he doesn't
    speak it** = capisce l'italiano, ma non lo
    parla

butcher *noun* ▶ 281 |
  a butcher = un macellaio/una macellaia

butter *noun*
  butter = il burro

butterfly *noun*
  a butterfly = una farfalla

button *noun*
  a button = un bottone

buy *verb*
  = comprare
  to buy a present for someone = comprare
    un regalo a qualcuno
  she bought herself a new coat = si è
    comprata un cappotto nuovo

by *preposition*
• **by** = da   ····▶

B

he was bitten by a dog = è stato morso
da un cane
- (on one's own)
by oneself = da solo/sola
- (using)
to travel by bus = viaggiare in autobus
we went there by bicycle = ci siamo
andati in bicicletta
to pay by cheque = pagare con un
assegno
to book by phone = prenotare per
telefono
to come in by the back door = entrare
dalla porta di dietro
- (as a result of)
she got in by breaking a window = è
entrata spaccando un vetro
- (beside) = vicino a
by the sea
(when it's a town) = sul mare
(when it's a house) = al mare
by the side of the road = sul ciglio della
strada
- (indicating the author or painter) = di
a book by Dickens = un libro di Dickens
- (when talking about time)
by next Thursday = per giovedì prossimo
he should be here by now = a quest'ora
dovrebbe essere qui
- (when talking about figures, rates)
to increase by 20% = aumentare del 20%
8 metres by 4 metres = 8 metri per 4
one by one = uno per uno

Cc

cab noun
a cab = un taxi

cabbage noun
cabbage = il cavolo

café noun
a café = un bar

cake noun
a cake = una torta

calculator noun
a calculator = una calcolatrice

calendar noun
a calendar = un calendario

calf noun
- (the animal)
a calf = un vitello
- (part of the leg) ▶ **137**|
the calf = il polpaccio

call verb
- = chiamare

to call the doctor = chiamare il dottore
he's called Michael = si chiama Michael
what's this called in Italian? = come si
chiama questo in italiano?
- (to phone) = chiamare
who's calling? = chi parla?
- (to pay a visit) = passare (**!** + essere)
they called yesterday = sono passati ieri
call back
- (to come back) = ripassare (**!** + essere)
- (to phone back) = richiamare
call off = annullare

call centre noun
a call centre = un call centre

calm
1 adjective
= calmo/calma
2 verb
= calmare
calm down = calmarsi (**!** + essere)

camcorder noun
a camcorder = una videocamera

camel noun
a camel = un cammello

camera noun
a camera (for taking photos) = una
macchina fotografica
(in a studio, for videos) = una telecamera

camp
1 noun
a camp = un campeggio
2 verb
= accamparsi (**!** + essere)
to go camping = andare in campeggio
(**!** + essere)

campsite noun
a campsite = un campeggio

can¹ verb
- (to have the possibility) = potere
can you come? = puoi venire?
where can I buy stamps? = dove posso
comprare dei francobolli?
he can't sleep when it's hot = non riesce
a dormire quando fa caldo
- (when talking about seeing, hearing,
understanding, can is not usually
translated)
I can hear you better now = ora ti sento
meglio
can they see us? = ci vedono?
- (to be allowed to)
can I smoke? = posso fumare?
we can't turn right here = qui non si può
girare a destra
- (to know how to) = sapere
she can swim = sa nuotare
can you speak Italian? = parli italiano?
- (when asking, offering or suggesting)
can we borrow your car? = possiamo
prendere la tua macchina?
can I help you? = posso esserti d'aiuto?

can² noun
a can   ····▶

(*for drinks*) = una lattina
(*for food*) = una scatoletta

Canada *noun* ► 151
Canada = il Canada

Canadian ► 199
1 *adjective*
= canadese
2 *noun*
the Canadians = i canadesi

canal *noun*
a canal = un canale

cancel *verb*
= annullare

cancer *noun* ► 193
cancer = il cancro

candle *noun*
a candle = una candela

candy *noun* (*US English*)
• candy = i dolciumi
• (*a sweet*)
a candy = una caramella

canoe *noun*
a canoe = una canoa

canoeing *noun* ► 178
canoeing = il canottaggio

can-opener *noun*
a can-opener = un apriscatole

canteen *noun*
a canteen = una mensa

cap *noun*
a cap = un berretto
a baseball cap = un berretto da baseball

capable *adjective*
• to be capable of looking after oneself
= essere capace di badare a se stesso
• (*having ability, skill*) = abile

capital
1 *noun*
the capital = la capitale
Rome is the capital of Italy = Roma è la
capitale d'Italia
2 *adjective*
= maiuscolo/maiuscola
capital P = P maiuscola

captain *noun*
a captain = un capitano

car *noun*
a car = una macchina

caravan *noun* (*British English*)
a caravan = una roulotte

card *noun*
• (*for sending to someone*)
a card = un biglietto
• (*for playing games*)
a card = una carta
to play cards = giocare a carte

care
1 *noun*
• to take care = fare attenzione
take care crossing the street! = fai
attenzione quando attraversi la strada!
• to take care of someone = prendersi cura
di qualcuno (**!** + *essere*)
to take care of something = trattare bene
qualcosa
2 *verb*
I don't care = non me ne importa
to care about the environment = tenere
all'ambiente

career *noun*
a career = una carriera

careful *adjective*
to be careful = stare attento/attenta
be careful crossing the street! = stai
attento quando attraversi la strada!
to be careful not to make mistakes
= stare attento a non fare errori

careless *adjective*
= incurante

carnival *noun*
• (*British English*) (*a festival*)
a carnival = un carnevale
• (*US English*) (*a fair*)
a carnival = un luna park

car park *noun* (*British English*)
a car park = un parcheggio

carpet *noun*
the carpet = la moquette

carrot *noun*
a carrot = una carota

carry *verb*
= portare
carry on = continuare

cartoon *noun*
a cartoon (*a comic strip*) = un fumetto
(*a film*) = un cartone animato

case¹: in case *conjunction*
= in caso
keep the bike in case you need it = tieni
la bici in caso ti serva

> **!** *Note that the subjunctive is used after*
> *in caso.*

case² *noun*
• (*a box*)
a case = una cassa
• (*a suitcase*)
a case = una valigia

cash
1 *noun*
• (*coins or bills*)
I don't have any cash on me = non ho
contanti
to pay in cash = pagare in contanti
• (*money in general*)
cash = soldi (*masculine plural*)   ····►

C

2 *verb*
 = incassare

cash dispenser *noun*
 a cash dispenser = un Bancomat®

cassette *noun*
 a cassette = una cassetta

cassette player *noun*
 a cassette player = un mangiacassette

castle *noun*
 a castle = un castello

cat *noun*
 a cat = un gatto/una gatta

catch *verb*
• (*to capture, to hold*) = prendere
 to catch a fish = prendere un pesce
• (*to pinch, to stick*)
 he caught his finger in the door = si è
  chiuso un dito nella porta
• to catch the train = prendere il treno
• (*to become ill with*)
 to catch flu = prendere l'influenza
• to catch fire = prendere fuoco
 catch up
 to catch up with someone = raggiungere
  qualcuno

caterpillar *noun*
 a caterpillar = un bruco

cathedral *noun*
 a cathedral = una cattedrale

cauliflower *noun*
 cauliflower = il cavolfiore

cause *verb*
 = causare
 to cause damage = fare dei danni

cautious *adjective*
 = cauto/cauta

cave *noun*
 a cave = una caverna

CD *noun*
 a CD = un CD
 a CD player = un lettore CD

ceiling *noun*
 the ceiling = il soffitto

celebrate *verb*
 = festeggiare

cellar *noun*
 a cellar = una cantina

cell phone, cellular phone
 (*US English*) *noun*
 a cell phone = un (telefono) cellulare,
  un telefonino

cement *noun*
 cement = il cemento

cemetery *noun*
 a cemetery = un cimitero

cent *noun*
 a cent (*of dollar*) = un centesimo
 (*of euro*) = un cent, un centesimo

centimetre (*British English*),
 centimeter (*US English*) *noun* ▶ 202 |
 a centimetre = un centimetro

central heating *noun*
 central heating = il riscaldamento
  autonomo

centre (*British English*), **center** (*US
 English*) *noun*
• (*a place for activities, meetings*)
 a centre = un centro
 a leisure centre = un centro sportivo
• (*the middle*)
 the centre = il centro

century *noun* ▶ 267 |
 a century = un secolo

certain *adjective*
 = certo/certa

certainly *adverb*
 = certamente

chain *noun*
 a chain = una catena

chair *noun*
 a chair = una sedia

chalk *noun*
 chalk = il gesso

champion *noun*
 a champion = un campione/una
  campionessa
 a tennis champion = un campione/una
  campionessa di tennis

chance *noun*
• (*when talking about a possibility*)
 there is a chance that she'll get a job in
  Turin = c'è la possibilità che trovi un
  lavoro a Torino

 > ! *Note that the subjunctive is used after*
 c'è la possibilità che.

• (*an opportunity*)
 a chance = un'occasione
 to have the chance to meet people
  = avere l'opportunità di incontrare della
  gente
• by chance = per caso

change
1 *noun*
• a change = un cambiamento
• (*a different experience*)
 let's go to the beach for a change = per
  cambiare andiamo al mare
• (*cash*)
 change = gli spiccioli
 have you got change for 10 euros? = ha
  da cambiare 10 euro?
• (*money given back after paying*)
 the change = il resto
2 *verb*
• (*to make different, to replace*) = cambiare
  (**!** + *avere*)   ····▶

I've changed my mind = ho cambiato idea
she keeps changing channels = continua a cambiare canale
to change dollars into lire = cambiare i dollari in lire
• (to become different) = cambiare (! + essere)
the town has changed a lot = la città è molto cambiata
• (to exchange in a shop) = cambiare (! + avere)
change a shirt for a smaller size piccola
• (when talking about one's clothes)
to get changed = cambiarsi (! + essere)
• (when using transport) = cambiare (! + avere)

channel noun
a TV channel = un canale televisivo

Channel noun
the (English) Channel = la Manica

chapter noun
a chapter = un capitolo

charge
1 verb
they'll charge you for the damage = ti faranno pagare i danni
2 noun
• (a price, a fee)
a charge = una tariffa
there's no charge = è gratis
3 in charge = responsabile
to be in charge of the money = essere responsabile dei soldi

charming adjective
= incantevole

chase verb
= inseguire

chat
1 verb
• (face to face, on the telephone)
= chiacchierare
• (on the Internet) = chattare
2 noun
a chat = una chiacchierata
chat up (British English) = abbordare

cheap adjective
• (not expensive) = economico/economica
it's cheap = non costa molto
it's cheaper to take the bus = costa meno prendere l'autobus
• (of poor quality) = scadente

cheat verb
= imbrogliare

check
1 verb
= controllare
you should check whether it's true = dovresti controllare se è vero

2 noun
• (US English) (a bill)
a check = un conto
• (US English) (a cheque)
a check = un assegno
check in
• (at the airport) = fare il check-in
• (at a hotel) = firmare il registro
check out = andare via (! + essere)

checkbook noun (US English)
a checkbook = un libretto degli assegni

checkers noun ▶ 178 | (US English)
checkers = la dama

check-in noun
the check-in = il check-in

checkout noun
the checkout = la cassa

cheek noun ▶ 137 |
the cheek = la guancia

cheeky adjective
= sfacciato/sfacciata

cheerful adjective
= allegro/allegra

cheese noun
cheese = il formaggio

chef noun ▶ 281 |
a chef = un cuoco/una cuoca

chemist noun ▶ 281 |
• (in a shop)
a chemist = un/una farmacista
• (the shop)
a chemist = una farmacia
• (in a laboratory)
a chemist = un chimico/una chimica

chemistry noun
chemistry = la chimica

cheque noun (British English)
a cheque = un assegno
to write a cheque for £50 = fare un assegno da 50 sterline

cheque book noun (British English)
a cheque book = un libretto degli assegni

cherry noun
a cherry = una ciliegia

chess noun ▶ 178 |
chess = gli scacchi

chest noun ▶ 137 |
the chest = il petto

chew verb
= masticare

chewing gum noun
chewing gum = il chewing-gum

chicken noun
a chicken = un pollo
chicken = il pollo

chickenpox noun
chickenpox = la varicella

child *noun*
a child = un bambino/una bambina

chilly *adjective*
it's chilly = fa freddo

chimney *noun*
a chimney = un camino

chin *noun* ▶ 137|
the chin = il mento

China *noun* ▶ 151|
China = la Cina

Chinese ▶ 199|
1 *adjective*
= cinese
2 *noun*
• (*the people*)
the Chinese = i cinesi
• (*the language*)
Chinese = il cinese

chips *noun*
• (*British English*) (*French fries*)
chips = le patate fritte
• (*US English*) (*crisps*)
(potato) chips = le patatine

chocolate *noun*
chocolate = il cioccolato
a chocolate = un cioccolatino
a box of chocolates = una scatola di
cioccolatini

choice *noun*
a choice = una scelta
we had no choice = non avevamo scelta

choir *noun*
a choir = un coro

choke *verb*
= soffocare

choose *verb*
= scegliere

chore *noun*
to do the chores = fare le faccende

Christian *adjective*
= cristiano/cristiana

Christian name *noun*
a Christian name = un nome di battesimo

Christmas *noun*
Christmas (Day) = il Natale
merry Christmas!, happy Christmas!
= buon Natale!

Christmas Eve *noun*
Christmas Eve = la Vigilia di Natale

Christmas tree *noun*
a Christmas tree = un albero di Natale

church *noun*
a church = una chiesa

cider *noun*
cider = il sidro

cigar *noun*
a cigar = un sigaro

cigarette *noun*
a cigarette = una sigaretta

cinema *noun* (*British English*)
a cinema = un cinema

circle *noun*
a circle = un cerchio
we were sitting in a circle = eravamo
seduti in cerchio

circus *noun*
a circus = un circo

citizen *noun*
a citizen = un cittadino/una cittadina

city *noun*
a city = una città

civil servant *noun* ▶ 281|
a civil servant = un
impiegato/un'impiegata statale

clap *verb*
= applaudire

class *noun*
• (*a group of students*)
a class = una classe
• (*a lesson*)
a class = una lezione
a history class = una lezione di storia
• (*a social group*)
a (social) class = una classe (sociale)

classical music *noun*
classical music = la musica classica

classmate *noun*
a classmate = un compagno/una
compagna di classe

classroom *noun*
a classroom = un'aula

clean
1 *adjective*
= pulito/pulita
my hands are clean = ho le mani pulite
to keep the house clean = tenere la casa
pulita
2 *verb*
= pulire
to have a jacket cleaned = far lavare una
giacca

clear
1 *adjective*
• = chiaro/chiara
is that clear? = è chiaro?
a clear voice = una voce chiara
your writing must be clear = la calligrafia
deve essere chiara
• (*with no rain or cloud*) = sereno/serena
on a clear day = quando è sereno
2 *verb*
• (*to empty, to remove from*)
to clear the table = sgombrare la tavola
to clear the snow off the road
= sgombrare la strada dalla neve
• (*if it's fog, mist*) = schiarire (! + *essere*)

clever *adjective*
- (*intelligent*) = intelligente
- (*smart*) = furbo/furba

click *verb*
= cliccare

cliff *noun*
a cliff = una scogliera

climate *noun*
a climate = un clima

climate change *noun*
climate change = il cambiamento climatico

climb *verb*
- to climb (up) a tree = arrampicarsi su un albero (**!** + *essere*)
  to climb a mountain = scalare una montagna
  to climb over a wall = scavalcare un muro
- (*to rise higher*) = salire (**!** + *essere*)

climbing *noun* ▶ **178|**
climbing = l'arrampicata

clinic *noun*
a clinic = una clinica

clock *noun*
a clock = un orologio
(*in sporting events*) = un cronometro

close¹
1 *adjective*
- = vicino/vicina
  the station is quite close = la stazione è abbastanza vicina
  is the house close to the school? = la casa è vicina alla scuola?
- (*as a friend*) = intimo/intima
2 *adverb*
  to live close (by) = abitare vicino

close² *verb*
= chiudere
close your eyes = chiudi gli occhi
the shop closes at noon = il negozio chiude a mezzogiorno
the door closed = la porta si è chiusa
close down = chiudere

closed *adjective*
= chiuso/chiusa

cloth *noun*
- (*material*)
  cloth = la stoffa
- a cloth = uno straccio

clothes *noun*
clothes = i vestiti
to put on one's clothes = vestirsi (**!** + *essere*)
to take off one's clothes = spogliarsi (**!** + *essere*)
to have no clothes on = essere nudo/nuda

cloud *noun*
a cloud = una nuvola

clown *noun*
a clown = un pagliaccio

club *noun*
- a club = un circolo
  a tennis club = un circolo di tennis
  to be in a club = essere socio/socia di un club
- (*a nightclub*)
  a club = un locale

clue *noun*
a clue = un indizio

clumsy *adjective*
= goffo/goffa

coach
1 *noun* (*British English*)
- (*a bus*)
  a coach = un pullman
  a coach station = una stazione dei pullman
- (*of a train*)
  a coach = una carrozza
2 *verb*
= allenare

coal *noun*
coal = il carbone

coast *noun*
the coast = la costa

coat *noun*
- a coat = un cappotto
- (*of an animal*)
  the coat = il pelo

coat hanger *noun*
a coat hanger = un attaccapanni

cock *noun*
a cock = un gallo

cocoa *noun*
- (*the drink*)
  cocoa = la cioccolata calda
- (*the product*)
  cocoa = il cacao

coconut *noun*
coconut = il cocco
a coconut = una noce di cocco

cod *noun*
cod = il merluzzo

coffee *noun*
coffee = il caffè
a coffee = un caffè

coin *noun*
a coin = una moneta
a 2 euro coin = una moneta da 2 euro

coincidence *noun*
a coincidence = una coincidenza

cold
1 *adjective*
= freddo/fredda
to be cold, to feel cold = avere freddo
I'm very cold = ho molto freddo
it's cold = fa freddo
to go cold = raffreddarsi (**!** + *essere*) ····▶

C

The clock

What time is it?

what time is it?	= che ore sono?
could you tell me the time?	= mi sa dire che ore sono?
it's exactly four o'clock	= sono le quattro in punto
it's 1.00	= è l'una
it's 4.00	= sono le quattro
it's 4 am	= sono le quattro di mattino
it's 4 pm	= sono le quattro di pomeriggio
it's 8 pm	= sono le otto di sera
it's 4.05	= sono le quattro e cinque
it's 4.10	= sono le quattro e dieci
it's 4.15	= sono le quattro e un quarto
it's 4.20	= sono le quattro e venti
it's 4.25	= sono le quattro e venticinque
it's 4.30	= sono le quattro e mezzo
it's 4.35	= sono le quattro e trentacinque
it's 4.40	= sono le quattro e quaranta
it's 4.45	= sono le quattro e quarantacinque
it's 4.50	= sono le quattro e cinquanta
it's 4.55	= sono le quattro e cinquantacinque
it's 12 (noon)	= è mezzogiorno
it's midnight	= è mezzanotte

The twenty-four hour clock is always used in timetables and fairly often in speech, so that **5.00 pm** is **le diciassette**.

When?

Italian uses the preposition **a** to say what time something happens:

at one	= **all**'una
at five	= **alle** cinque
at midnight	= **a** mezzanotte

Italian always uses the preposition **a** (or another preposition like **verso** or **dopo**) even where it is often omitted in English:

what time did it happen?	= **a** che ora è successo?
*it happened **at** two*	= è successo **alle** due
*he'll come **at** one*	= verrà **all**'una
at about five	= **verso** le cinque
*it must be ready **by** ten*	= deve essere pronto **per** le dieci
*closed **from** 1.00 **to** 2.00*	= chiuso **dall**'una **alle** due

---

2 *noun*
* (*the lack of heat*)
  the cold = il freddo
* (*a common illness*)
  a cold = un raffreddore

collapse *verb*
  (*if it's a building, a wall*) = crollare (**!** + *essere*)
  (*if it's a chair*) = cadere (**!** + *essere*)

collar *noun*
* (*on a shirt or jacket*)
  a collar = un collo
* (*for a pet*)
  a collar = un collare

colleague *noun*
  a colleague = un/una collega

collect *verb*
* (*to gather*) = raccogliere

  to collect the exercise books
    = raccogliere i quaderni
* (*to make a collection of*) = collezionare
  he collects stamps = colleziona francobolli
* (*to take away*)
  to collect the post = ritirare la posta
  to collect the rubbish = portare via la spazzatura

collection *noun*
* (*a set*)
  a collection = una collezione
* (*money collected*)
  a collection = una colletta

college *noun*
  a college = un istituto superiore
  I'm at college = vado all'università

colour (*British English*), **color** (*US English*) *noun*   ····▸

Colours

Most colours agree with the noun they are describing:

a *red* hat	= un cappello **rosso**
a *red* shirt	= una camicia **rossa**
a *green* shoe	= una scarpa **verde**
green shoes	= scarpe **verdi**

There are exceptions, labelled (**!** *never changes*) in the dictionary. Even with a plural noun, this type of adjective remains the same:

a **blue** jacket	= una giacca **blu**
a **pink** dress	= un vestito **rosa**

Describing the colour of something

what colour is your car?	= di che colore è la tua macchina?
it's green	= è verde

---

a colour = un colore
what colour is the car? = di che colore è la macchina?

colourful (*British English*), **colorful** (*US English*) *adjective*
  a colourful shirt = una camicia dai colori vivaci

comb
1 *noun*
  a comb = un pettine
2 *verb*
  to comb one's hair = pettinarsi (**!** + *essere*)

come *verb*
• to come = venire (**!** + *essere*)
  she's coming today = viene oggi
  come to Padua with us = vieni a Padova con noi
  we came by bike = siamo venuti in bicicletta
  come and see! = vieni a vedere!
  I'm coming! = vengo!
  is the bus coming? = sta arrivando l'autobus?
  be careful when you come down the stairs = stai attento quando scendi le scale
  he came into the house = è entrato in casa
• (*to reach*)
  turn left when you come to the traffic lights = gira a sinistra quando arrivi al semaforo
• (*to be a native or a product of*)
  she comes from Italy = è italiana
  I come from Dublin = sono di Dublino
  where do you come from? = di dove sei?
  the strawberries come from Spain = le fragole vengono dalla Spagna
• (*in a contest*)
  to come first = arrivare primo/prima (**!** + *essere*)
come around ▶ come round
come back = tornare (**!** + *essere*)
  she came back home = è tornata a casa

come in
• (*to enter*) = entrare (**!** + *essere*)
• (*if it's a plane, a train*) = arrivare (**!** + *essere*)
• the tide's coming in = si sta alzando la marea
come off
  (*if it's a cover, a lid*) = venire via (**!** + *essere*)
  (*if it's a button, a label*) = staccarsi (**!** + *essere*)
come on
• (*to start to work*) = accendersi (**!** + *essere*)
• (*when encouraging someone*)
  come on, hurry up! = dai, sbrigati!
  come on, you can do better than that! = forza, puoi fare meglio di così
come out
• (*to leave a place*) = uscire (**!** + *essere*)
  I saw him as I was coming out of the shop = l'ho visto mentre uscivo dal negozio
• (*if it's a film, a book*) = uscire (**!** + *essere*)
• (*to wash out*) = venire via (**!** + *essere*)
• (*if it's a photo*) = venire (**!** + *essere*)
come round
• (*to visit*) = passare (**!** + *essere*)
• (*after a faint*) = rinvenire (**!** + *essere*)
come to
  lunch came to 40 euros = il pranzo è costato 40 euro
  how much does it come to? = quant'è?

comfortable *adjective*
• (*if it's a chair, a bed*) = comodo/comoda
  are you comfortable? = stai comodo?
• (*relaxed*)
  I don't feel comfortable here = non mi sento a mio agio qui
• (*having enough money*) = agiato/agiata

comic strip *noun*
  a comic strip = un fumetto

commercial
1 *adjective*
  = commerciale

····▶

2 *noun*
a commercial = uno spot pubblicitario

commit *verb*
to commit a crime = commettere un crimine

common *adjective*
= comune

communicate *verb*
= comunicare

community *noun*
a community = una comunità

company *noun*
• (*a business*)
a company = una ditta
• (*a group of actors*)
a theatre company = una compagnia teatrale
• (*other people*)
company = la compagnia
to keep someone company = fare compagnia a qualcuno

compare *verb*
to compare France with Italy
= paragonare la Francia all'Italia

competition *noun*
• competition = la concorrenza
there's a lot of competition between the schools = c'è molta concorrenza tra le scuole
• (*a contest*)
a competition = un concorso

competitive *adjective*
to be competitive = avere spirito di competizione

complain *verb*
• = lamentarsi (**!** + *essere*)
to complain about the weather
= lamentarsi del tempo
• (*to make a complaint*) = fare reclamo
he complained about the service = ha fatto reclamo per il servizio

complete
1 *adjective*
it was a complete disaster = è stato un disastro totale
this is a complete waste of time = è una totale perdita di tempo
2 *verb*
= finire
she completed the course = ha finito il corso

completely *adverb*
= completamente

complicate *verb*
= complicare

complicated *adjective*
= complicato/complicata

✱ in informal situations

compliment
1 *noun*
a compliment = un complimento
2 *verb*
to compliment someone = congratularsi con qualcuno (**!** + *essere*)

comprehensive *noun* (*British English*)
a comprehensive = una scuola superiore statale

compulsory *adjective*
= obbligatorio/obbligatoria

computer *noun*
a computer = un computer

computer game *noun*
a computer game = un gioco per computer

computer studies *noun*
computer studies = l'informatica

concentrate *verb*
= concentrarsi (**!** + *essere*)

concert *noun*
a concert = un concerto

concrete *noun*
concrete = il cemento

condition
1 *noun*
a condition = una condizione
in a terrible condition = in pessime condizioni
the car is in good condition = la macchina è in buone condizioni
2 on condition that = a condizione che
you can go on condition that her parents drive you home = puoi andare a condizione che i suoi genitori ti riaccompagnino a casa
> **!** *Note that the subjunctive is used after* a condizione che.

condom *noun*
a condom = un preservativo

conductor *noun* ▶ 281|
a conductor = un direttore d'orchestra

cone *noun*
a cone = un cono

conference *noun*
a conference = una conferenza

confidence *noun*
• confidence = la sicurzza
• (*trust*)
to have confidence in someone = avere fiducia in qualcuno

confident *adjective*
= sicuro/sicura di sé
she's a confident girl = è una ragazza sicura di sé
> **!** *Note that* **sé** *will change to* **me, te,** *etc, depending on the person or people being described.*

confidential adjective
= riservato/riservata

conflict noun
a conflict = un conflitto

confused adjective
= confuso/confusa
to get confused = confondersi (**!** +
essere)

congratulate verb
= congratularsi con (**!** + essere)

congratulations noun (also
exclamation)
congratulations! = congratulazioni!

connection noun
a connection = una relazione
it has no connection with the strike
= non ha nessuna relazione con lo
sciopero

conscientious adjective
= diligente

conscious adjective
• (aware) = consapevole
• (after an operation) = cosciente

construct verb
= costruire

consult verb
= consultare

contact
1 noun
to be in contact with someone = essere in
contatto con qualcuno
to lose contact = perdere contatto
2 verb
= contattare

contact lens noun
a contact lens = una lente a contatto

contain verb
= contenere

content adjective
= soddisfatto/soddisfatta

contest noun
a contest = un concorso

continent noun
• (a large mass of land)
a continent = un continente
• (British English) (Europe)
the Continent = l'Europa continentale

continue verb
to continue to talk, to continue talking
= continuare a parlare

continuous adjective
= continuo/continua
the continuous noise of the traffic = il
continuo rumore del traffico

contraception noun
contraception = la contraccezione

contract noun
a contract = un contratto

contradict verb
= contraddire

contradiction noun
a contradiction = una contraddizione

contrast noun
a contrast = un contrasto

contribute verb
• (to give money) = contribuire
• to contribute to the discussion
= partecipare alla discussione

control
1 noun
to take control of a situation = prendere il
controllo della situazione
to lose control of a car = perdere il
controllo della macchina
2 verb
to control a region = controllare una
regione

convenient adjective
• (useful, practical) = comodo/comoda
it's more convenient to take the bus
= conviene prendere l'autobus
• (suitable) = adatto/adatta
it's a convenient place to meet = è un
posto adatto per incontrarsi
it's not convenient for me = a me non va
bene

conversation noun
a conversation = una conversazione
to have a conversation = parlare

convince verb
= convincere

cook
1 verb
• (to prepare food) = cucinare
to cook a meal = fare da mangiare
• (to boil, fry, roast) = cuocere
to cook vegetables = cuocere le verdure
2 noun ▶ 281 |
a cook = un cuoco/una cuoca

cooker noun (British English)
a cooker = una cucina

cookie noun (US English)
a cookie = un biscotto

cooking noun
cooking = la cucina
to do the cooking = cucinare

cool adjective
• (fresh, not hot) = fresco/fresca
a cool drink = una bibita fresca
it's much cooler today = oggi fa più
fresco
• (calm) = calmo/calma
• (fashionable) = figo/figa**✶**
• (relaxed) = calmo/calma
cool down = raffreddarsi (**!** + essere)

cooperate verb
= collaborare

cope *verb*
- (*to manage*) = cavarsela (**!** + *essere*)
- **to cope with pain** = sopportare il dolore

copy
1 *noun*
  a copy = una copia
2 *verb*
  = copiare
copy down, copy out = ricopiare

cork *noun*
- **a cork** = un tappo
- **cork** = il sughero

corkscrew *noun*
  a corkscrew = un cavatappi

corner *noun*
- (*of a street, a building*)
  the corner = l'angolo
  the shop on the corner = il negozio
    all'angolo
  to go around the corner = girare l'angolo
- (*in football*)
  a corner = un calcio d'angolo

correct
1 *adjective*
  = esatto/esatta
  the correct answer = la risposta esatta
  that's correct! = esatto!
2 *verb*
  = correggere

correction *noun*
  a correction = una correzione

corridor *noun*
  a corridor = un corridoio

cost *verb*
  = costare (**!** + *essere*)
  how much does it cost? = quanto costa?
  it costs a lot of money = costa tanto

costume *noun*
  a costume = un costume

cosy *adjective* (*British English*)
  a cosy room = una stanza accogliente

cot *noun* (*British English*)
  a cot = un lettino

cottage *noun*
  a cottage = una villetta

cotton *noun*
  cotton = il cotone

cotton wool *noun* (*British English*)
  cotton wool = il cotone idrofilo

couch *noun*
  a couch = un divano

cough
1 *verb*
  = tossire
2 *noun*
  to have a cough = avere la tosse

could *verb*
- (*had the possibility*)
  I couldn't move = non potevo muovermi
  he couldn't sleep for weeks = non ha
    potuto dormire per settimane
- (*knew how to*)
  she could read at the age of three
    = sapeva leggere all'età di tre anni
  he couldn't type = non sapeva battere a
    macchina
  I couldn't speak any German = non
    sapevo parlare tedesco
- (*when talking about* **seeing, hearing,**
  understanding, could *is not translated*)
  I couldn't see a thing = non vedevo
    niente
  he could hear them = li sentiva
  they couldn't understand me = non mi
    capivano
- (*when implying that something did not*
  happen)
  she could have become a doctor
    = poteva diventare un medico
  you could have apologized! = potevi
    scusarti!
- (*when indicating a possibility*)
  they could be wrong = potrebbero
    sbagliarsi
- (*when asking, offering or suggesting*)
  could I speak to Annie? = posso parlare
    con Annie?
  could you help me? = può darmi una
    mano?

count *verb*
  = contare
count on
  to count on someone = contare su
    qualcuno

counter *noun*
  a counter (*in a shop*) = un banco
  (*in a bank, a post office*) = uno sportello
  (*in a bar*) = un banco

country *noun*
- (*a state*)
  a country = un paese
- (*the countryside*)
  the country = la campagna
  to live in the country = vivere in
    campagna

countryside *noun*
  the countryside = la campagna

couple *noun*
- **a couple of days**
  (*a few days*) = un paio di giorni
- (*two people*)
  a couple = una coppia

courage *noun*
  courage = il coraggio

course
1 *noun*
- (*a series of lessons or lectures*)
  a course = un corso   ····▶

Countries, cities, and continents

Countries and continents

The definite article **il/la**, etc is used when talking about countries and continents in Italian:

I like Italy/Japan	= mi piace l'Italia/**il** Giappone
to visit the United States	= visitare **gli** Stati Uniti

Names of countries and continents can be masculine or feminine, and some are plural.

C

In, to, and from somewhere

In is used in Italian for both **in** and **to** in English. When **in** is used the article is generally omitted:

*to live **in** Italy*	= vivere **in** Italia
*to go **to** China*	= andare **in** Cina
*to live **in** Mexico*	= vivere **in** Messico
*to go **to** Brazil*	= andare **in** Brasile

but note:

*to live **in the** United States*	= vivere **negli** Stati Uniti
*to go **to the** United States*	= andare **negli** Stati Uniti
*to live **in the** Czech Republic*	= vivere **nella** Repubblica Ceca

Da followed by the definite article is used to express **from**:

__from__ France	= **dalla** Francia
__from__ Australia	= **dall'**Australia

Towns and cities

For **in** and **to** with the name of a town, use **a** (or **ad** before a vowel). For **from** use **da**. If the Italian name includes the definite article, it combines with **a** or **da**:

*to live **in** Pavia*	= vivere **a** Pavia
*to go **to** Ancona*	= andare **ad** Ancona
*to live **in La** Spezia*	= vivere **alla** Spezia
*to arrive **from** Cairo*	= arrivare **dal** Cairo

---

an Italian course = un corso d'italiano
• (*part of a meal*)
  a course = una portata
  what's the main course? = cosa c'è come piatto principale?
2 of course = certo
  of course not! = certo che no!

court *noun*
• (*of law*)
  a court = un tribunale
• (*for playing sports*)
  a tennis court = un campo da tennis
  a basketball court = un campo di pallacanestro

cousin *noun*
  a cousin = un cugino/una cugina

cover
1 *verb*
  to cover = coprire
  to be covered in spots = essere coperto/coperta di brufoli
2 *noun*
• (*a lid*)
  a cover = un coperchio
• (*for a cushion, a quilt*)
  a cover = una fodera

• (*a blanket*)
  a cover = una coperta
• (*on a book, a magazine*)
  the cover = la copertina

coverage *noun*
  (*of mobile phone networks*)
  coverage = la copertura di rete

cow *noun*
  a cow = una mucca

coward *noun*
  a coward = un vigliacco/una vigliacca

cozy *adjective* (*US English*)
  a cozy room = una stanza accogliente

crab *noun*
  a crab = un granchio

crack *verb*
  = incrinarsi (**!** + *essere*)

cramp *noun*
  a cramp = un crampo

crash
1 *noun*
  a crash = uno scontro   ····▶

2 *verb*
to crash into a tree = andare a sbattere contro un albero (**!** + *essere*)
the plane crashed = l'aereo è precipitato

crazy *adjective*
= pazzo/pazza

cream *noun*
cream = la panna

create *verb*
= creare

credit card *noun*
a credit card = una carta di credito

cricket *noun* ▶ 178 |
cricket = il cricket

crime *noun*
a crime = un crimine
crime = la crminalità

criminal
1 *noun*
a criminal = un/una criminale
2 *adjective*
= criminale

crisis *noun*
a crisis = una crisi

crisps *noun* (*British English*)
crisps = le patatine

critical *adjective*
= critico/critica

criticize *verb*
= criticare

crocodile *noun*
a crocodile = un coccodrillo

crooked *adjective*
= storto/storta
the picture is crooked = il quadro è storto

cross
1 *verb*
• (*to go across*) = attraversare
to cross the road = attraversare la strada
to cross the Channel = attraversare la Manica
• (*other uses*)
to cross one's legs = accavallare le gambe
our letters crossed = le nostre lettere si sono incrociate
2 *noun*
a cross = una croce
3 *adjective*
= arrabbiato/arrabbiata
to get cross = arrabbiarsi (**!** + *essere*)
cross out = cancellare

crossroads *noun*
a crossroads = un incrocio

crossword puzzle *noun*
a crossword puzzle = un cruciverba

crowd *noun*
• (*a large number of people*)

a crowd = una folla
crowds of people = una gran folla
• (*watching a game*)
the crowd = il pubblico

crown *noun*
a crown = una corona

cruel *adjective*
= crudele

cruelty *noun*
cruelty = la crudeltà

cruise *noun*
a cruise = una crociera

crush *verb*
= schiacciare

crutch *noun*
a crutch = una stampella

cry
1 *verb*
= piangere
2 *noun*
a cry = un grido

cub *noun*
a cub = un cucciolo

cucumber *noun*
a cucumber = un cetriolo

cuddle *noun*
to give someone a cuddle = fare le coccole a qualcuno

culprit *noun*
the culprit = il/la colpevole

cultural *adjective*
= culturale

culture *noun*
culture = la cultura

cunning *adjective*
(*describing a person*) = astuto/astuta
(*describing a plan*) = ingegnoso/ingegnosa

cup *noun*
• a cup = una tazza
a cup of coffee = un caffè
• (*in sport*)
a cup = una coppa

cupboard *noun*
a cupboard = un armadio

curb *noun* (*US English*)
the curb = il bordo del marciapiede

cure
1 *verb*
= guarire
2 *noun*
a cure = una cura

curious *adjective*
= curioso/curiosa

curly *adjective*
= riccio/riccia
to have curly hair = avere i capelli ricci

currency *noun*
a currency = una valuta

curry *noun*
a curry = una pietanza al curry

curtain *noun*
a curtain = una tenda

cushion *noun*
a cushion = un cuscino

custard *noun* (*British English*)
custard = la crema

custom *noun*
a custom = un'usanza

customer *noun*
a customer = un/una cliente

customs *noun*
customs = la dogana
to go through customs = passare la dogana

customs officer *noun* ▶ 281 |
a customs officer = un doganiere

cut
1 *verb*
= tagliare
to cut an apple in half = tagliare una mela a metà
to cut [one's finger | one's knee | one's foot] = tagliarsi [un dito | un ginocchio | un piede] (! + *essere*)
she cut herself = si è tagliata
to have one's hair cut = tagliarsi i capelli (! + *essere*)
I got my hair cut = mi sono tagliata i capelli
2 *noun*
a cut = un taglio
cut down = tagliare
cut out
to cut a photo out of a magazine = ritagliare una foto da una rivista
cut up = fare a pezzetti

cute *adjective*
= carino/carina

CV *noun*
a CV = un curriculum

cycle *verb*
I cycle to school = vado a scuola in bicicletta
to go cycling = andare in bicicletta (! + *essere*)

cycling *noun* ▶ 178 |
cycling = il ciclismo

cyclist *noun*
a cyclist = un/una ciclista

cynical *adjective*
= cinico/cinica

Czech Republic *noun* ▶ 151 |
the Czech Republic = la Repubblica Ceca

Dd

D

dad, Dad *noun*
a dad = un papà

damage
1 *verb*
• to damage = danneggiare
the building was damaged by the fire = l'edificio è stato danneggiato dall'incendio
• (*to harm*) = nuocere a
it can damage your health = può nuocere alla salute
2 *noun*
damage = i danni
to cause damage = danneggiare

damp *adjective*
= umido/umida

dance
1 *verb*
= ballare
2 *noun*
a dance = un ballo

dancer *noun* ▶ 281 |
a dancer = un ballerino/una ballerina

dancing *noun*
dancing = il ballo

danger *noun*
danger = il pericolo
to be in danger = essere in pericolo

dangerous *adjective*
= pericoloso/pericolosa

Danish ▶ 199 |
1 *adjective*
= danese
2 *noun*
Danish = il danese

dare *verb*
• (*to have the courage*) = osare
• (*when testing someone*)
to dare someone to play a trick = sfidare qualcuno a fare uno scherzo
• (*when expressing anger*)
don't dare speak to me like that! = come ti permetti di usare questo tono con me?

dark
1 *adjective*
• (*lacking light*) = buio/buia
it's getting dark = si sta facendo buio
• (*describing a colour, clothes*) ▶ 147 |
= scuro/scura
a dark blue dress = un vestito blu scuro
• (*describing a person*) = bruno/bruna
2 *noun*
the dark = il buio

darts noun ▶ 178 |
  darts = le freccette

date ▶ 155 | noun
- (in a calendar)
  a date = una data
  what date is today? = quanti ne abbiamo oggi?
- (with a friend)
  a date = un appuntamento

daughter noun
  a daughter = una figlia

daughter-in-law noun
  a daughter-in-law = una nuora

dawn noun
  dawn = l'alba
  at dawn = all'alba

day noun ▶ 267 |

> ! Note that **day** is usually translated by **giorno** in Italian. However it is sometimes translated by **giornata**, which refers to all the things that happen during the day.

  a day = un giorno
  what day is it today? = che giorno è oggi?
  during the day = durante il giorno
  we had a very nice day = abbiamo passato una bella giornata
  the next day, the day after = il giorno dopo
  the day before = il giorno prima

daylight noun
  daylight = la luce del giorno

dazzle verb
  = abbagliare

dead adjective
  = morto/morta
  he is dead = è morto

deaf adjective
  = sordo/sorda

deal
1 noun
- **a deal** = un affare
- **a great deal** [of money | of time | of energy] = [molti soldi | molto tempo | molta energia]
2 verb
  to deal the cards = dare le carte
  deal with = occuparsi di (! + essere)
  to deal with a problem = affrontare un problema

dear
1 adjective
- (in letters) = caro/cara
  Dear Anne = Cara Anne
  Dear Anne and Paul = Cari Anne e Paul
  Dear Sir/Madam = Gentile Signore/Signora
- (expensive) = caro/cara
2 exclamation
  oh dear! = oh Dio!

death noun
  death = la morte

debate noun
  a debate = un dibattito

debt noun
  a debt = un debito
  to be in debt = avere dei debiti

decade noun
  a decade = un decennio

decaffeinated adjective
  = decaffeinato/decaffeinata

deceive verb
  = ingannare

December noun ▶ 155 |
  December = dicembre (masculine)

decide verb
  = decidere
  he decided [to accept | to stay | to get married] = ha deciso [di accettare | di restare | di sposarsi]

decision noun
  a decision = una decisione
  to make a decision = prendere una decisione

deck noun
  a deck = un ponte
  on deck = sul ponte

deckchair noun
  a deckchair = una sedia a sdraio

decorate verb
- (with ornaments) = decorare
- (with wallpaper) = mettere la carta da parati
  (to paint) = dipingere

decoration noun
  a decoration = una decorazione

deed noun
  (of a house)
  a deed = un atto di trasferimento di proprietà

deep adjective ▶ 202 |
  = profondo/profonda
  how deep is the lake? = quanto è profondo il lago?

deer noun
  a deer = un cervo

defeat
1 verb
  = sconfiggere
  the team was defeated = la squadra è stata sconfitta
2 noun
  a defeat = una sconfitta

defence (British English), **defense** (US English) noun
  defence = la difesa

defend verb
  = difendere

Dates, days, and months

The days of the week

Note that Italian uses lower-case letters for the names of the days. All the days are masculine except **domenica**.

Monday	= lunedì
Tuesday	= martedì
Wednesday	= mercoledì
Thursday	= giovedì
Friday	= venerdì
Saturday	= sabato
Sunday	= domenica

In the examples below, **lunedì** can be replaced by any day (but be careful with **domenica**, which the adjective and the article should agree with). Note the use of **il** for weekly occurrences and no article for one-off occurrences:

on Monday	= lunedì
on Mondays	= il lunedì
every Monday	= ogni lunedì
Monday evening	= lunedì sera
last/next Monday	= lunedì scorso/prossimo
early on Monday	= lunedì presto

The months of the year

As with the days of the week, do not use capitals to spell the names of the months in Italian. All the months are masculine.

January	= gennaio
February	= febbraio
March	= marzo
April	= aprile
May	= maggio
June	= giugno
July	= luglio
August	= agosto
September	= settembre
October	= ottobre
November	= novembre
December	= dicembre

May in the notes below stands for any month: they all work the same way.

in *May*	= a maggio
the middle of May	= metà maggio
the end of May	= fine maggio

Dates

On is not translated when giving dates:

(on) May 1	= il primo maggio
(on) May 2	= il due maggio
(on) May 8	= l'otto maggio
from 3rd to 11th May	= dal tre all'undici maggio
Monday May 1st	= lunedì primo maggio
what's the date?	= quanti ne abbiamo oggi?
it's the tenth of May	= è il 10 maggio
in 1968	= nel 1968 (*say* millenovecentosessantotto)
in the year 2000	= nel duemila

Centuries

There are two ways to refer to centuries in Italian. The first is as in English **the 20th century**. The second is similar to the English **the 1900s** and can be used only for the centuries from the 13th to the 20th:

the 20th century	= il ventesimo secolo
in the 15th century	= nel Quattrocento

definite adjective
• (obvious, visible) = netto/netta
  a definite improvement = un netto
  miglioramento
• (describing a plan) = preciso/precisa

definitely adverb
  = di sicuro
  they're definitely lying = stanno
  mentendo di sicuro
  I'm definitely coming = vengo di sicuro
  definitely! = certamente!

defy verb
  = sfidare

degree noun
• (from a university)
  a degree = una laurea
• (in measurements)
  a degree = un grado

delay
1 verb
  = ritardare
2 noun
  a delay = un ritardo

deliberately adverb
  = apposta
  he did it deliberately = l'ha fatto apposta

delicious adjective
  = squisito/squisita

delighted adjective
  = contentissimo/contentissima
  I'm delighted with the present = sono
  contentissimo del regalo

deliver verb
  = consegnare

demand verb
  = esigere

demolish verb
  = demolire

demonstration noun
  a demonstration = una manifestazione

denim noun
  a denim jacket = un giubbotto di jeans

Denmark noun ▶ 151 |
  Denmark = la Danimarca

dentist noun ▶ 281 |
  a dentist = un/una dentista

deny verb
  = negare

department noun
  a department (in a firm, a store) = un
  reparto
  (in a school, university) = un dipartimento

department store noun
  a department store = un grande
  magazzino

depend verb
  = dipendere

to depend on someone = dipendere da
  qualcuno
  it depends = dipende

depressed adjective
  = depresso/depressa

depressing adjective
  = deprimente

depth noun ▶ 202 |
  depth = la profondità

describe verb
  = descrivere

description noun
  a description = una descrizione

desert noun
  a desert = un deserto

deserve verb
  = meritare
  he deserves to be punished = si merita
  di essere punito

design
1 verb
• (to plan) = progettare
  the house was designed for a hot climate
  = la casa è stata progettata per un clima
  caldo
• (in fashion)
  to design clothes = disegnare degli abiti
2 noun
• (a subject of study)
  (fashion) design = la moda
• (a pattern)
  a design = un motivo

desk noun
  a desk = una scrivania
  (at school) = un banco

desperate adjective
  = disperato/disperata

dessert noun
  a dessert = un dessert

destroy verb
  = distruggere

detail noun
  a detail = un particolare

detective noun ▶ 281 |
  a detective = un
  investigatore/un'investigatrice
  a private detective = un investigatore
  privato/un'investigatrice privata

detective story noun
  a detective story = un poliziesco

determined adjective
  = deciso/decisa
  to be determined to go = essere deciso ad
  andare

develop verb
• (when it's a photograph) = sviluppare
• (to change) = svilupparsi (**!** + essere)

development *noun*
  a development = uno sviluppo

diagram *noun*
  a diagram = uno schema

dial *verb*
  to dial a number = fare un numero

dialling code *noun* (*British English*)
  a dialling code = un prefisso telefonico

dialling tone (*British English*), **dial
tone** (*US English*) *noun*
  a dialling tone = un segnale di libero

diamond *noun*
  a diamond = un diamante

diary *noun*
  • (*for personal thoughts*)
  a diary = un diario
  • (*for appointments*)
  a diary = un'agenda

dice *noun*
  a dice = un dado

dictionary *noun*
  a dictionary = un dizionario

die *verb*
  • to die = morire (**!** + *essere*)
  he died in the war = è morto in guerra
  • (*used for emphasis*)
  I'm dying to go on holiday = muoio dalla
  voglia di andare in ferie**✗**

diet *noun*
  a diet = una dieta
  to go on a diet = mettersi a dieta (**!** +
  essere)

difference *noun*
  a difference = una differenza
  I can't tell the difference = non vedo la
  differenza
  it won't make any difference = non farà
  nessuna differenza

different *adjective*
  = diverso/diversa

difficult *adjective*
  = difficile
  Spanish is not difficult to learn = lo
  spagnolo non è difficile da imparare
  he's difficult to get along with = è
  difficile andarci d'accordo

difficulty *noun*
  a difficulty = una difficoltà
  to have difficulty concentrating = avere
  difficoltà a concentrarsi

dig *verb*
  = scavare

digital *adjective*
  = digitale

diner *noun* (*US English*)
  a diner = una tavola calda

dinghy *noun*
  a dinghy = un gommone

dining room *noun*
  a dining room = una sala da pranzo

dinner *noun*
  a dinner = una cena
  dinner's ready! = è pronto!

dip *verb*
  = immergere

direct
  1 *adjective*
  = diretto/diretta
  2 *verb*
  • (*when talking about directions*)
  could you direct me to the station?
  = potrebbe indicarmi la strada per la
  stazione?
  • (*in cinema or theatre*) = dirigere

direction *noun*
  a direction = una direzione
  is this the right direction? = è questa la
  direzione giusta?
  they were going in the other direction
  = andavano nell'altra direzione

directions *noun*
  directions = le indicazioni
  to give someone directions = indicare la
  strada a qualcuno
  to ask someone for directions = chiedere
  la strada a qualcuno

director *noun* ▶ **281** |
  • (*of a film or play*)
  a director = un/una regista
  • (*of a company*)
  a director = un direttore/una direttrice

dirt *noun*
  dirt = lo sporco

dirty
  1 *adjective*
  = sporco/sporca
  to get dirty = sporcarsi (**!** + *essere*)
  2 *verb*
  = sporcare

disabled *adjective*
  = disabile

disadvantage *noun*
  a disadvantage = uno svantaggio

disagree *verb*
  = non essere d'accordo
  I disagree with you = non sono d'accordo
  con te

disappear *verb*
  = scomparire (**!** + *essere*)

disappoint *verb*
  = deludere

disappointed *adjective*
  = deluso/delusa

disappointing *adjective*
  = deludente

disappointment noun
  disappointment = una delusione

disapprove verb
  to disapprove of someone = disapprovare
  qualcuno

disaster noun
  a disaster = un disastro

discipline noun
  discipline = la disciplina

disco noun
  a disco = una discoteca

disconnect verb
  • (to pull out a plug) = staccare
  • (to cut off) = tagliare

discourage verb
  = scoraggiare

discover verb
  = scoprire

discovery noun
  a discovery = una scoperta

discreet adjective
  = discreto/discreta

discrimination noun
  discrimination = la discriminazione

discuss verb
  = discutere di
  to discuss politics = discutere di politica

discussion noun
  a discussion = una discussione

disease noun ▶ 193 |
  a disease = una malattia

disguise
1 noun
  a disguise = un travestimento
  to wear a disguise = essere
  travestito/travestita
2 verb
  to disguise oneself as a woman
  = travestirsi da donna (! + essere)

disgusting adjective
  = disgustoso/disgustosa

dish noun
  • (food)
  a dish = un piatto
  • the dishes = i piatti
  to wash the dishes = lavare i piatti

dishonest adjective
  = disonesto/disonesta

dishwasher noun
  a dishwasher = una lavapiatti

dislike verb
  I dislike him = non mi piace

dismiss verb
  = licenziare

disobedient adjective
  = disobbediente

disobey verb
  to disobey someone = disobbedire a
  qualcuno

dispute noun
  a dispute = una disputa

disqualify verb
  = squalificare

disrupt verb
  = disturbare

dissatisfied adjective
  = scontento/scontenta

distance noun
  a distance = una distanza
  in the distance = in lontananza
  to keep one's distance = mantenere le
  distanze

distinct adjective
  = distinto/distinta

distinguish verb
  = distinguere

distract verb
  = distrarre
  to distract someone from working
  = distrarre qualcuno dal lavoro

distressed adjective
  = angosciato/angosciata

distribute verb
  = distribuire

disturb verb
  = disturbare

disturbing adjective
  = inquietante

dive verb ▶ 178 |
  = tuffarsi (! + essere)
  to go diving = fare delle immersioni

divide verb
  = dividere

diving board noun
  a diving board = un trampolino

divorce
1 noun
  a divorce = un divorzio
2 verb
  = divorziare

DIY noun (British English)
  DIY = il fai da te

dizzy adjective
  I feel dizzy = mi gira la testa

do verb
  ▶ See the boxed note on **do** for more
  information and examples.
  • to do = fare
  to do the cooking = fare da mangiare
  to do one's homework = fare i compiti
  what has he done with the newspaper?
  = cosa ne ha fatto del giornale?
  what has she done to her hair? = cosa si
  è fatta ai capelli?   ····➤

do

Usually the Italian equivalent of **do** is **fare**:

*what **are** you **doing?***   = cosa **stai facendo?**
*I'm **doing** a crossword*   = **sto facendo** le parole crociate

As an auxiliary verb

English uses **do** to form questions, negative statements and other constructions; Italian has no equivalent for this.

D

do you come here often?   = ci vieni spesso?
*yes, I **do**/no, I **don't***   = sì/no
*I **don't** remember*   = non mi ricordo
*so **do** I*   = anch'io
*nor **do** I*   = neanch'io
*I **do** like it!*   = come mi piace!
***don't** shout!*   = non gridare!
*you cheated, **didn't** you?*   = hai imbrogliato, non è vero?
*you **don't** eat meat, **do** you?*   = non mangi la carne, vero?
***do** sit down!*   = si accomodi!

---

do as you're told = fai come ti si dice
• (*in questions, negatives*)
do you like cats? = ti piacciono i gatti?
I don't like cats = non mi piacciono i gatti
I didn't do anything = non ho fatto niente
don't shout! = non gridare!
• (*in short answers and tag questions*)
'do you like strawberries?'—**'yes, I do'** = 'ti piacciono le fragole?'—'sì'
'I never said I liked him'—**'yes, you did'** = 'non ho mai detto che mi piaceva'—'sì che l'hai detto'
'I live in the country'—**'so do I'** = 'vivo in campagna'—'anch'io'
'who wrote it?'—**'I did'** = 'chi l'ha scritto?'—'io'
he lives in London, doesn't he? = abita a Londra, no?
Martina didn't phone, did she? = Martina non ha mica telefonato?
'may I sit down?'—**'yes, please do'** = 'posso sedermi?'—'prego'
• (*to be enough*) = bastare (**!** + *essere*)
ten pounds will do = dieci sterline basteranno
• (*to be suitable*) = andare bene (**!** + *essere*)
that box will do = quella scatola andrà bene
• (*to perform*)
he did well = se l'è cavata bene
he did badly = gli è andata male
do up (*British English*)
to do up one's buttons = abbottonarsi (**!** + *essere*)
to do up a house = rimettere a nuovo una casa
do with
it's got something to do with computers = ha qualcosa a che fare con i computer
it has nothing to do with him = lui non c'entra niente

do without = fare a meno di
I can do without a television = posso fare a meno della televisione

dock noun
a dock = una darsena

doctor noun ▶ 281 |
a doctor = un dottore

document noun
a document = un documento

documentary noun
a documentary = un documentario

dog noun
a dog = un cane

doll noun
a doll = una bambola

dollar noun
a dollar = un dollaro

dolphin noun
a dolphin = un delfino

dominoes noun ▶ 178 |
dominoes = il domino

donkey noun
a donkey = un asino

door noun
a door = una porta

doorbell noun
a doorbell = un campanello

dose noun
a dose = una dose

double

1 *adjective*   ....➤
- (*of an amount*) = doppio/doppia
  a double helping of strawberries = una
  doppia porzione di fragole
- (*when spelling or giving a number*)
  Anna is spelled with a double 'n' = Anna
  si scrive con due 'n'
  three double five (*British English*)
  = trecentocinquantacinque
2 *verb*
  = raddoppiare

double bass *noun*
  a double bass = un contrabbasso

double bed *noun*
  a double bed = un letto matrimoniale

double-decker *noun*
  a double-decker = un autobus a due
  piani

double room *noun*
  a double room = una camera doppia

doubt

1 *noun*
  a doubt = un dubbio
  I've no doubt that it's true = sono certo
  che è vero
2 *verb*
  = dubitare
  I doubt if she'll come = dubito che venga
  ! *Note that the subjunctive is used after*
  dubitare che.

doughnut, donut (*US English*) *noun*
  a doughnut = un bombolone

down

  ! *Often* **down** *occurs in combinations*
  with verbs, for example: **calm down, let**
  down, slow down *etc. To find the*
  correct translations for this type of
  verb, look up the separate dictionary
  entries at **calm, let, slow** *etc.*

1 *preposition*
  he ran down the hill = è corso giù per la
  collina
  the kitchen is down those stairs = la
  cucina è in fondo alle scale
2 *adverb*
  she's down in the cellar = è giù in
  cantina
  down in Brighton = a Brighton
  to go down = scendere (**!** + *essere*)
  to fall down = cadere (**!** + *essere*)
  down there = laggiù

downstairs *adverb*
  = di sotto
  I'm going downstairs = vado giù
  to bring the boxes downstairs = portare
  giù le scatole

dozen *noun* ▶ **233|**
  a dozen = una dozzina
  a dozen eggs = una dozzina di uova

draft *noun* (*US English*)
  a draft = una corrente d'aria

drag *verb*
  = trascinare

drain *verb*
- (*when cooking*) = scolare (**!** + *avere*)
- (*if it's water*)
  to drain (away) = scolare (**!** + *essere*)

drama *noun*
  drama = l'arte drammatica

dramatic *adjective*
  = spettacolare

drapes *noun* (*US English*)
  the drapes = le tende

draught *noun* (*British English*)
  a draught = una corrente d'aria

draughts *noun* ▶ **178|** (*British English*)
  draughts = la dama

draw

1 *verb*
- (*with a pen or pencil*) = disegnare
  to draw a rabbit = disegnare un coniglio
  to draw a picture = fare un disegno
  to draw a line = tracciare una riga
  she drew his portrait = gli ha fatto il
  ritratto
- (*to pull*) = tirare
  to draw the curtains = tirare le tende
- (*to take out*) = tirare fuori
  to draw a knife = tirare fuori un coltello
- (*to attract*) = attirare
- (*British English*) (*in sport*) = pareggiare
- **Christmas is drawing near** = il Natale si
  avvicina
2 *noun*
- (*in sport*)
  a draw = un pareggio
- (*in a lottery*)
  a draw = un'estrazione a sorte
draw aside
  to draw someone aside = tirare qualcuno
  in disparte

drawer *noun*
  a drawer = un cassetto

drawing *noun*
  drawing = il disegno
  a drawing = un disegno

dread *verb*
  = avere il terrore di

dreadful *adjective*
  = spaventoso/spaventosa

dream

1 *noun*
  a dream = un sogno
  to have a dream = fare un sogno
2 *verb*
  = sognare
  to dream of going to Japan = sognare di
  andare in Giappone